THE ART AND SCIENCE
of Track and Field Marking

Dr S. Saraboji, Ph.D.,
Dr E. Amudhan, Ph.D.,
Dr S. Sethu, Ph.D.,

Clever Fox® PUBLISHING
Chennai • Bangalore

CLEVER FOX PUBLISHING
Chennai, India

Published by CLEVER FOX PUBLISHING 2025
Copyright © S. SARABOJI, E. AMUDHAN, S. SETHU 2025

All Rights Reserved.
ISBN: 978-93-67078-17-4

This book has been published with all reasonable efforts taken to make the material error-free after the consent of the author. No part of this book shall be used, reproduced in any manner whatsoever without written permission from the author, except in the case of brief quotations embodied in critical articles and reviews.

The Authors of this book is solely responsible and liable for its content including but not limited to the views, representations, descriptions, statements, information, opinions and references ["Content"]. The Content of this book shall not constitute or be construed or deemed to reflect the opinion or expression of the Publisher or Editor. Neither the Publisher nor Editor endorse or approve the Content of this book or guarantee the reliability, accuracy or completeness of the Content published herein and do not make any representations or warranties of any kind, express or implied, including but not limited to the implied warranties of merchantability, fitness for a particular purpose. The Publisher and Editor shall not be liable whatsoever for any errors, omissions, whether such errors or omissions result from negligence, accident, or any other cause or claims for loss or damages of any kind, including without limitation, indirect or consequential loss or damage arising out of use, inability to use, or about the reliability, accuracy or sufficiency of the information contained in this book.

BANGLADESH KRIRA SHIKKHA PROTISHTAN (BKSP)
Zirani, Savar, Dhaka

Dr Kalyan Chaudhuri
Foreign Coach (BKSP, Dhaka)
'KRIRA GURU' Recipient (West Bengal)
Former Deputy Chief Athletic Coach, Team India.
Former Chief Coach, Sports Authority of India.

FOREWORD

Track and Field marking is much more than a technical task; it is a precise art that requires a deep understanding, meticulous attention, and unwavering dedication. For students pursuing Physical Education and Sports, mastering the nuances of Track and Field marking is essential. Educational institutions incorporate Annual Track & Field Meets into their academic calendar and host inter-institutional competitions, where accurate markings are pivotal to ensuring fair play and seamless execution.

The **"The Art and Science of Track and Field Marking"** is a definitive guide for Physical Education and Sports students and professionals, offering an exhaustive resource on track and field event markings, Authored by Dr S. Saraboji, Dr E. Amudhan, and Dr S. Sethu. This manual is a testament to their vast expertise, meticulous craftsmanship, and commitment to excellence in sports education.

What truly distinguishes this manual is the clarity and precision of its diagrams, thoughtfully designed to be systematic and easy to comprehend. Each aspect of event marking is detailed thoroughly, making the manual a valuable reference for both seasoned professionals and those new to the field.

The authors have put forth an extraordinary effort in compiling this guide, showcasing their dedication to creating a practical and reliable resource. I am confident this manual will become an indispensable tool for physical education teachers, coaches, and sports administrators, aiding them in organizing flawless athletic events with confidence.

With immense pride and admiration, I extend my heartfelt congratulations to Dr S. Saraboji, Dr E. Amudhan, and Dr S. Sethu for their remarkable contribution to the field of Sports Education through this outstanding publication.

(Dr Kalyan Chaudhuri)

Author's Foreword

The creation of **The Art and Science of Track and Field Marking** has been a long-cherished dream, nurtured over two decades. Our vision has always been to provide a comprehensive and practical guide that not only supports professionals in Physical Education but also benefits coaches, athletes, sports administrators, and enthusiasts who are deeply involved in athletics.

One of the primary objectives of this manual is to demystify the complexities of track and field construction and event organization. This book offers clear and precise guidelines on designing a 200m Oval Track and a 400m Standard Oval Track, along with step-by-step instructions for accurately drawing throwing circles, landing areas, and runways essential for field events. By presenting technical concepts in an accessible manner, we aim to empower readers with confidence and clarity, ensuring that they can apply this knowledge effectively in their respective roles.

We are profoundly honored that Dr. Kalyan Chaudhuri, Foreign Coach (BKSP, Dhaka), 'KRIRA GURU' Recipient (West Bengal), Former Deputy Chief Athletic Coach, Team India, and Former Chief Coach, Sports Authority of India, has graciously written the foreword for this book. His vast experience, wisdom, and invaluable insights add immense depth and credibility to our work.

This book is a humble tribute to our loving parents, whose unwavering support, encouragement, and sacrifices have been the foundation of our journey. Without their belief in us, this endeavor would not have been possible.

We also extend our deepest gratitude and respect to the scholars, experts, and professionals in the field who may offer constructive feedback. Their critical insights and suggestions will be invaluable in further refining and enhancing future editions of this book, ensuring that it continues to evolve as a definitive resource in the field of athletics.

It is our sincere hope and aspiration that Track and Field Marking Manual serves as a cornerstone of knowledge and inspiration, helping athletes and professionals alike to build a stronger, more scientifically informed foundation in the world of track and field.

Authors

THE ART AND SCIENCE OF TRACK AND FIELD MARKING

Sl No	Content	Page No
	400 Metre Standard Oval Track – Track Events	
1.	Guidelines for Layout a 400 Metre Standard Oval Track	1
2.	World Athletics Approved Synthetic Running Track Colors for 400 Metre Standard Oval Track	2
3.	400 Metre Standard Oval Track - Requirements of Construction Categories	3
4.	Competition Categories and Recommended Track Construction Category	4
5.	Calculation of Kerb Line Radius (KLR) / Construction Line Radius (CLR) and Running Line Radius (RLR) for 400 Metre Standard Oval Track	5
6.	Kerb Line Radius (KLR) / Construction Line Radius (CLR) and Running Line Radius (RLR) for 400 Metre Standard Oval Track	6
7.	400 Metre Standard Oval Track Set Out Measurement	7
8.	Calculation of the Track Length of the 400 Metre Standard Oval Track	8
9.	Setting Out Plan and Dimensions of the 400 Metre Standard Oval Track	9-10
10.	28 - Point Control Measurement of 400 Metre Standard Oval Track	11
11.	Width of the Running Lane	12

THE ART AND SCIENCE OF TRACK AND FIELD MARKING

Sl No	Content	Page No
	400 Metre Standard Oval Track – Track Events	
12.	Measurement of Race Distance	13
13.	Black Rectangles	14
14.	Measurement of Race Distance (200 Metres)	15
15.	Measurement of Race Distance (400 Metres)	16
16.	Calculation of Staggers (For the track with raised kerb)	17
17.	Calculation of Breakline Distance (For the track with raised kerb)	18
18.	Breakline Marking (For the track with raised kerb)	19
19.	Staggered Start Data for the 400 Metre Standard Oval Track	20
20.	Track Markings	21-25
21.	Marking of the Straight Incorporated within the 400 Metre Standard Oval Track Layout Plan	26-27
22.	Olympics Track Circumferences	28
23.	100 Metres	29
24.	200 Metres	30
25.	400 Metres	31
26.	800 Metres	32

THE ART AND SCIENCE OF TRACK AND FIELD MARKING

Sl No	Content	Page No
	400 Metre Standard Oval Track – Track Events	
27.	1500 Metres	33
28.	1 Mile	34
29.	1000 Metres, 3000 Metres, 5000 Metres	35
30.	1000 Metres, 3000 Metres, 5000 Metres Group Start	36
31.	800 Metres, 2000 Metres, 10,000 Metres	37
32.	800 Metres, 2000 Metres, 10,000 Metres Group Start	38
33.	Technical Rule 17.5.2 Group Start	39
34.	4 x 100 Metres Relay Take Over Zone	40
35.	4 x 400 Metres Relay First Take Over Zone	41
36.	4 x 400 Metres Relay Second and Third Take Over Zone	42
37.	4 x 100 Metres Relay	43
38.	4 x 100 Metres Relay Third Take Over Zone	44
39.	4 x 100 Metres Relay Second Take Over Zone	45
40.	4 x 100 Metres Relay First Take Over Zone	46
41.	4 x 100 Metres Relay - Diagram	47

THE ART AND SCIENCE OF TRACK AND FIELD MARKING

Sl No	Content	Page No
	400 Metre Standard Oval Track – Track Events	
42.	4 x 400 Metres Relay	48
43.	100 Metres and 110 Metres Hurdle - Height, Position and Number	49
44.	Hurdle Positions	50
45.	100 Metres Hurdles	51
46.	110 Metres Hurdles	52
47.	400 Metres Hurdles – Height, Position and Number	53
48.	80 Metres Hurdles – Height, Position and Number	54
49.	400 Metres Hurdles Positions	55-56
50.	Hurdle Measurements Diagram	57
51.	Calculation for Placing the First Hurdles in Lanes 2 to 8 for the 400 Metres Hurdles	58
52.	Calculation for Placing the Fourth and Fifth Hurdles in Lanes 2 to 8 for the 400 Metres Hurdles	59
53.	Hurdles Position Table	60
54.	Placement of the First Hurdles in Lanes 2 to 8 for the 400 Metres Hurdles on a Standard 400 Metre Oval Track	61
55.	Placement of the Fourth and Fifth Hurdles in Lanes 2 to 8 for the 400 Metres Hurdles on a Standard 400 Metre Oval Track	62

THE ART AND SCIENCE OF TRACK AND FIELD MARKING

Sl No	Content	Page No
	400 Metre Standard Oval Track – Track Events	
56.	Steeplechase Track with Water Jump Inside the Bend of the 400 Metre Standard Oval Track	63-65
57.	Steeplechase Track with Water Jump Inside the Bend Integrated Into the 400 Metre Standard Oval Track Calculation of the Length of Running (Lr)	66-67
58.	Steeplechase Track with Water Jump Outside the Bend of the 400 Metre Standard Oval Track	68-69
59.	Steeplechase Track with Water Jump outside the Bend Integrated Into the 400 Metre Standard Oval Track Calculation of the Length Of Running (Lr)	70-71
60.	Height and Number of Hurdles for Steeplechase Track with Water Jump Inside and Outside the Bend Integrated Into the 400 Metre Standard Oval Track	72
61.	Steeplechase Hurdle Measurements	73

THE ART AND SCIENCE OF TRACK AND FIELD MARKING

Sl No	Content	
	Field Events	
62.	Long Jump Runway and Landing Area	77
63.	Triple Jump Runway and Landing Area	78
64.	High Jump Runway and Landing Area	79-82
65.	Pole Vault Runway and Landing Area	83-86
66.	Throwing Events Official Implements	87
67.	How to Lay Out a 34.92° Sector	88
68.	Shot Put Circle and Landing Sector	89
69.	Shot Put Circle and Stop Board	90
70.	Discus Throw Circle and Landing Sector	91
71.	Cage for Discus Throw Only (with cage dimensions to netting)	92
72.	Cage for Hammer and Discus Throw with Concentric Circles (Discus Throw configuration, with cage dimensions to netting)	93
73.	Hammer Throw Circle and Landing Sector	94
74.	Cage for Hammer and Discus Throw with Concentric Circles (Hammer Throw configuration for anti clockwise thrower with cage dimensions to netting)	95
75.	Javelin Throw Runway and Landing Sector	96-97

THE ART AND SCIENCE OF TRACK AND FIELD MARKING

Sl No	Content	Page No
	200 Metre Oval Track – Track Events	
76.	Calculation of Kerb Line Radius (KLR) and Running Line Radius (RLR) for 200 Metre Oval Track	101
77.	Kerb Line Radius (KLR) and Running Line Radius (RLR) for 200 Metre Oval Track	102
78.	200 Metre Oval Track Set Out Measurement	103
79.	Calculation of the Track Length of the 200 Metre Oval Track	104
80.	Setting Out Plan and Dimensions of the 200 Metre Oval Track	105-107
81.	Calculation of Staggers (For the track without raised kerb)	108
82.	Calculation of Breakline Distance (For the track without raised kerb)	109
83.	Breakline Marking (For the track without raised kerb)	110
84.	100 Metres	111
85.	200 Metres	112
86.	400 Metres	113
87.	800 Metres	114
88.	1500 Metres	115
89.	800 Metres, 1000 Metres, 2000 Metres, 5000 Metres, 10,000 Metres	116

THE ART AND SCIENCE OF TRACK AND FIELD MARKING

Sl No	Content	Page No
	200 Metre Oval Track – Track Events	
90.	4 x 100 Metres Relay	117
91.	4 x 100 Metres Relay First Take Over Zone	118
92.	4 x 100 Metres Relay Second Take Over Zone	119
93.	4 x 100 Metres Relay Third Take Over Zone	120
94.	4 x 400 Metres Relay	121
95.	Athletics Technical Data	122-124
96.	Athletics Measurements: From 6 Millimetres to 100 Metres	125-128
97.	Olympic Oath	129
98.	Main Elements of Olympic Opening and Closing Ceremony	130
99.	Introduction of Athletics at the Summer Olympics	131
100.	Athletics Events in the Olympics and World Athletics Championships	132
101.	400 Metres - (the track without raised kerb)	133

400 METRE STANDARD OVAL TRACK

TRACK EVENTS

Guidelines for Layout a 400 Metre Standard Oval Track
(As per World Athletics Track and Field Facilities Manual 2024)

1. When installing all Track and Field facilities, careful consideration must be given to the position of the sun at critical times of day and the prevailing wind conditions. To avoid the dazzling effect of the sun when it is low, the longitudinal axis of arenas should lie along the north-south axis, although it is possible to deviate to the north-north-east and north-north-west. That said, there are very successful stadia which are oriented east-west because of topography and the prevailing breeze being from the west.

2. The 400m Standard Oval Track has 8, 6 or occasionally 4 lanes but the last is not used for international running competition. Nine (9) is the maximum number of oval lanes that should be provided at a facility as otherwise there is too much advantage gained by the athlete in the outside lane in a 200m race over the athlete in the inside lane.

3. Experience has shown that the most suitable 400m oval tracks are constructed with bend radii of between 35m and 38m, with an optimum of 36.50m. It is recommended that all future tracks are constructed to the latter specification and this will be referred to as the **"400m Standard Oval Track"**.

4. A track with a single bend radius less than 33.50m and where the running line radius of the outer lane exceeds 50m will not be certified.

5. Normally, there should be one finish line for all Track Events which is the prolongation of diameter D-A (see page 29). However, if site limitations dictate, a separate finish line for the 110m may be marked not more than 10m past the normal finish line with a minimum 17m run-out past the added finish line.

6. The Official synthetic surface Running Track's Colors for World Ranking Competitions are blue and red only.

World Athletics Approved Synthetic Running Track Colors for 400 Metre Standard Oval Track

400 Metre Standard Oval Track - Requirements of Construction Categories

Item	Competition Facilities	Construction Category				
		I	II	III	IV	V
1.	400m track as described under Chapter 2 in Track and Field facilities Manual with minimum 8 oval lanes and 8 straight lanes for 100m and 110m Hurdles	1	1	1	1	1
2.	400m track as item 1, but with min. 6 oval lanes and 6 straight lanes for 100m and 110m Hurdles	-	-	-	1	-
3.	400m track as item 1, but with min. 4 oval lanes and 6 straight lanes for 100m and 110m Hurdles	-	-	-	-	1
4.	Water jump for the Steeplechase	1	1	1	-	-
5.	Long and Triple Jump facility with landing area at each end	2	2	1	2	-
6.	Long and Triple Jump facility with landing area at one end	-	-	-	-	1
7.	High Jump facility	2	2	1	2	1
8	Pole Vault facility with provision for landing area at each end	2	2	1	2	-
9.	Pole Vault facility with provision for landing area at one end	-	-	-	-	1
10.	Discus and Hammer Throw combined facility (concentric or separate circles but concentric is preferred)	1	1	1	1	1
11.	Javelin Throw facility	2	2	2	1	1
12.	Shot Put facility	2	2	2	2	1

Competition Categories and Recommended Track Construction Category

Competition Category	Event	Recommended Construction Category
1.	World Championships and Olympic Games	I
2.	Area, Regional and Group Championshipsand and Games	II
3.	Continental / Regional /Area Cups	III
4.	Matches	III
5.	International Invitation Meetings specifically authorised by World Athletics	III
6.	International Invitation Meetings specifically authorised by an Area Association	III
7.	Other Meetings specifically authorised by an Area or a Member and National Championships	IV
8.	Combined Events	IV
9.	Other National Competitions	V

WORLD ATHLETICS MEMBER FEDERATIONS

CAA - Confederation of African Athletics

Atletismo Sudamericano (South America)

OAA - Oceania Athletics Association

AA - Asian Athletics

EA - European Athletics

NACAC - North American, Central American and Caribbean AA

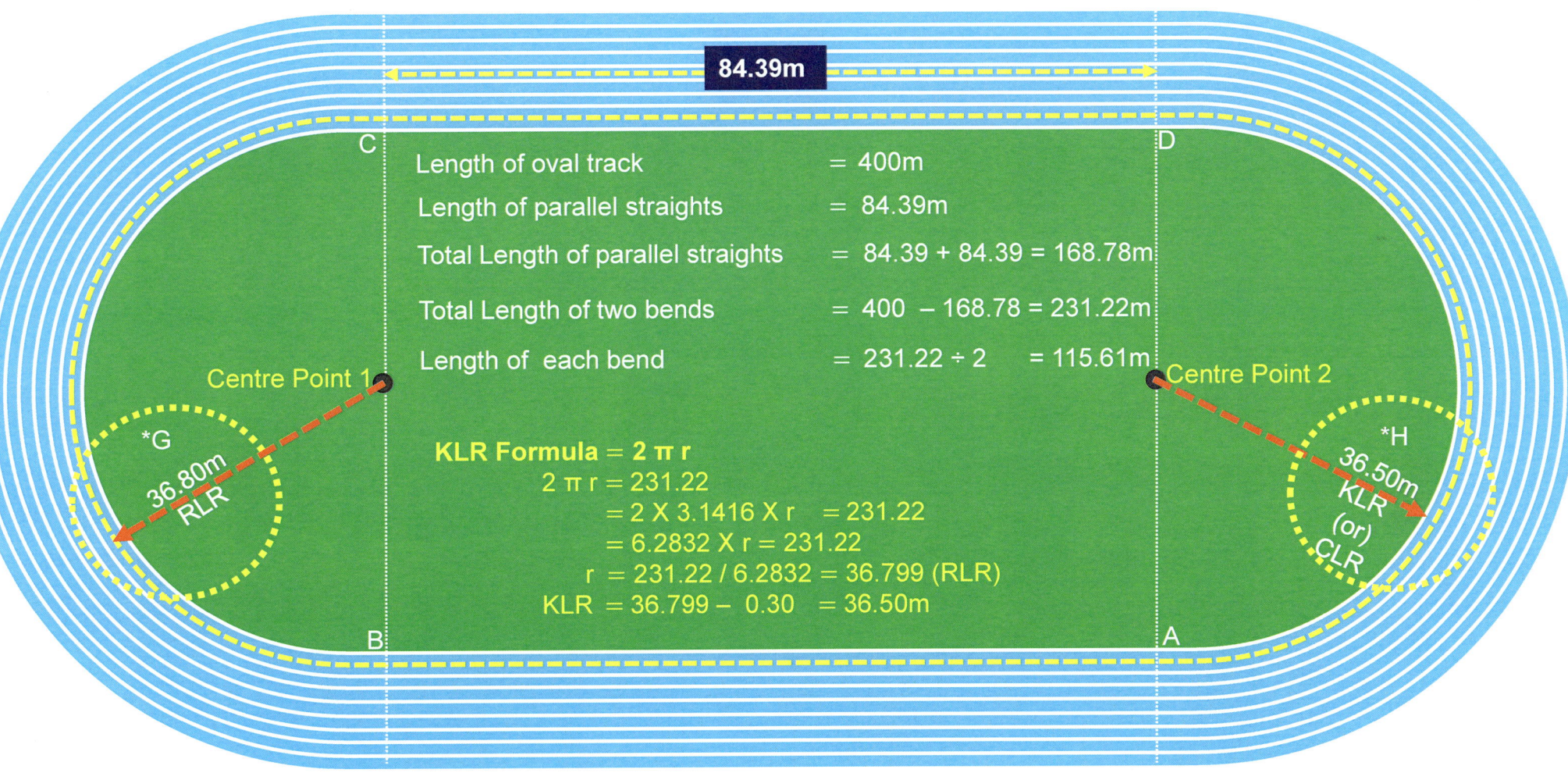

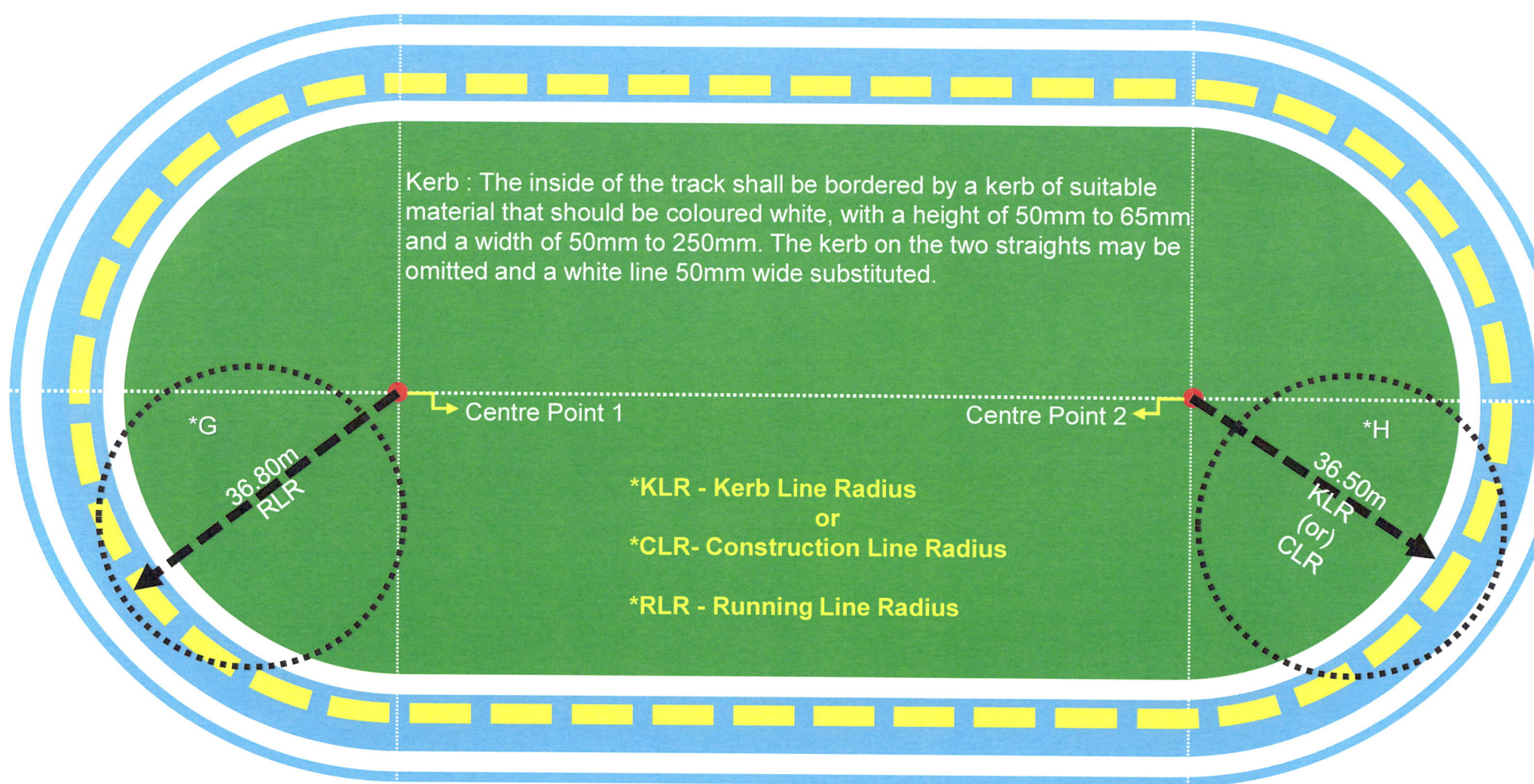

400 Metre Standard Oval Track Set Out Measurement

Set Out Measurement	Metre
Length of parallel straights	84.390
Construction radius of semicircle bend (including the raised kerb on inside edge of track)	36.500
Radius of measurement line (running line) in lane 1 (0.30m outside raised kerb)	36.800
Length of each bend on construction line (kerb line)	114.6681
Length of each bend along running line (nominal measuring length)	115.6106
Length of oval track on construction line (kerb line)	398.1163
Length of oval track along of running line (nominal measuring length)	400.0012
Width of the lane including the 0.05m line on the outside	1.22m ± 0.01
Length of Steeplechase lap along line of running where the water jump is inside the 400m track	396.085
Length of Steeplechase lap along line of running where the water jump is outside the 400m track	419.407

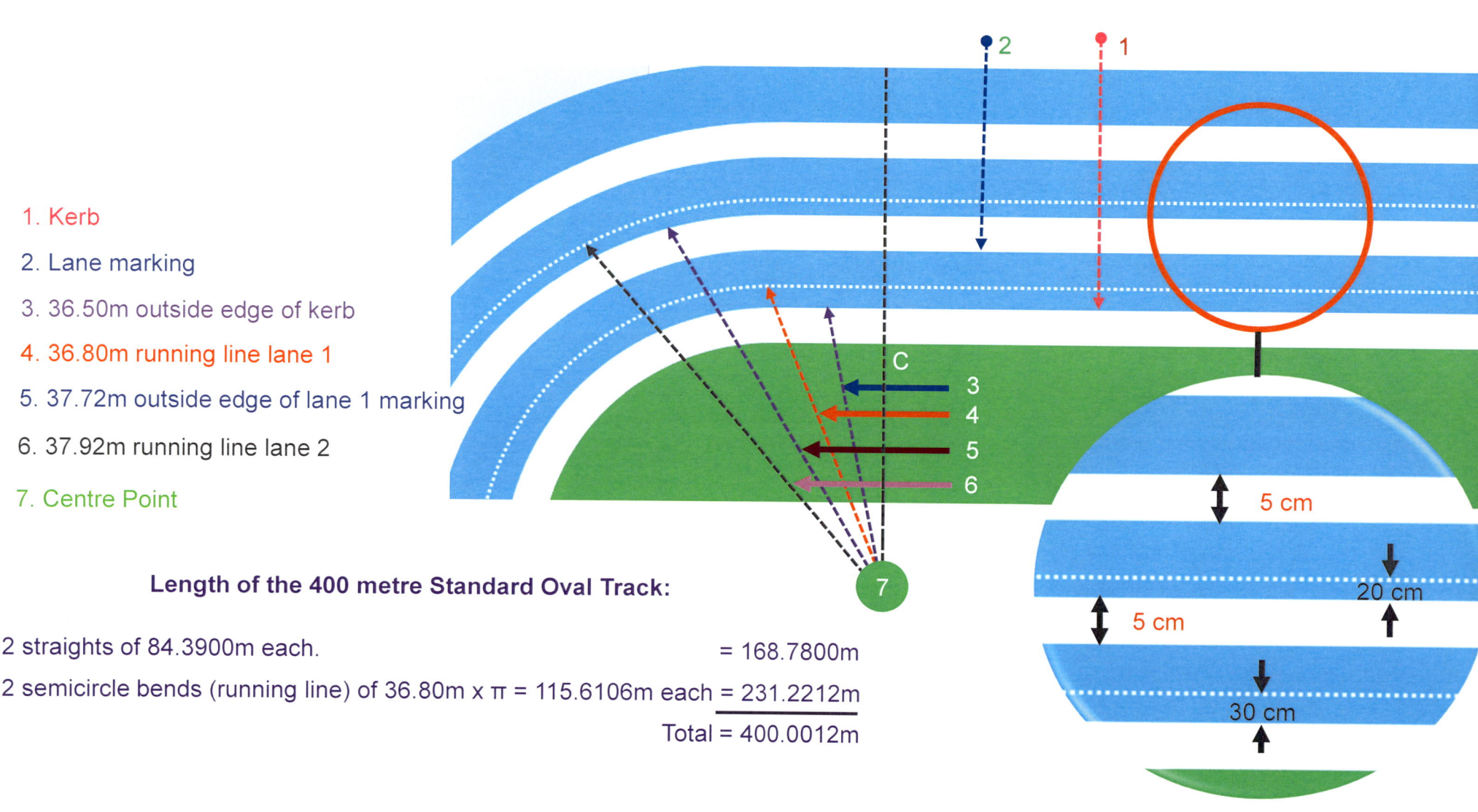

Setting Out Plan and Dimensions of the 400 Metre Standard Oval Track

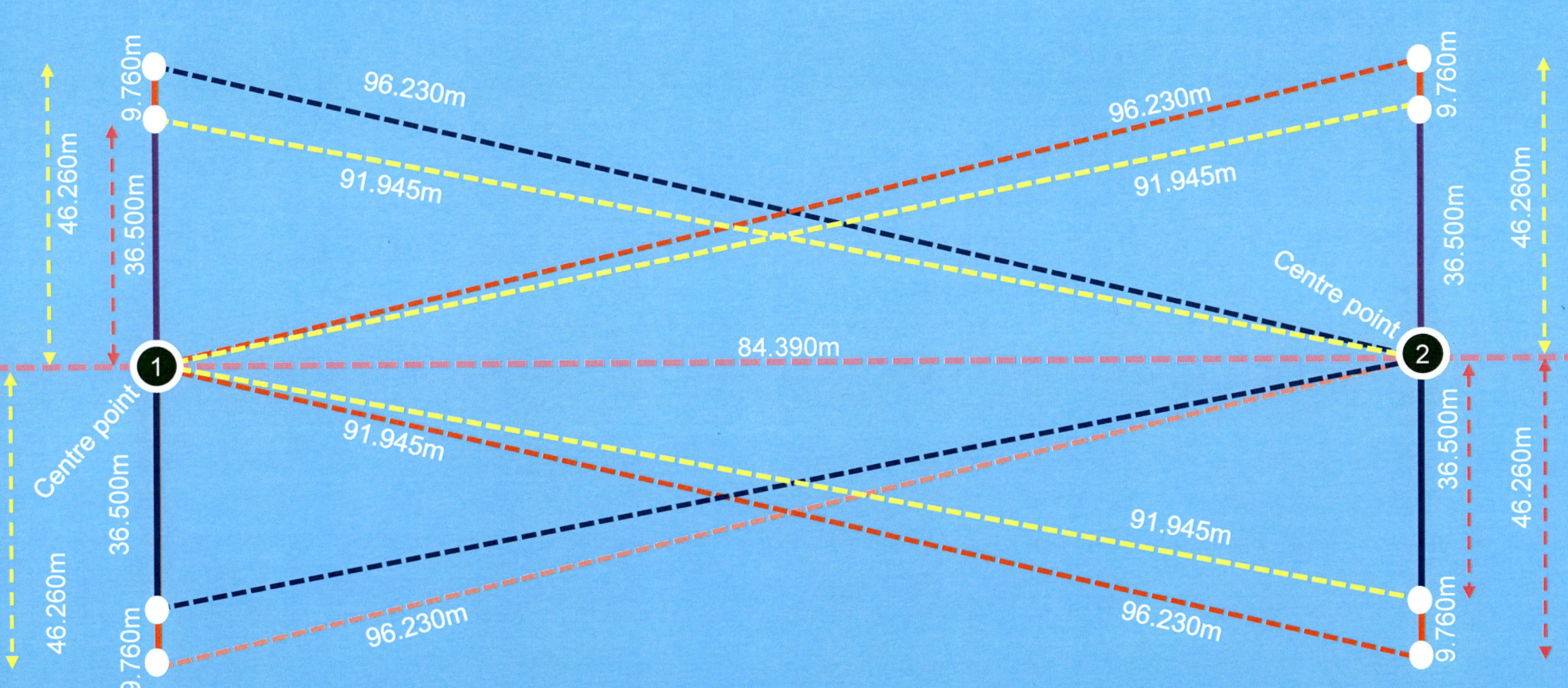

Setting Out Plan and Dimensions of the 400 Metre Standard Oval Track

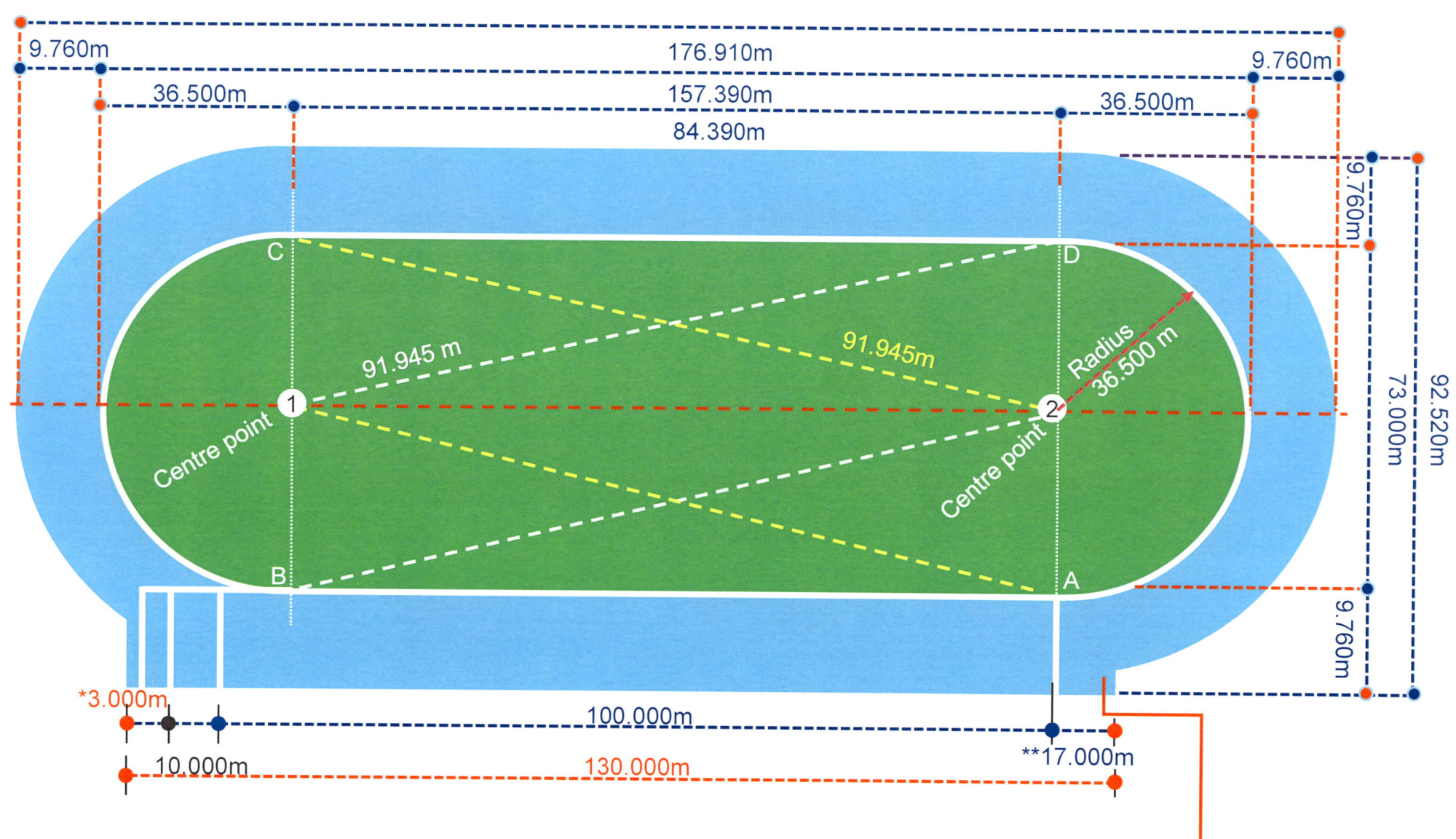

*The straight shall incorporate a starting area, *3m minimum., and run-out, **17m minimum

28 - Point Control Measurement of 400 Metre Standard Oval Track

The dimensional accuracy of the 400m Standard Track, required for all categories of competition, is deemed fulfilled if the following set values are attained in the "28-point control measurement" on the outside edge of the inner track border: 84.390m ± 0.005m for each of the two straights (2 readings). 36.500m ± 0.005m for 12 points per semicircle (including kerb) on the arc of the circle Approximately 10.42m apart (24 readings). Alignment of the kerb in the area of the two straights: no deviations greater than 0.010m (2 readings). Ideally, the length of the kerb in the straight and the length of the outer lane measured along the outside edge of the lane should be equal.

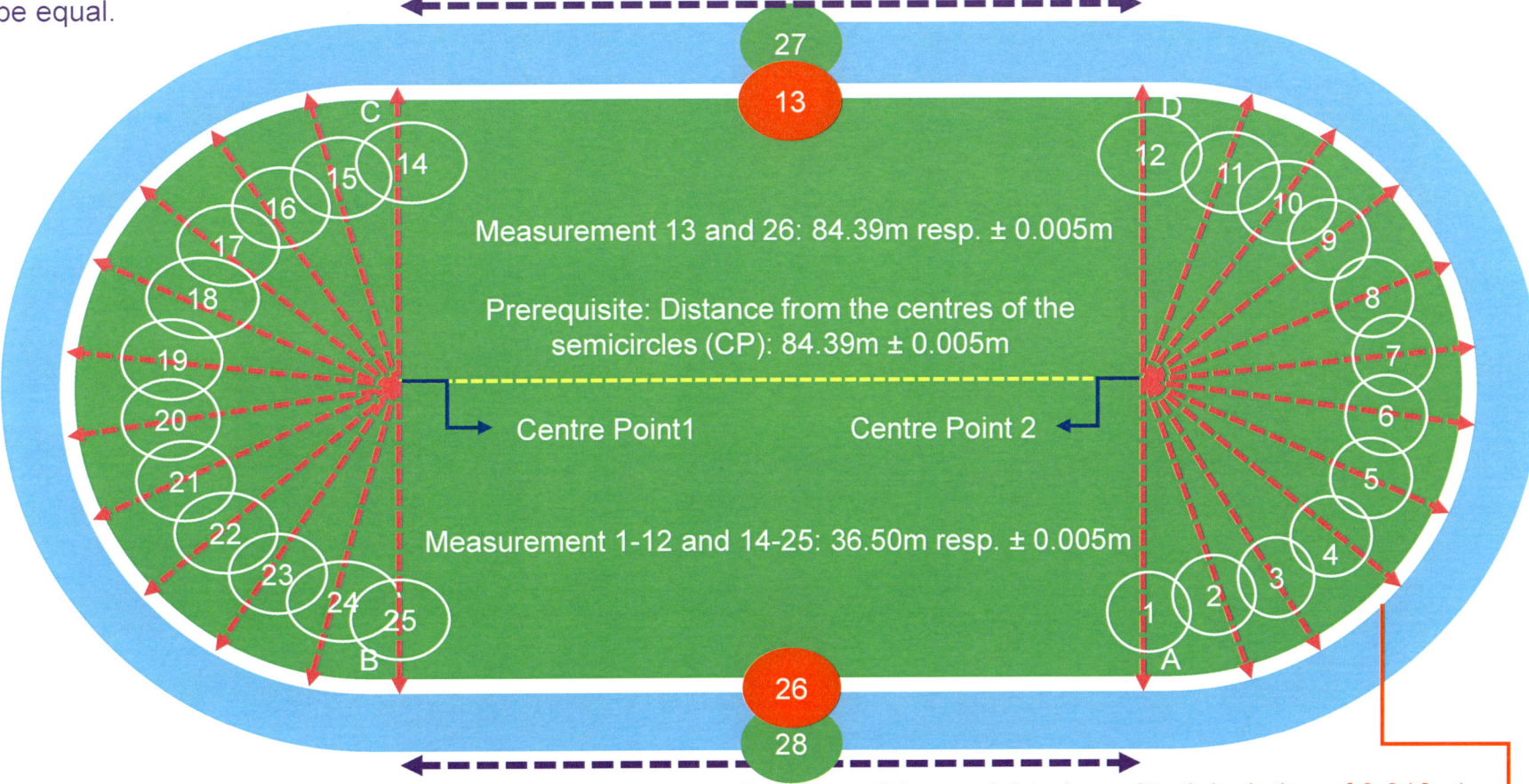

Measurement 13 and 26: 84.39m resp. ± 0.005m

Prerequisite: Distance from the centres of the semicircles (CP): 84.39m ± 0.005m

Centre Point 1 Centre Point 2

Measurement 1-12 and 14-25: 36.50m resp. ± 0.005m

Measurement 27 and 28: alignment of the straights (permitted deviation of 0.010m).

The readings ascertained for 1-12 and 14-25 must be equalized in the light of the record of 28 point control measurement.

The track length calculated after equalization may not be less than 400.000m or more than 400.040m.

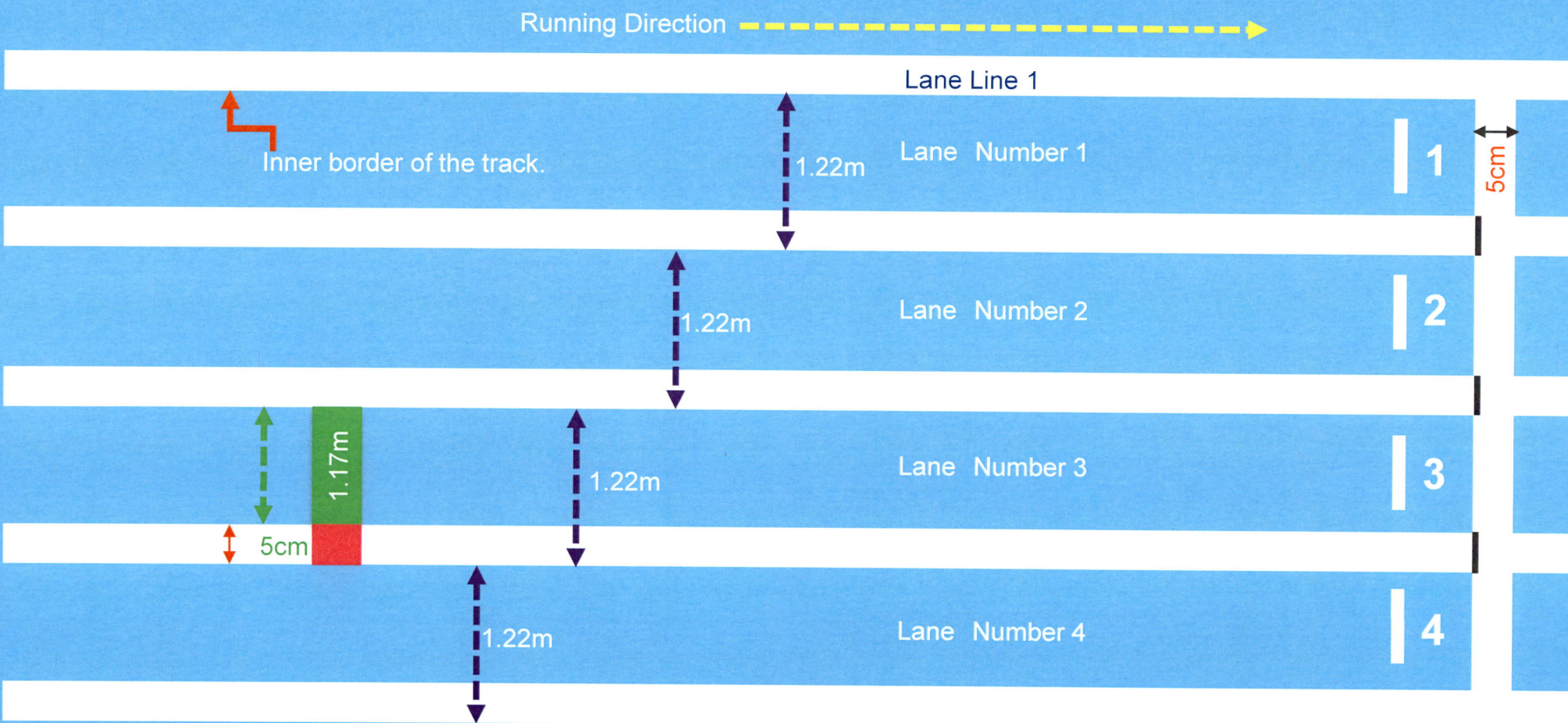

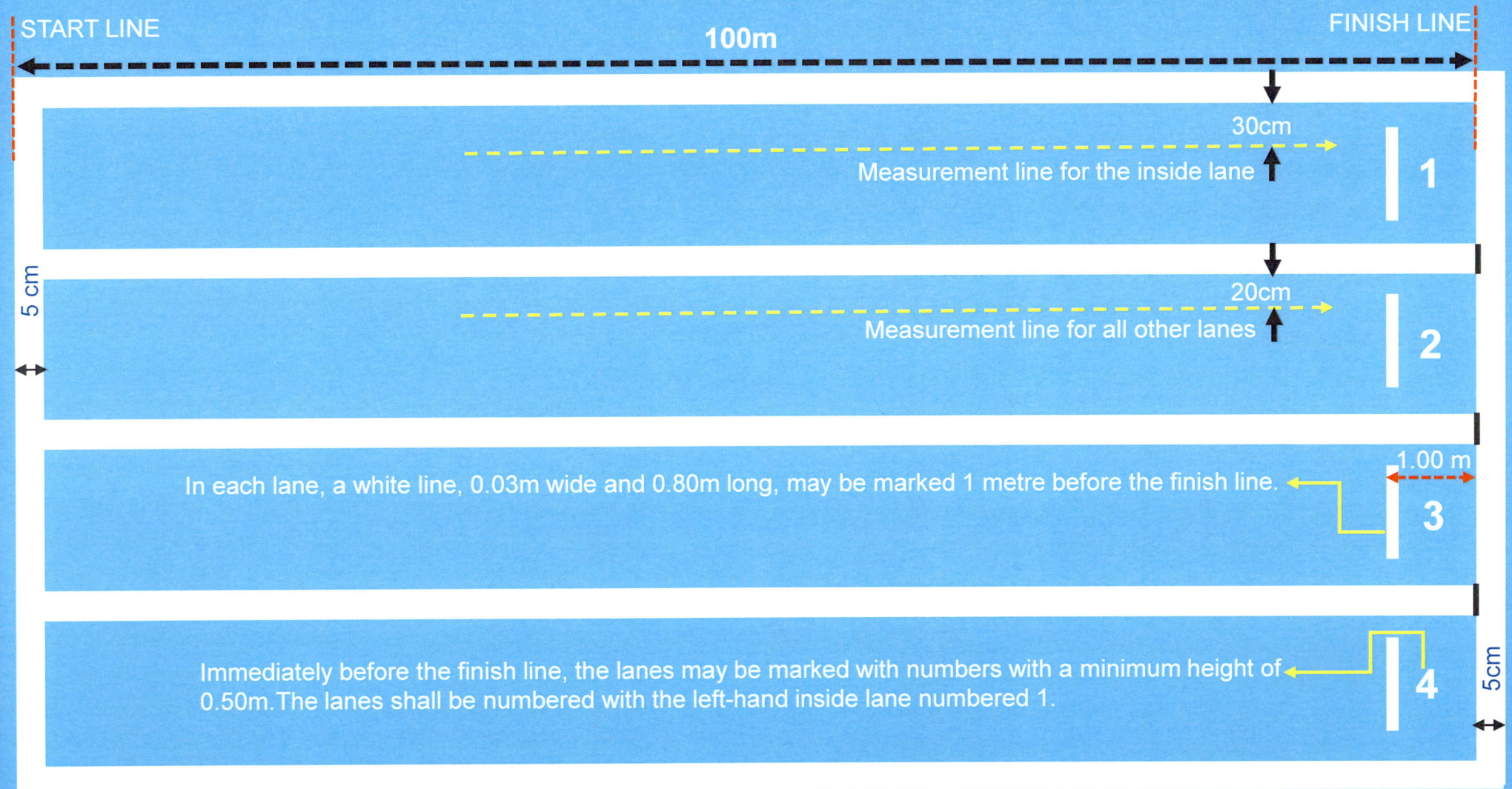

Black Rectangles

Finish line

*In order to confirm that the camera is correctly aligned and to facilitate the reading of the photo finish image, the intersection of the lane lines and the finish line shall be coloured black in a suitable design. Any such design must be solely confined to the intersection, for no more than 0.02m beyond, and not be extended before, the leading edge of the finish line. Similar black marks may be placed on each side of an appropriate lane line and the finish line to further facilitate reading.

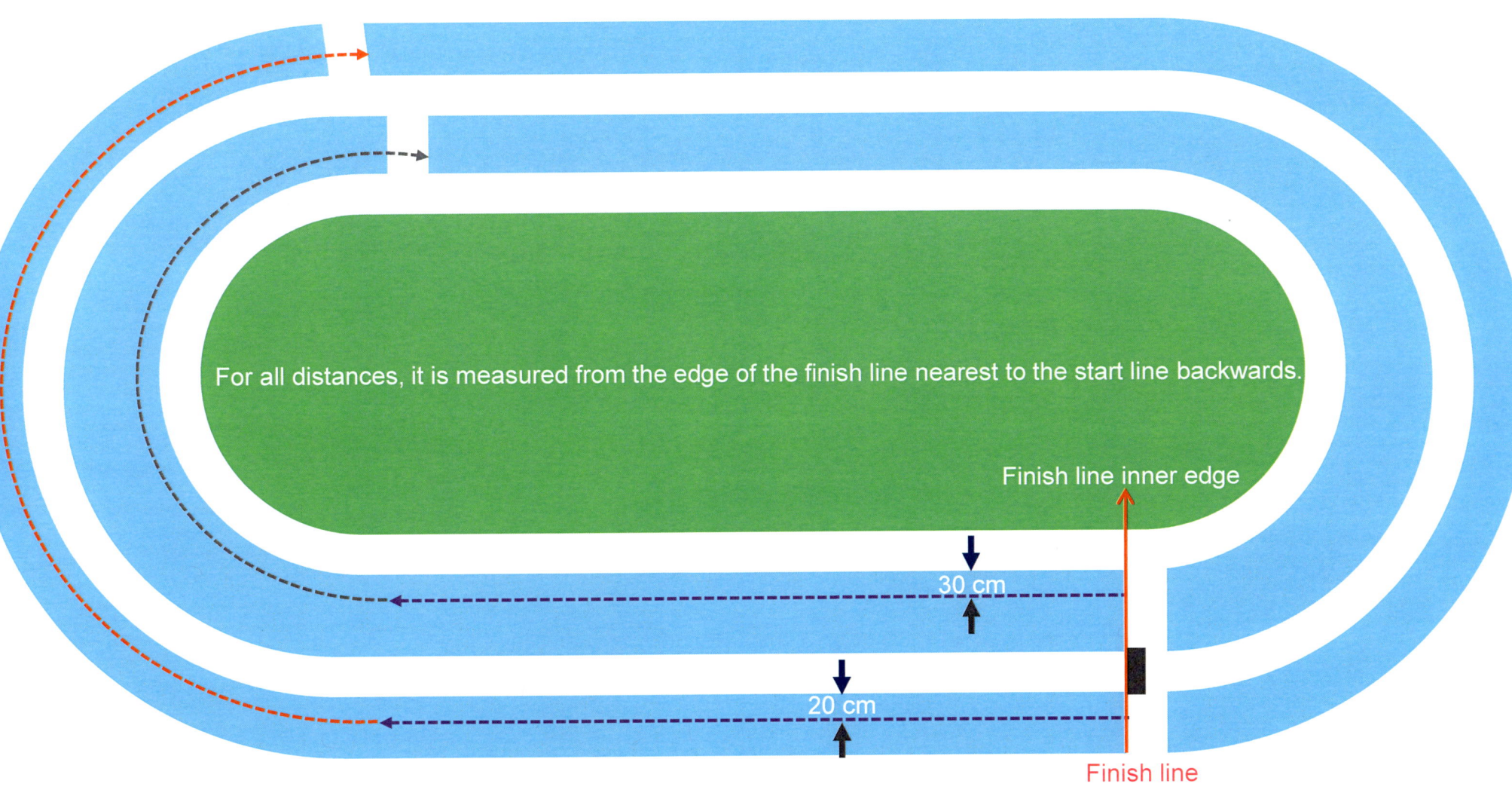

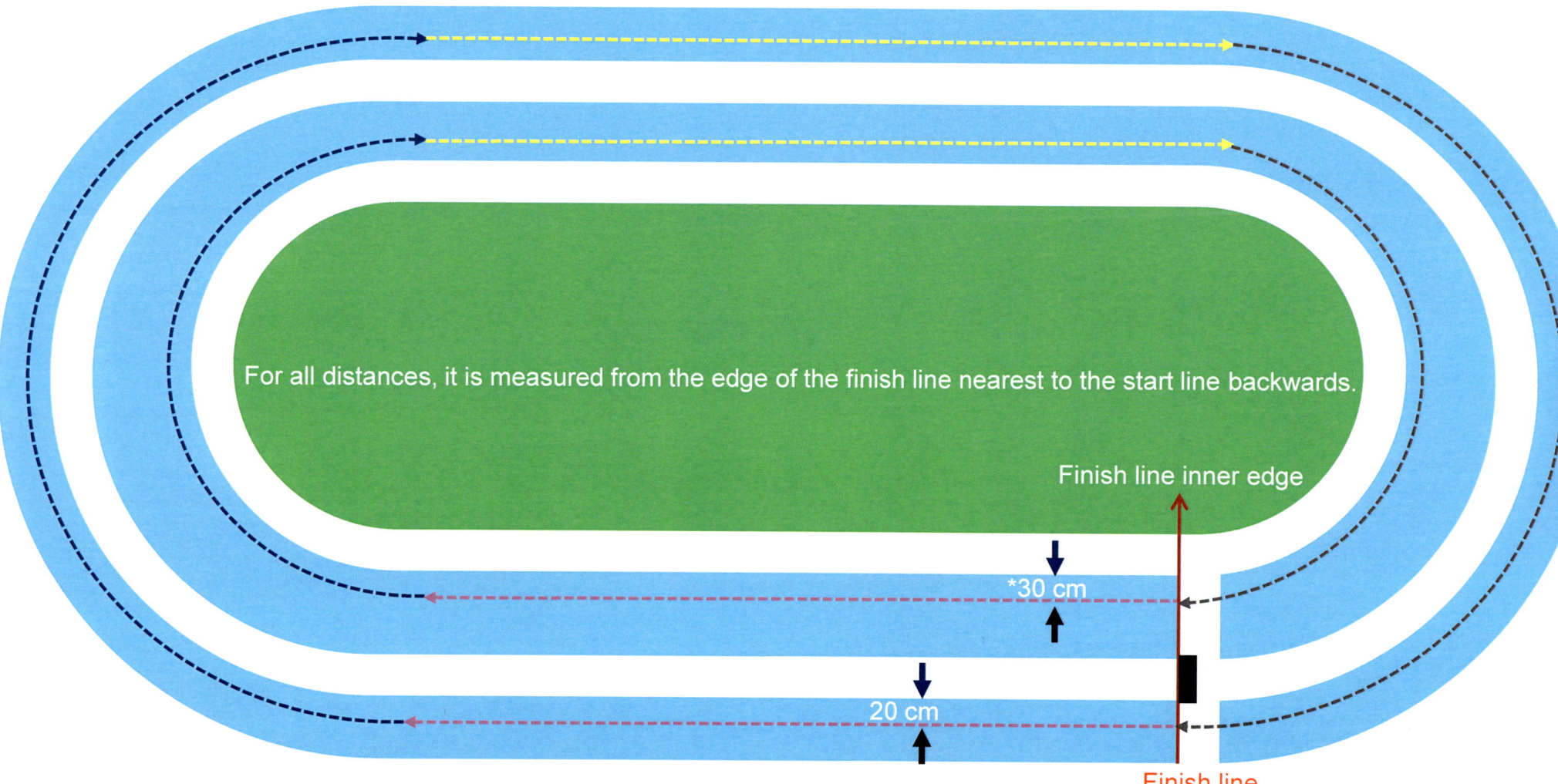

*The inner edge of the track is 398.116m in length (36.50m × 2 × π + 84.39m ×2). This length for the inner edge gives a length of 400.001m (36.80m × 2 × π + 84.39m × 2) for the theoretical running line (measurement line) at a distance of 0.30m outward from the kerb or the painted white line if the kerb is omitted from the straights only. The inside lane (lane 1) will, therefore, have a length of 400.001m along its theoretical running line. The length of each of the other lanes is measured along a theoretical running line 0.20m from the outer edge of the adjacent inside lane .

Calculation of Staggers (Measurements in Metres)
(For the track with raised kerb)

Stagger Formula W (n–1) – 0.10 X 2 π

W – Width of the lane

n – Number of the lane

π – Value 3.141

Example : Lane number 2 = 1.22 (2–1) – 0.10 X 2 X 3.1416 = 7.037

1 Stagger = 7.037

1/2 Stagger = 7.037 ÷ 2 = 3.519

1 1/2 Stagger = 7.037 + 3.519 = 10.556

Stagger	Lane Number 2	Lane Number 3	Lane Number 4	Lane Number 5	Lane Number 6	Lane Number 7	Lane Number 8
½	3.519	7.351	11.184	15.017	18.850	22.682	26.515
1	7.037	14.703	22.368	30.034	37.699	45.365	53.030
1 1/2	10.556	22.054	33.552	45.054	56.549	68.047	79.545

As per World Athletics suggestion, the π Value is 3.1416

Calculation of Breakline Distance
(For the track with raised kerb)

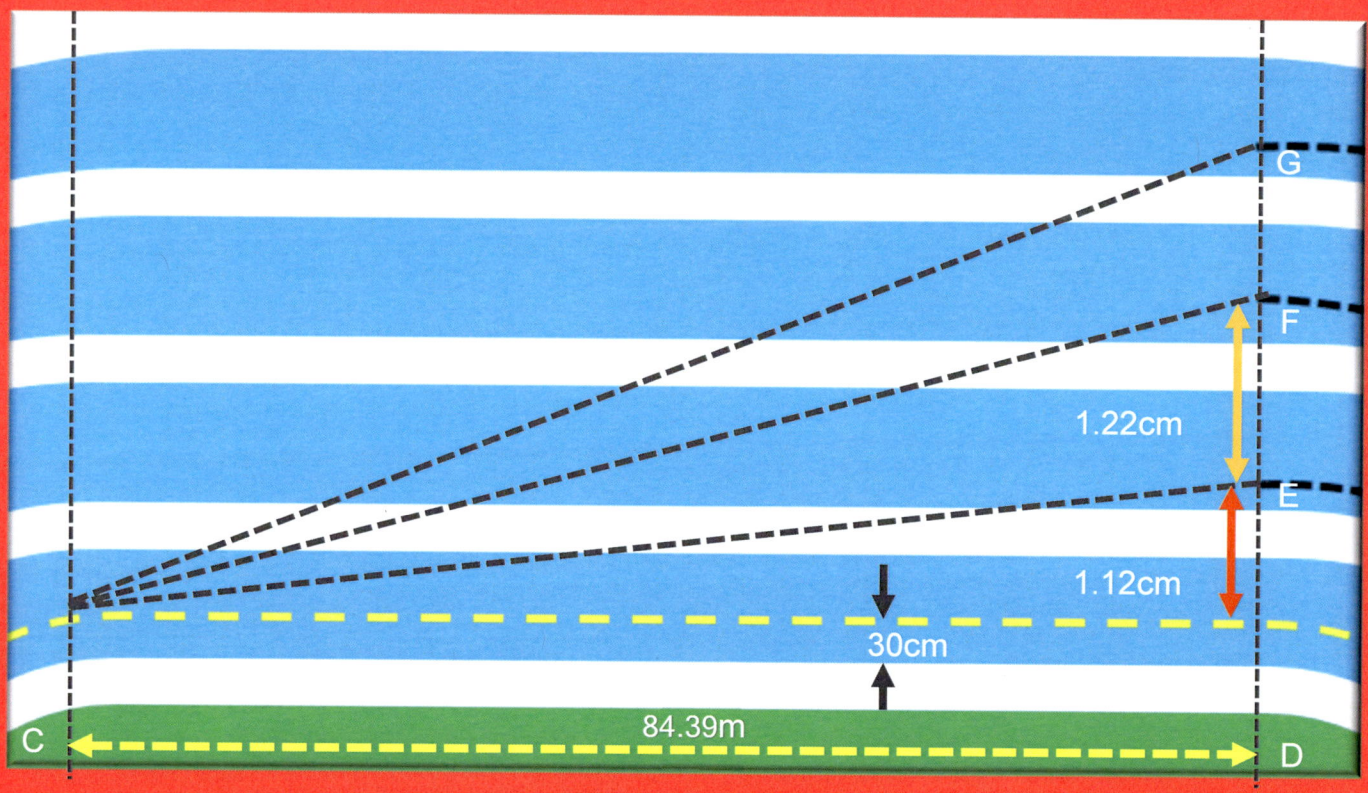

Example : Lane Number 3

$$CF = \sqrt{CD^2 + DF^2} - CD$$

$$= \sqrt{(84.39)^2 + (1.12+1.22)^2} - 84.39$$

$$= \sqrt{7121.6721 + 5.4756} - 84.39$$

$$= \sqrt{7127.1477} - 84.39$$

$$CF = 84.4224 - 84.39 = 0.032m$$

Lane Numbers	2	3	4	5	6	7	8
Breakline Distance	0.007m	0.032m	0.075m	0.134m	0.211m	0.305m	0.415m

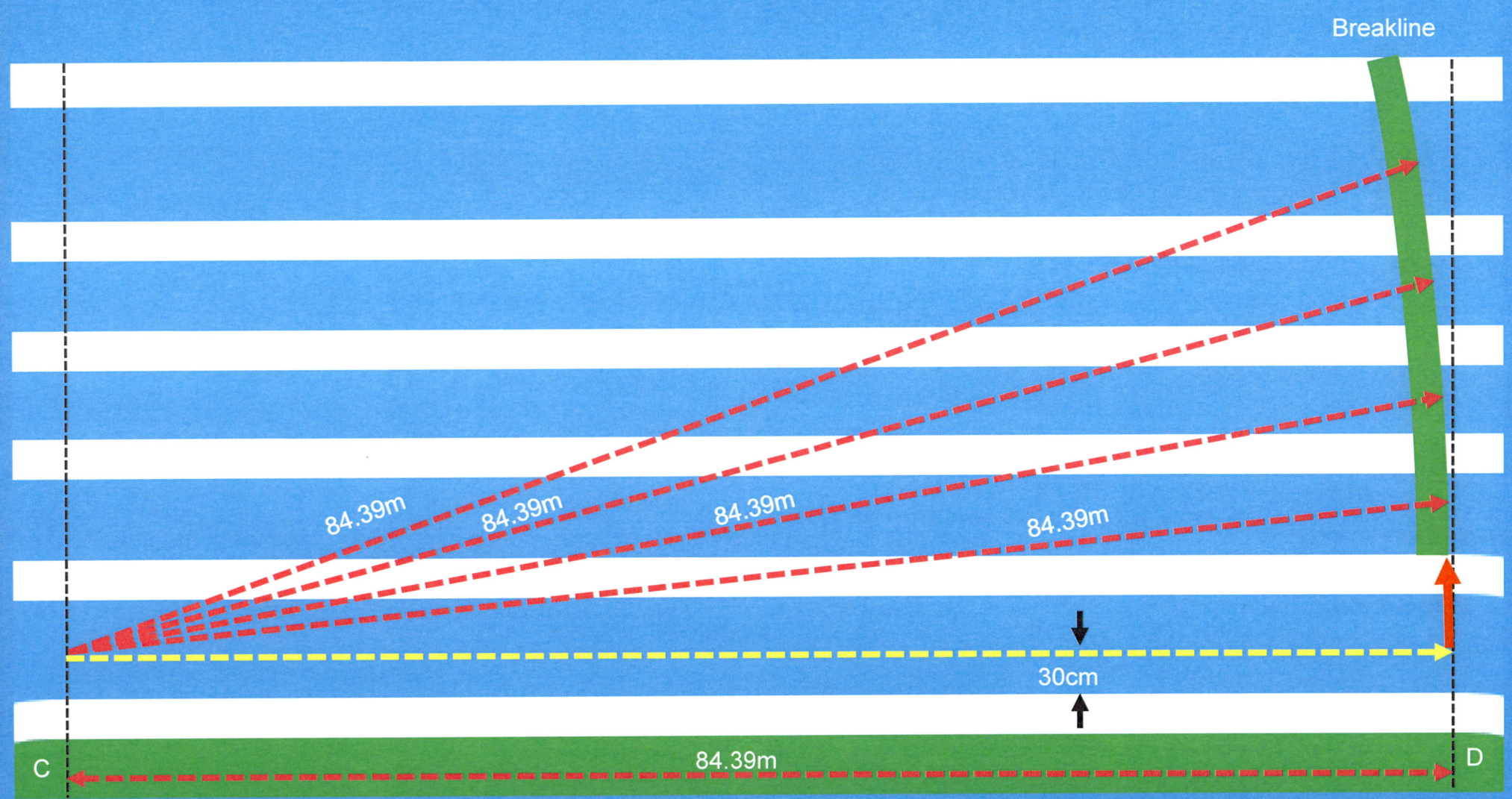

Staggered Start Data for the 400 Metre Standard Oval Track (Measurements in Metres)

Distance on Running Line	Marking Plan Area	Bends Run in Lanes	Lane Number 2	Lane Number 3	Lane Number 4	Lane Number 5	Lane Number 6	Lane Number 7	Lane Number 8
200	C	1	3.519	7.351	11.184	15.017	18.850	22.682	26.515
400	A	2	7.037	14.703	22.368	30.034	37.699	45.365	53.030
800	A	1	3.526	7.384	11.259	15.151	19.060	22.987	26.930
4X400	A	3	10.563	22.086	33.627	45.185	56.760	68.352	79.960

Distance measured on the running line.

Track Markings

Color	Symbol	Size (m), Position	Stage	Event	Marking Plan Area
White		Full track width	Finish	All events	A
White		1.17 (full lane width)	Start	400m, 4 x 100mR	A
White		1.17 (full lane width)	Start	100mH*, 110mH**	B
White		1.17 (full lane width)	Start	200m = SL, 4 x 100mR 3rd athletes	C

All lines width: 0.05m.

TERMS & ABBREVIATIONS

*100 Metres Hurdles -100mH

**110 Metres Hurdles -110mH

Track Markings

Color	Symbol	Size (m), Position	Stage	Event	Marking Plan Area
White		Curve (full track width)	Start	2000m, 10,000m	A
White		Curve (full track width)	Start	1 Mile	A
White		Curve (full track width)	Start	2000m Steeplechase	A
White		Curve (full track width)	Start	1000m, 3000m, 5000m	C
White		Curve (full track width)	Start	3000mSC	C
White		Curve (full track width)	Start	1500m	D

All lines width: 0.05m.

Track Markings

Color	Symbol	Size (m), Position	Stage	Event	Marking Plan Area
White		Lanes 5 to 8 (Curve)	Start	Group start: 2000m, 10,000m	A
White		Lanes 5 to 8 (Curve)	Start	Group starts: 1000m, 3000m, 5000m,	C
White		0.40 in the middle	Scratch line (SL)	4 x 100mR 2nd and 4th athletes	B, D
White with red* inset		1.17 (full lane width), 0.40 in the middle	Start	4 x 400mR	A
White with green inset		1.17 (full lane width), 0.40 in the middle	Start	800m = SL, 4 x 400mR 2nd athletes	A

All lines width: 0.05m.   * For red coloured tracks, blue should be used.

Track Markings

Color	Symbol	Size (m), Position	Stage	Event	Marking Plan Area
Red*	⌐	0.80 from inner line, hook in 45°, outside 0.15m	ZE End of takeover zone (10m after SL)	4 x 400mR 2nd athletes	A
Red*	⌐	0.80 from inner line, hook in 45°, outside 0.15m	ZS Start of takeover zone (10m before SL)	4 x 400mR 2nd athletes	A
Red*	▬	0.80 in the middle 10m after finish line, parallel to finish line in lanes 2 to 5	ZE End of takeover zone (10m after SL)	For Relay races or parts of races not run in lanes e.g. 4 x 400mR 3rd and 4th athletes	A
Red*	▬	0.80 in the middle 10m before finish line in lanes 2 to 8	ZS Start of takeover zone (10m before SL)	For Relay races or parts of races not run in lanes e.g. 4 x 400mR 3rd and 4th athletes	A

All lines width: 0.05m.   * For red coloured tracks, blue should be used.

Track Markings

Color	Symbol	Size (m), Position	Stage	Event	Marking Plan Area
Yellow		1.10 from inner line, hook in 45°, outside 0.15	ZE End of takeover zone (10m after SL)	4 x 100mR 2nd, 3rd and 4th athletes	B,C,D
Yellow		1.10 from inner line, hook in 45°, outside 0.15	ZS Start of takeover zone (20m before SL)	4 x 100mR* 2nd, 3rd and 4th athletes	B,C,D
Green		Curve, lanes 2 to 8	Breakline	800m, 4 x 400mR ** 2nd athletes	D
Green	Lane 4 — lane 5	0.05 x 0.05 on the line between lanes 4 and 5	Break point	1000m, 3000m, 5000m group start	B

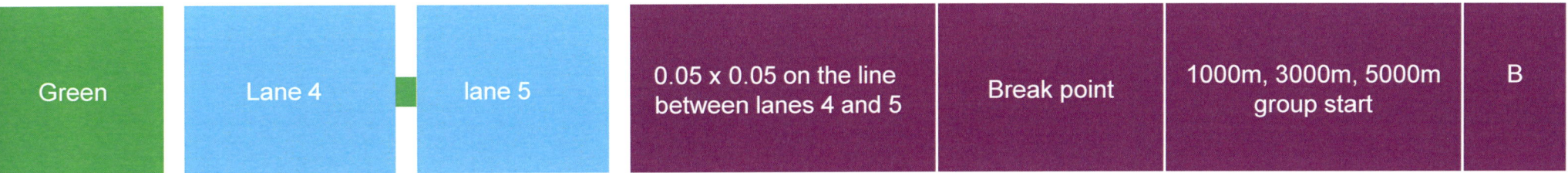

All lines width: 0.05m.

TERMS & ABBREVIATIONS

*4 × 100 Metres Relay - 4 × 100mR

**4 × 400 Metres Relay - 4 × 400mR

Marking of the Straight Incorporated within the 400 Metre Standard Oval Track Layout Plan
(Kerb width min. 0.05, dimensions in m)

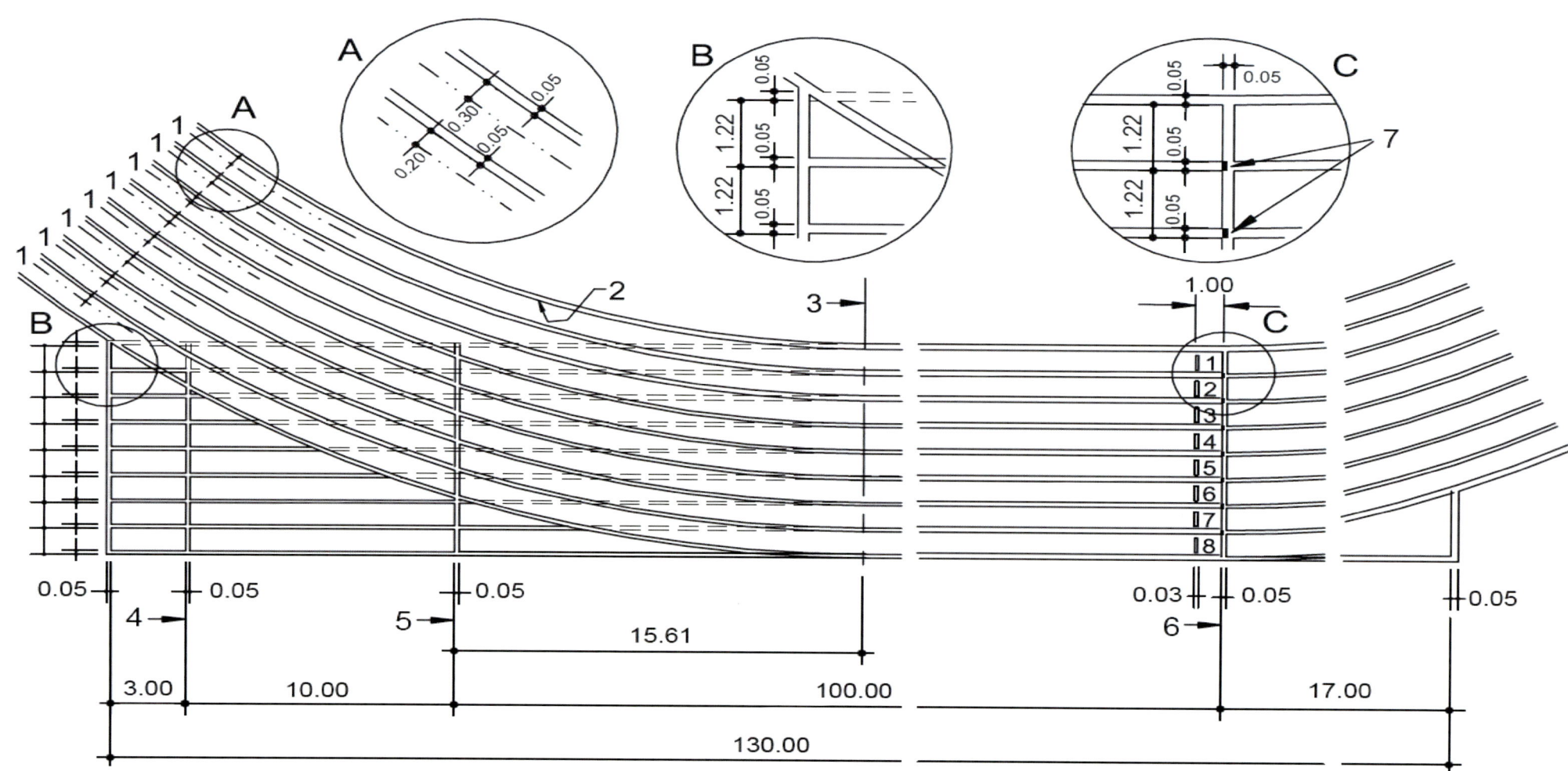

The straight as a component of the 400m standard Oval track

Marking of the Straight Incorporated within the 400 Metre Standard Oval Track Layout Plan
(Kerb width min. 0.05, dimensions in m)

1. Measurement line (running line) for oval track
2. Inside edge of track
3. Axis through semicircle centre
4. Start line for 110m Hurdles
5. Start line for 100m and Hurdlers
6. Finish line
7. Black rectangles 0.05m x 0.02m max.

Olympics Track Circumferences

Year	Circumference	Olympics Host
1896	400 Metre	Athens, Greece
1900	500 Metre	Paris France
1904	536.45 Metre	St. Louis, United States
1908	536.45 Metre	London, England
1912	383 Metre	Stockhlom, Sweden
1920	389.8 Metre	Antwerp, Belgium
1924	500 Metre	Paris France
1928 Onwards	400 Metre	Amsterdam, Netherlands

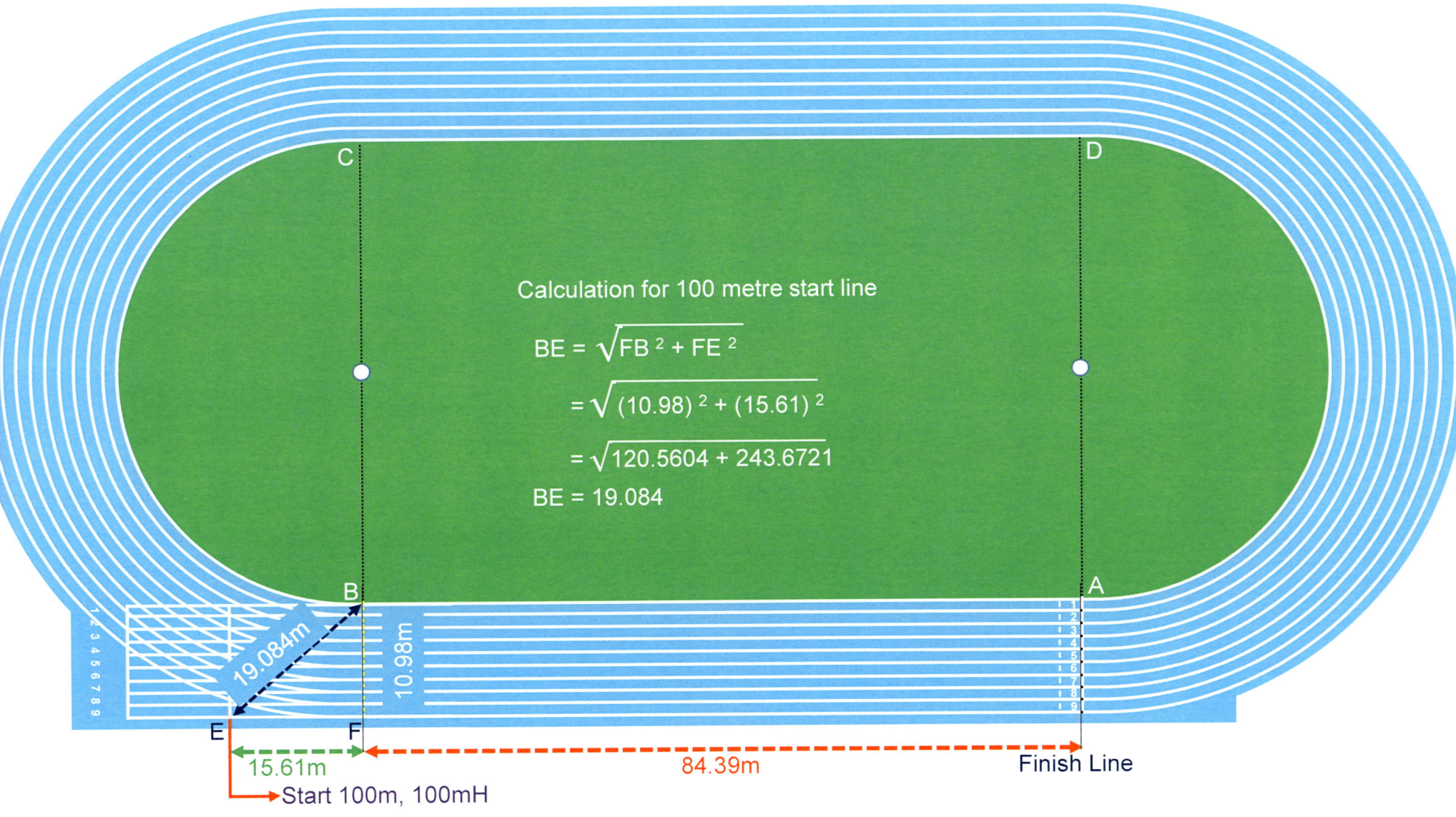

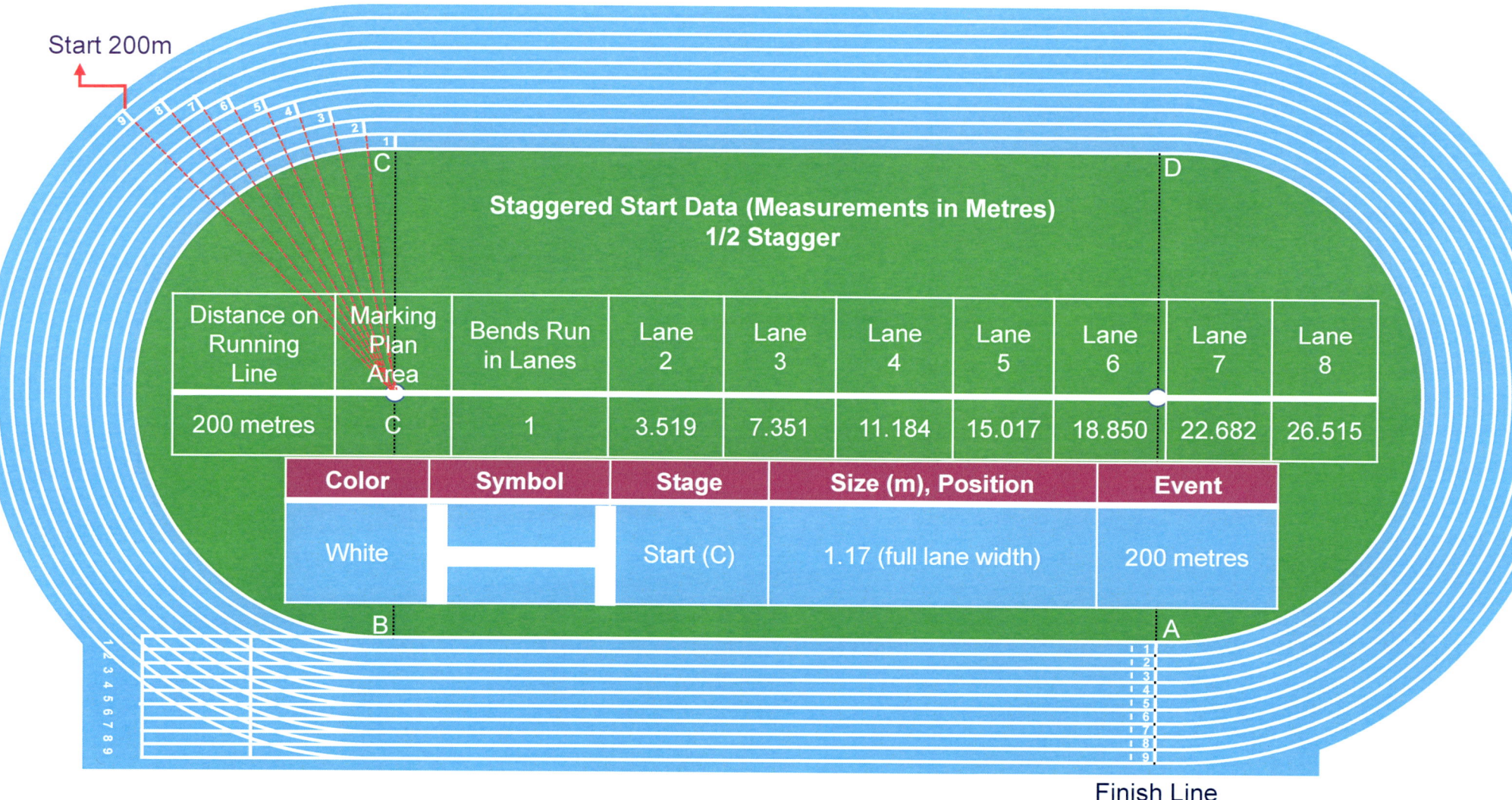

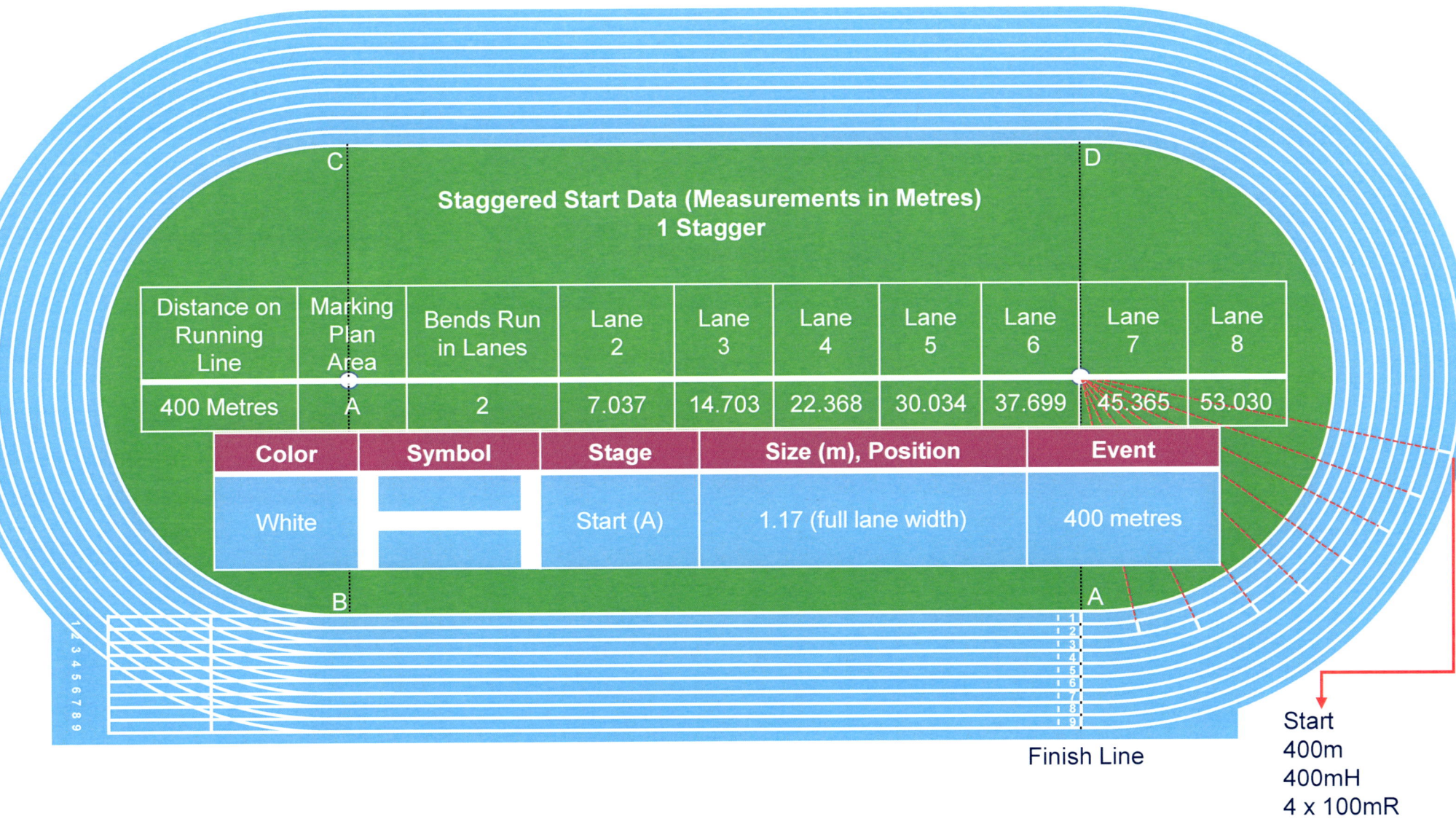

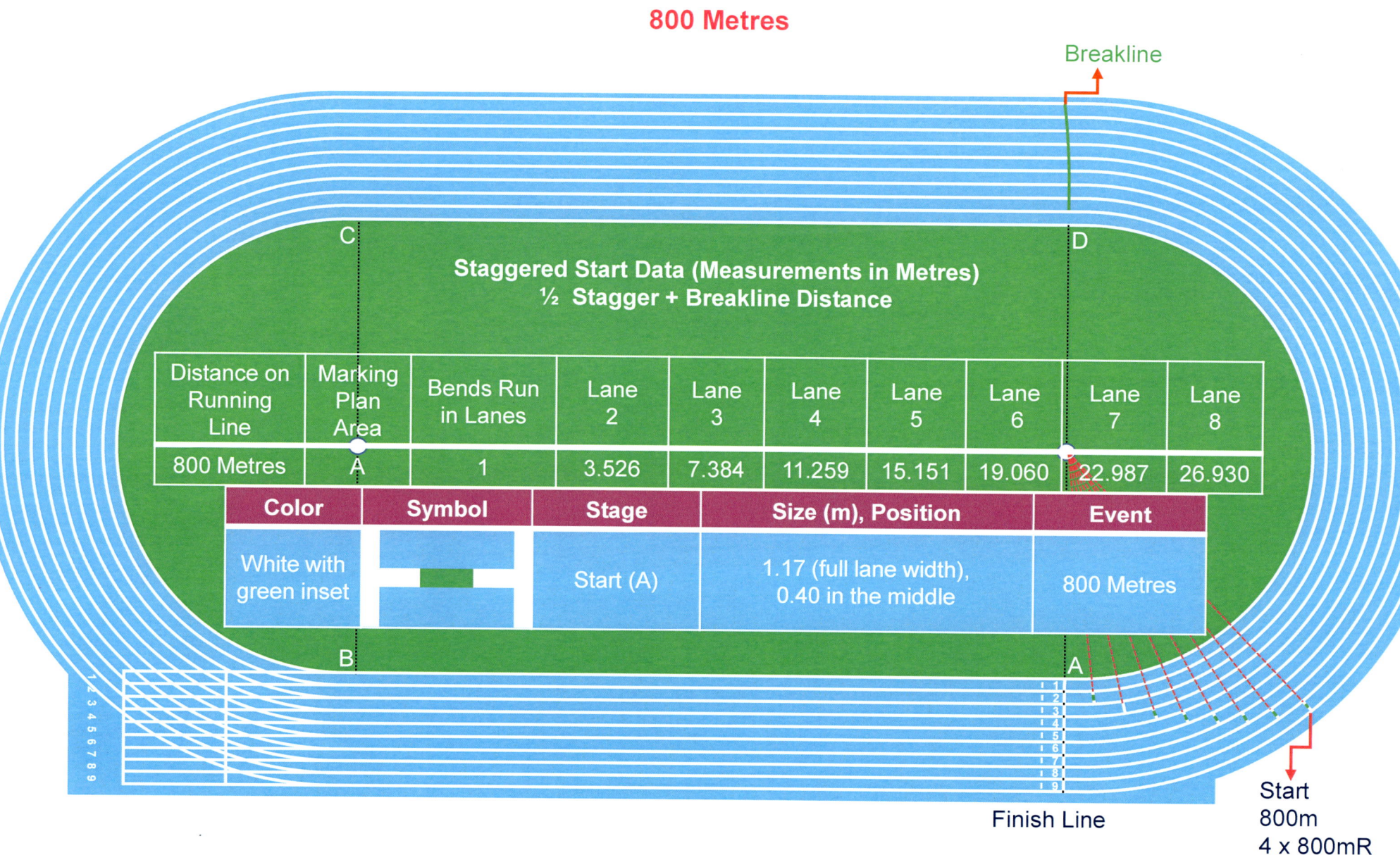

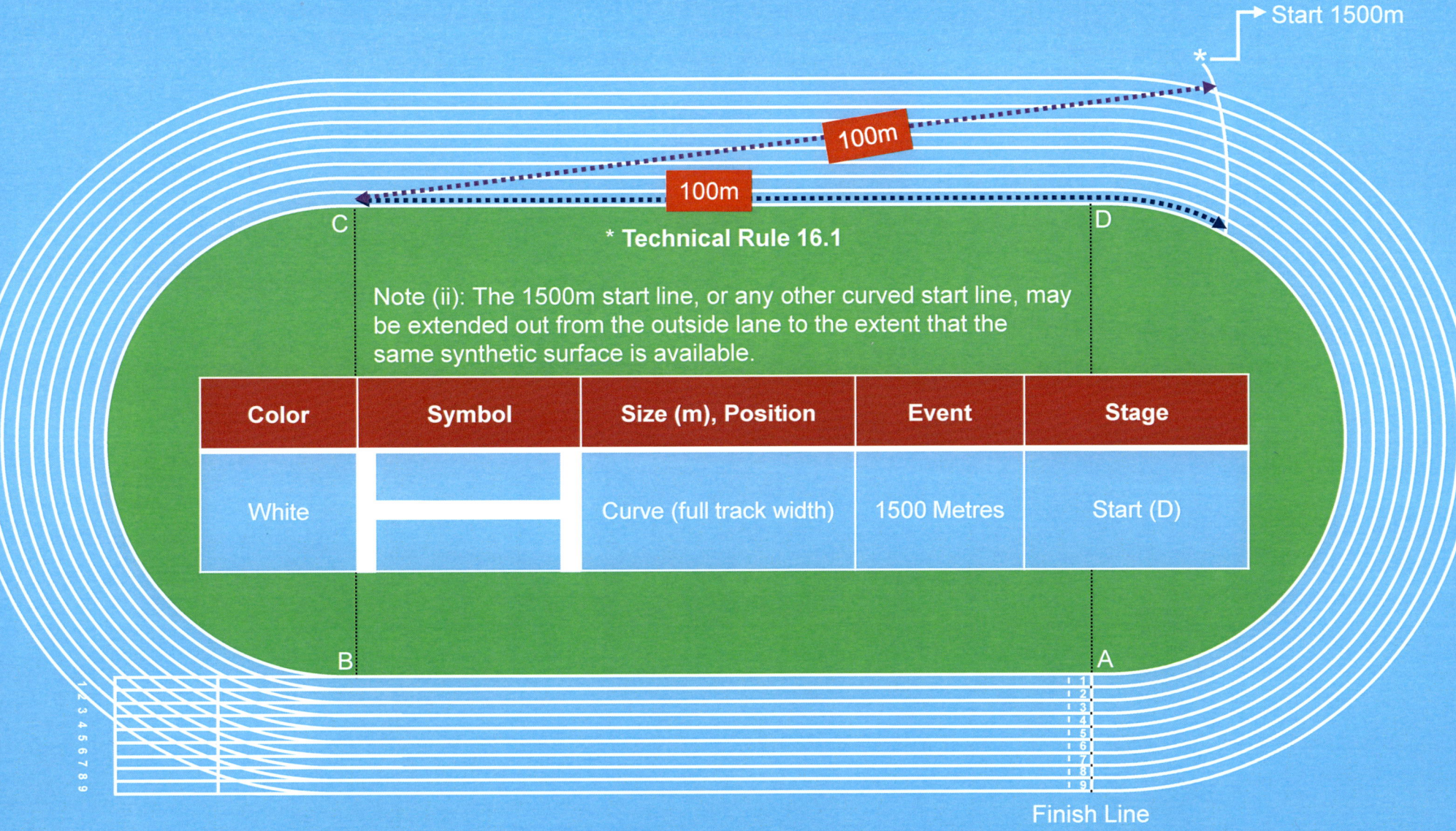

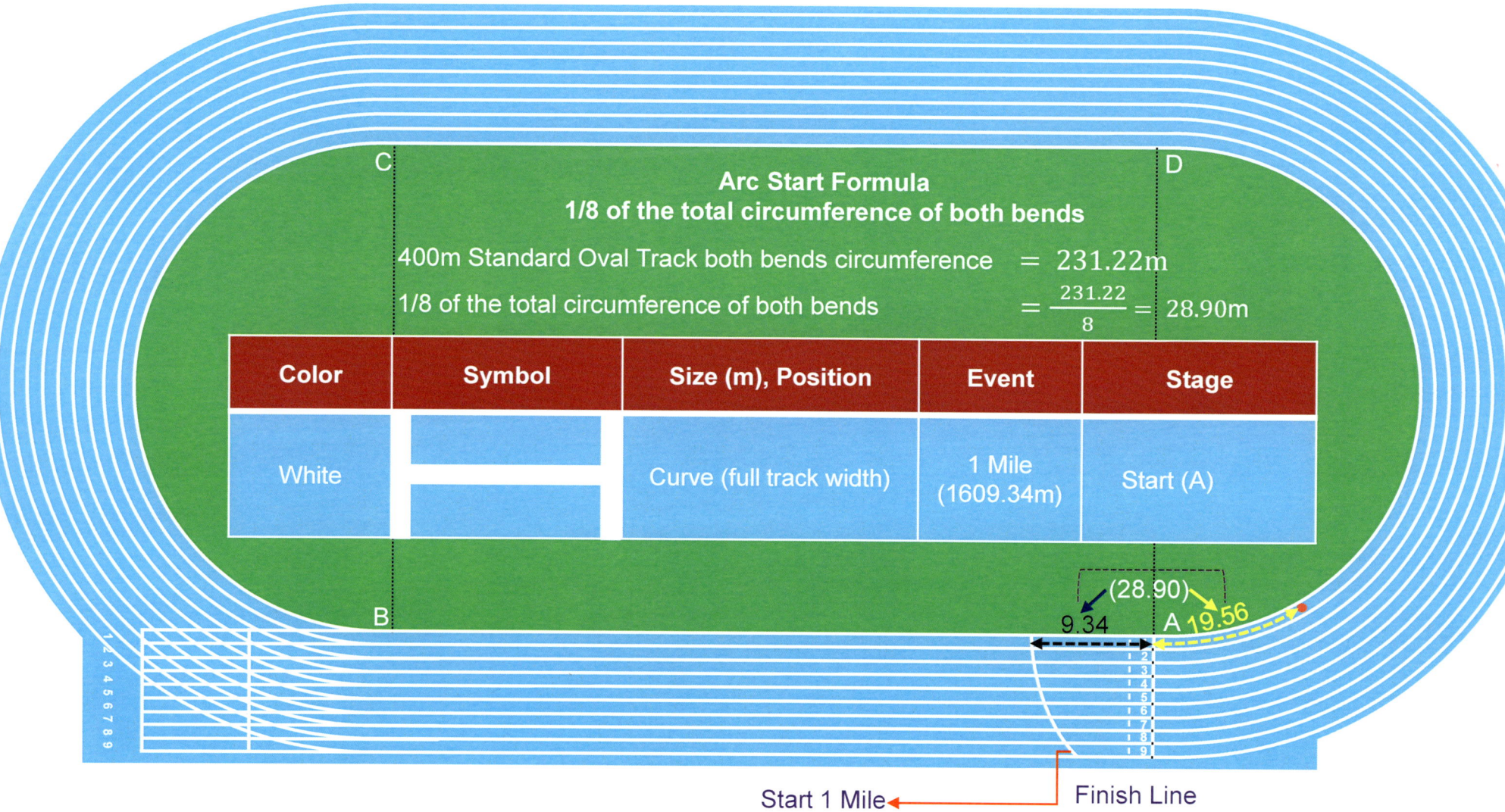

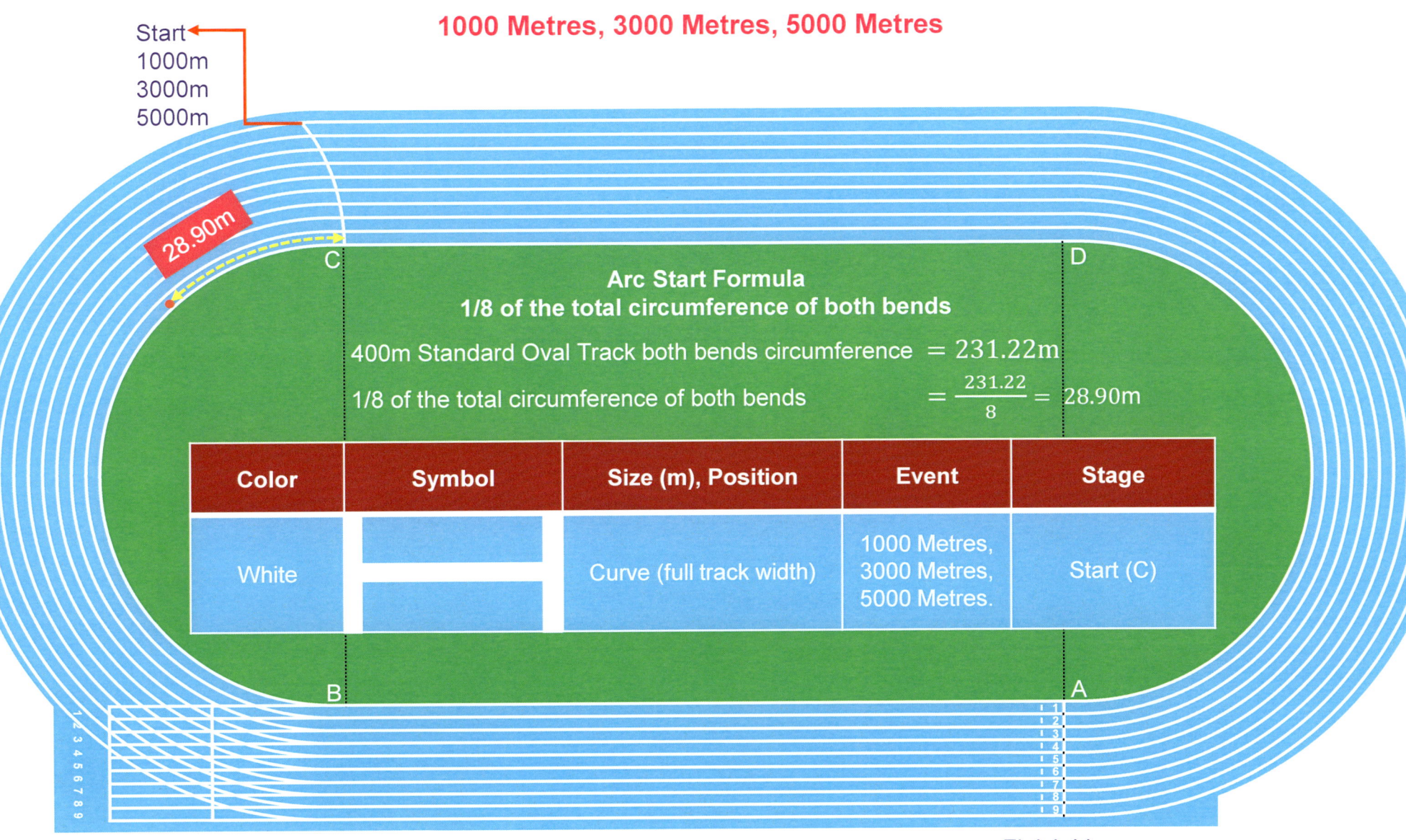

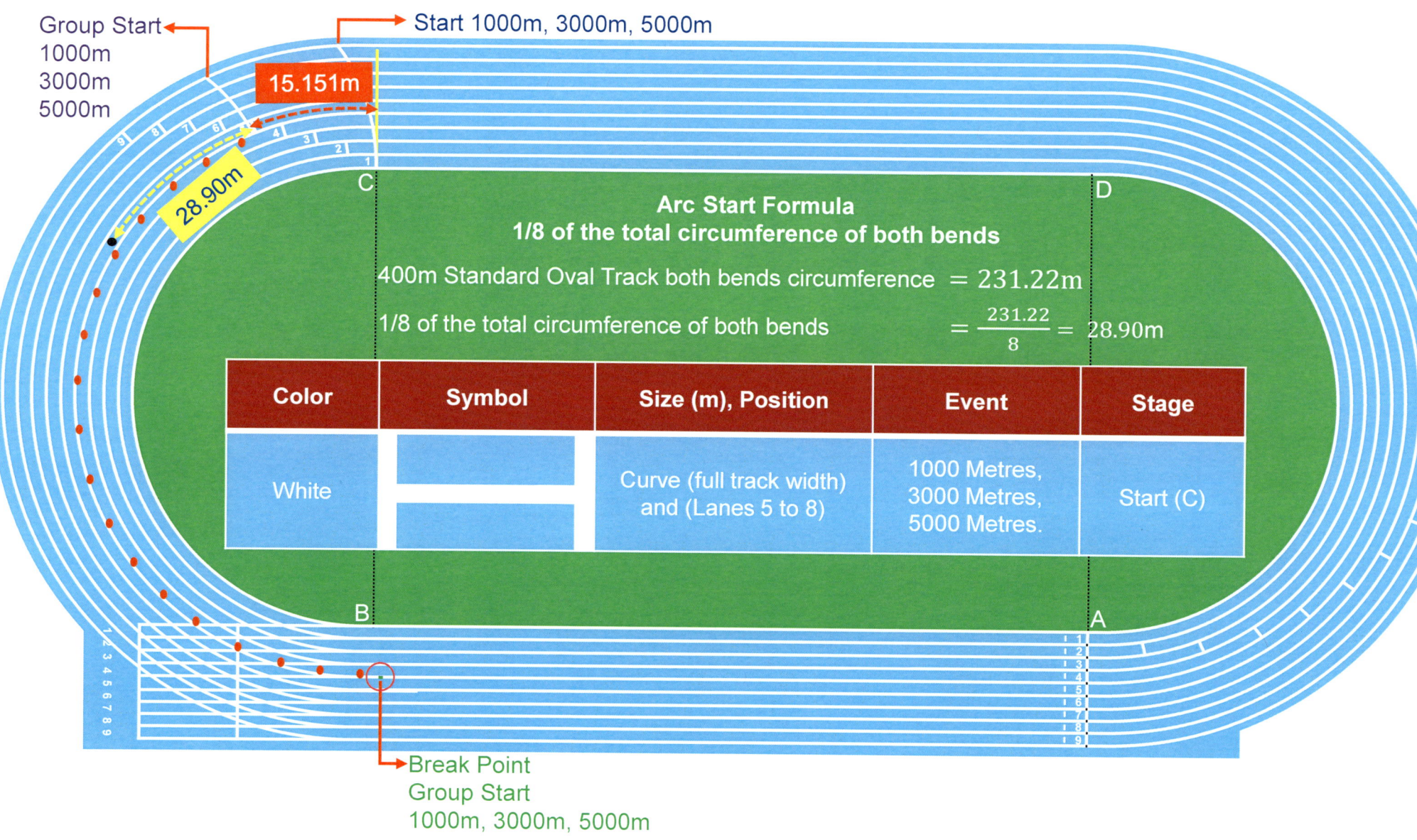

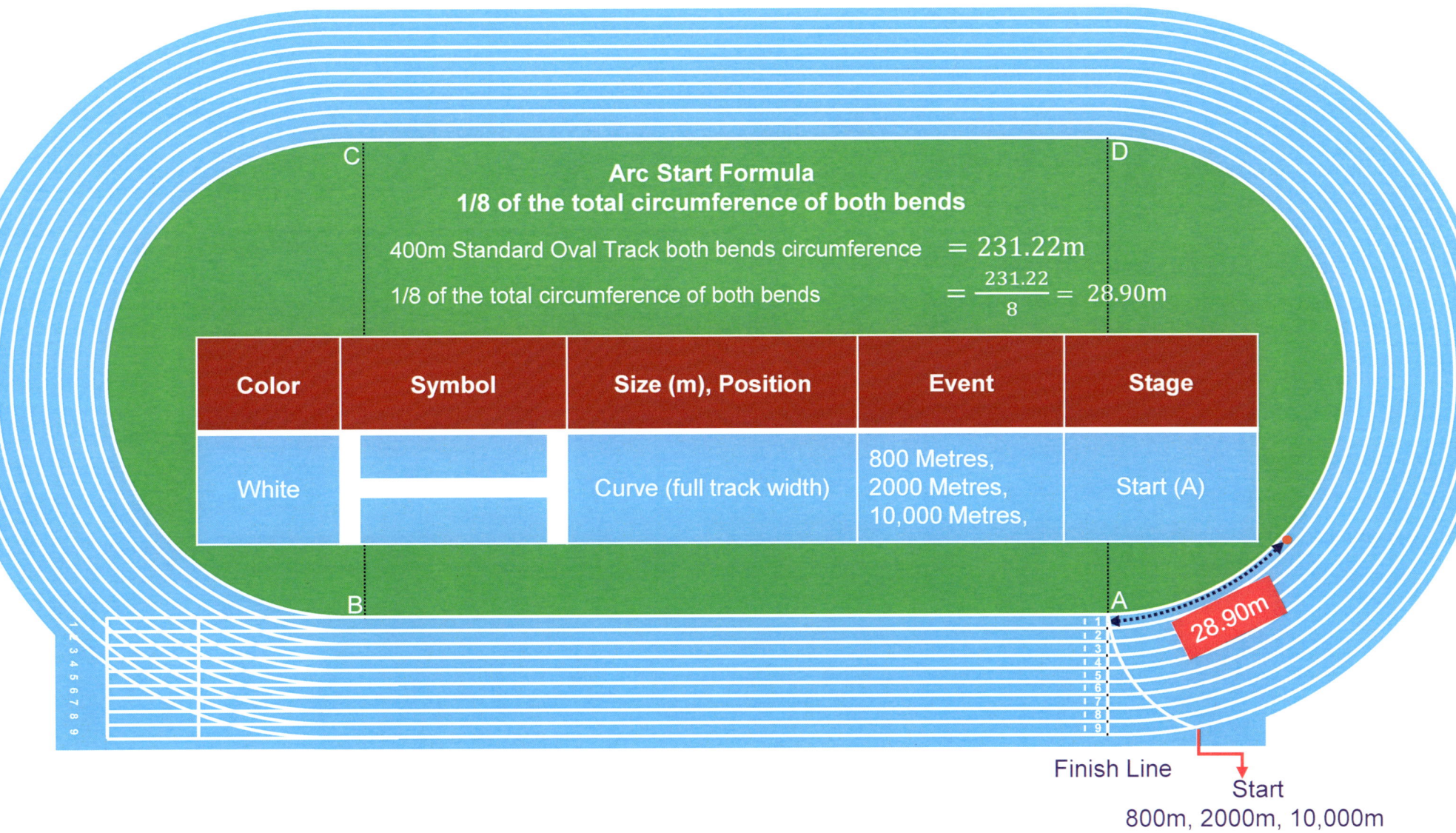

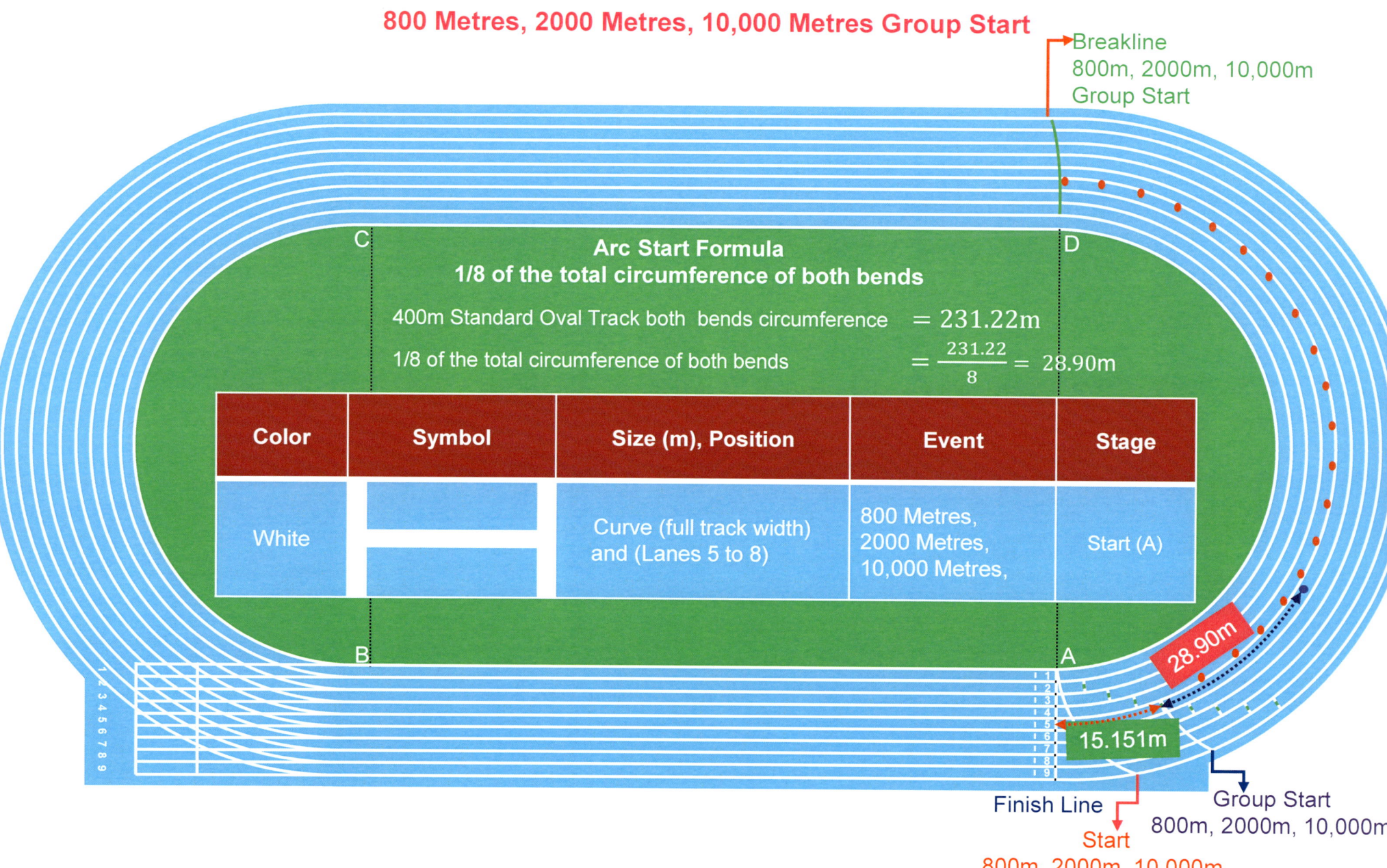

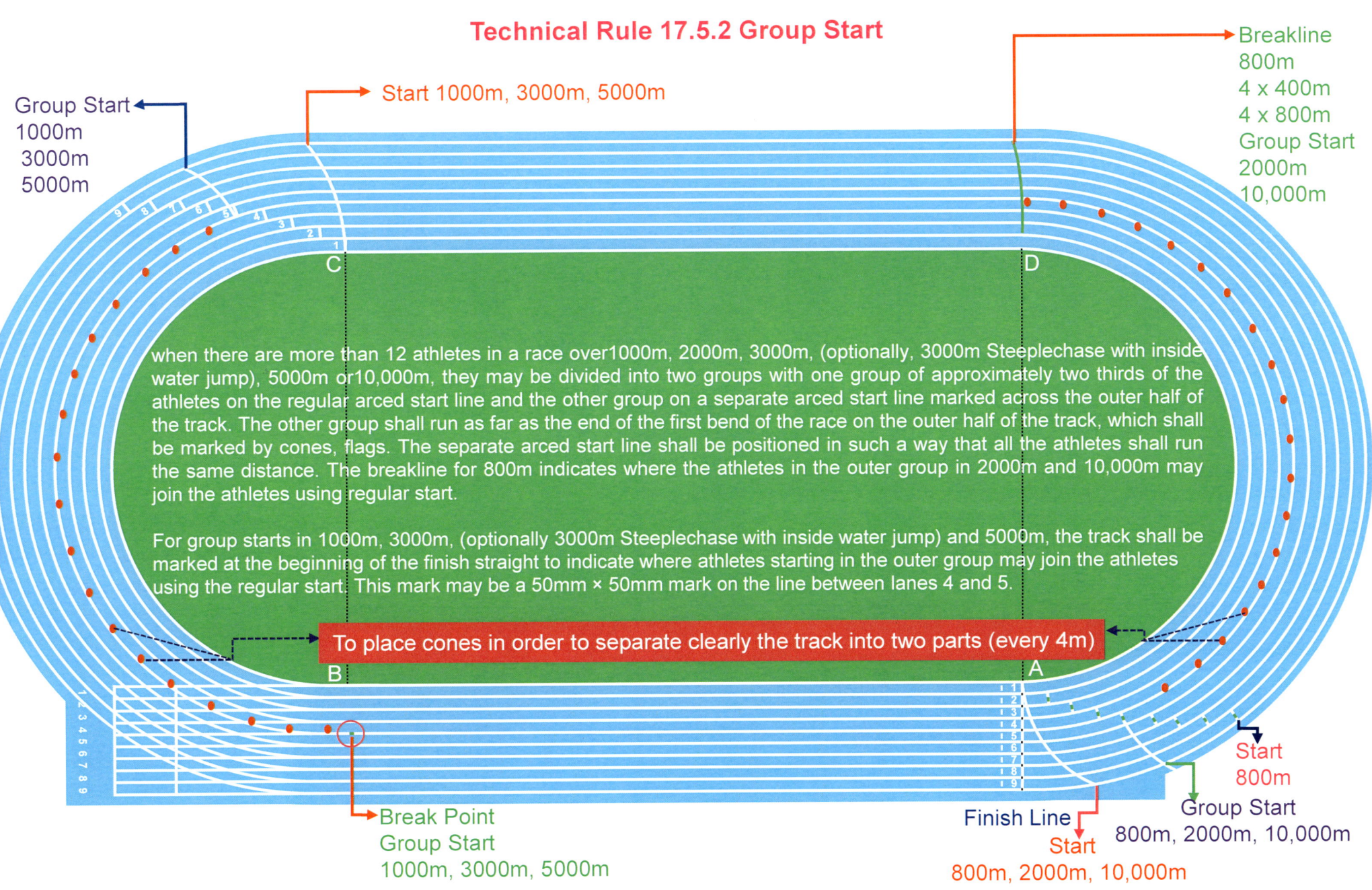

4 x 100 Metres Relay - Take Over Zone

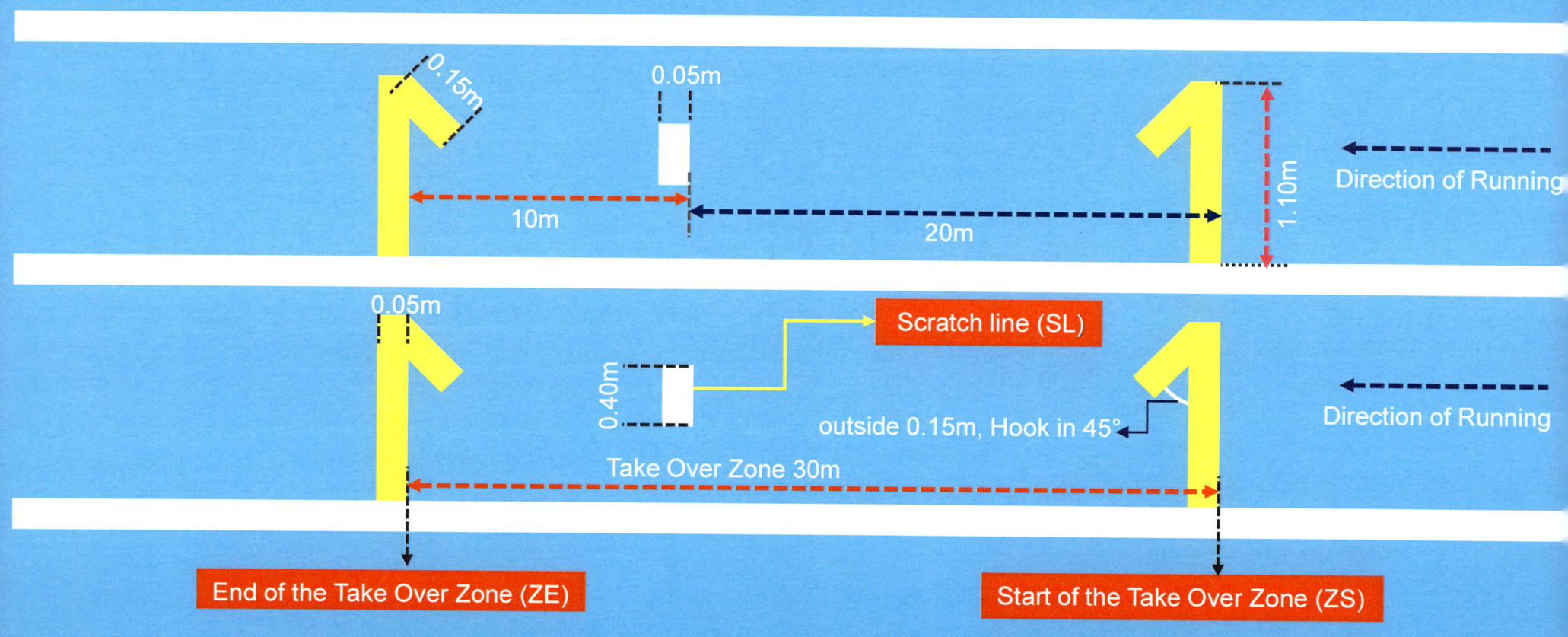

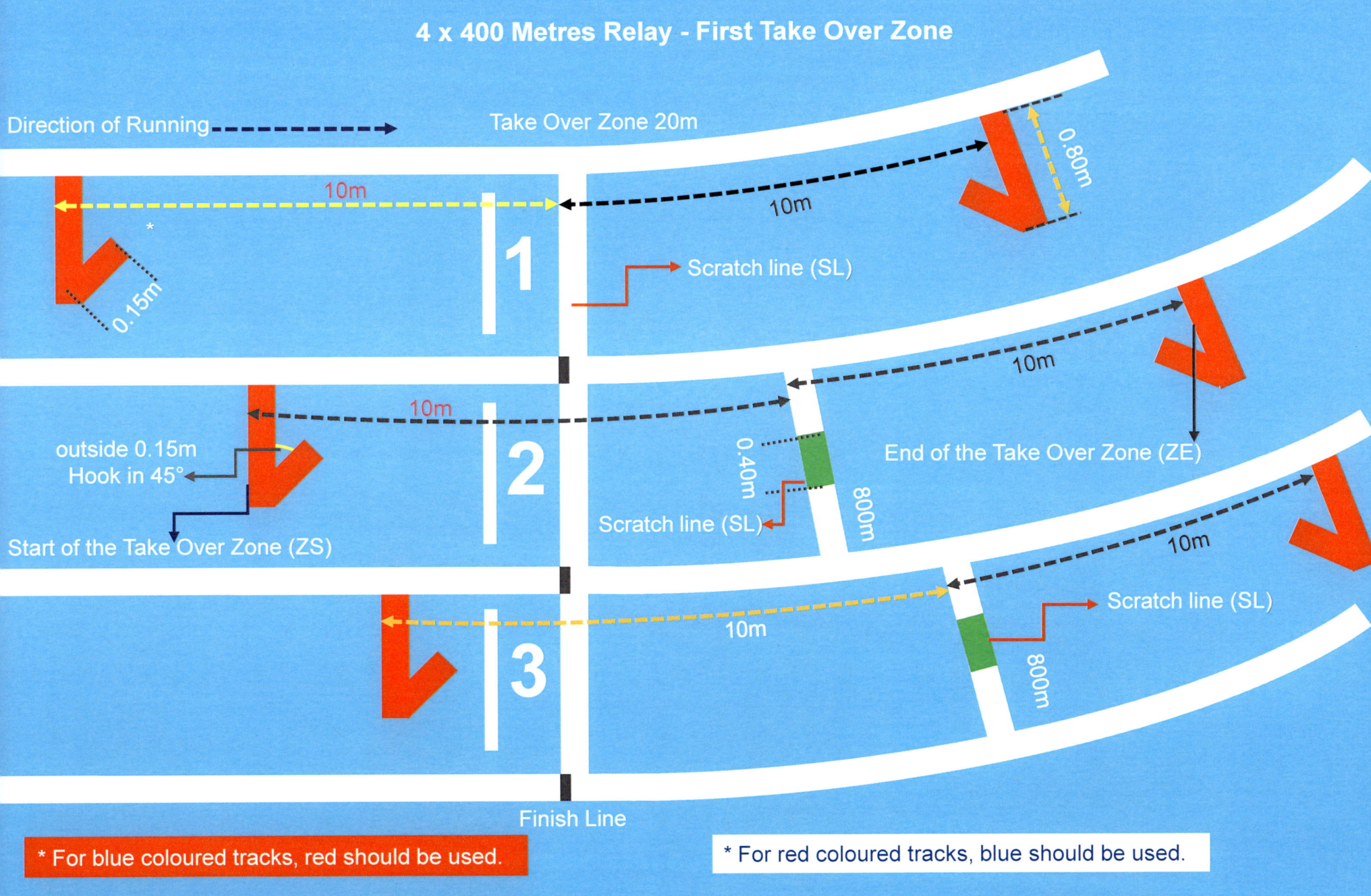

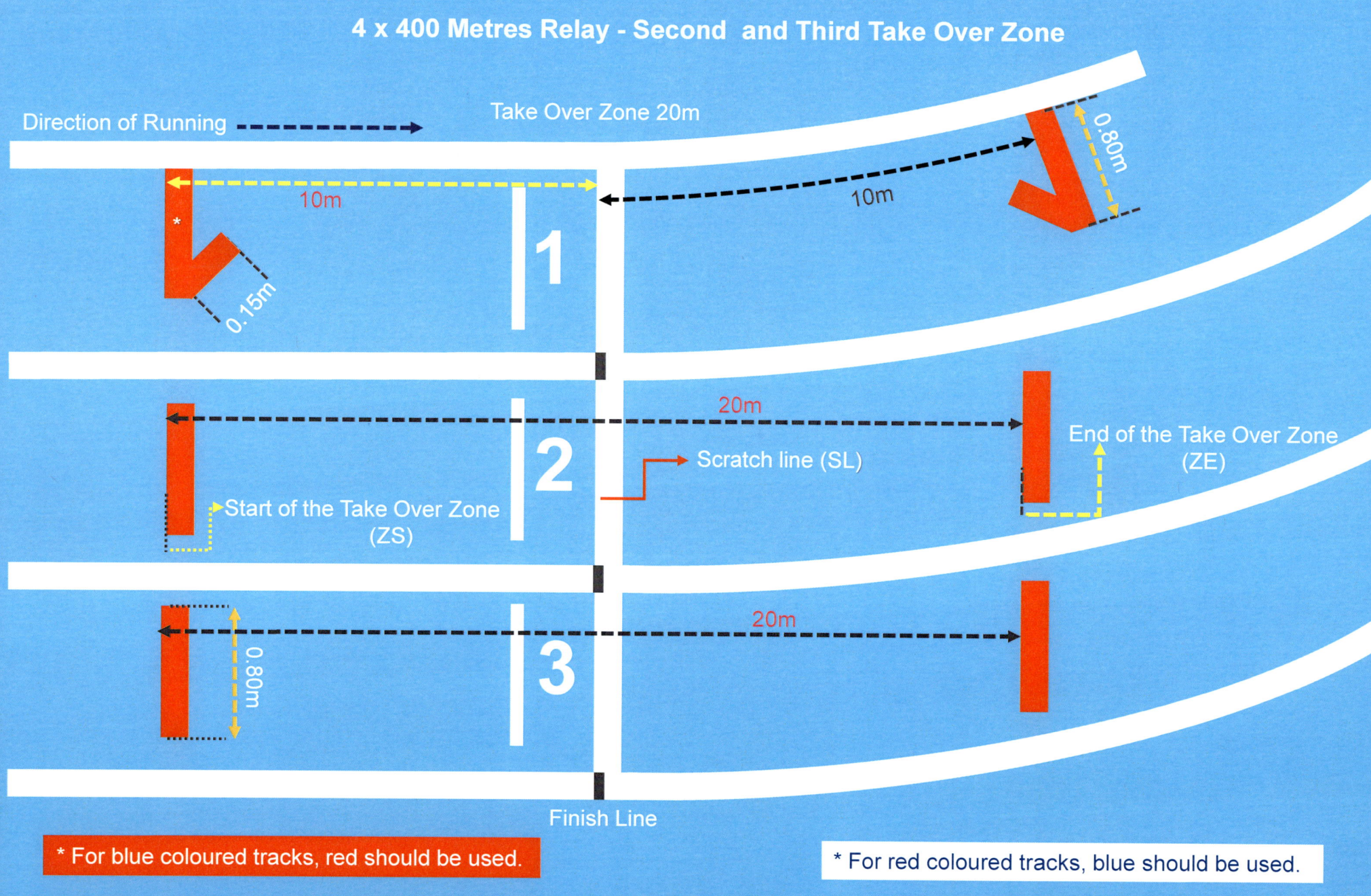

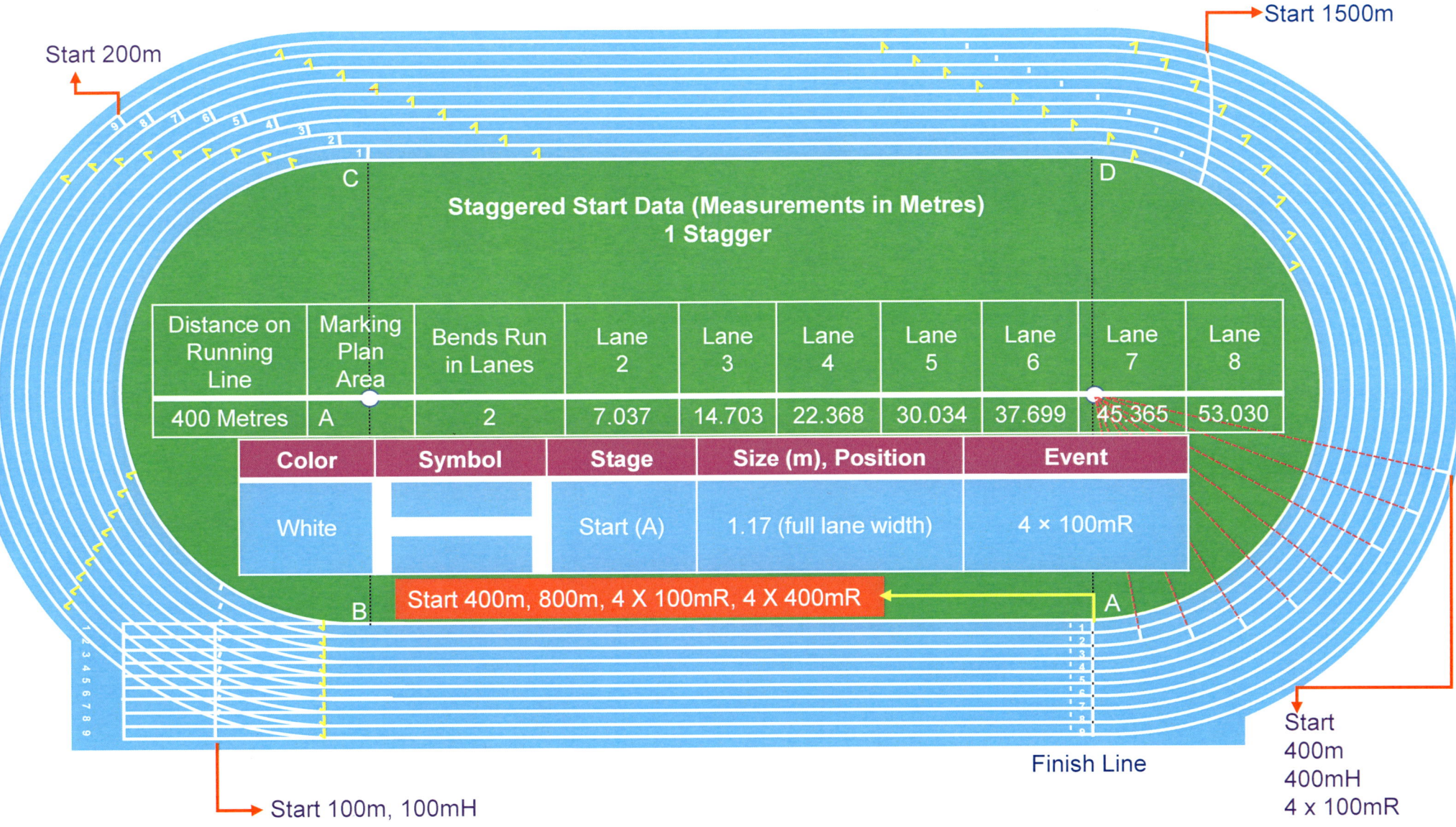

4 x 100 Metres Relay - Third Take Over Zone

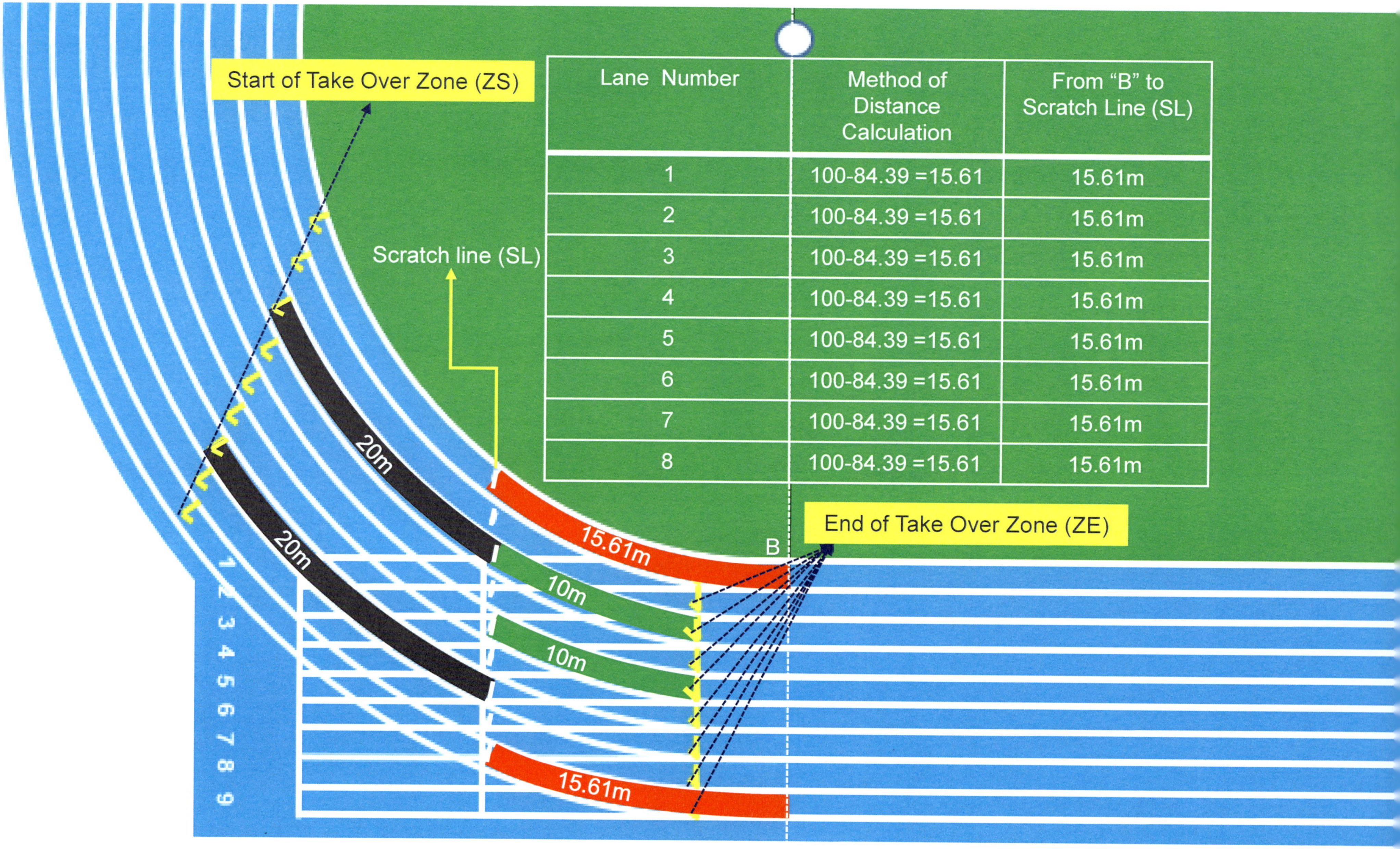

Start of Take Over Zone (ZS)

Scratch line (SL)

End of Take Over Zone (ZE)

Lane Number	Method of Distance Calculation	From "B" to Scratch Line (SL)
1	100-84.39 =15.61	15.61m
2	100-84.39 =15.61	15.61m
3	100-84.39 =15.61	15.61m
4	100-84.39 =15.61	15.61m
5	100-84.39 =15.61	15.61m
6	100-84.39 =15.61	15.61m
7	100-84.39 =15.61	15.61m
8	100-84.39 =15.61	15.61m

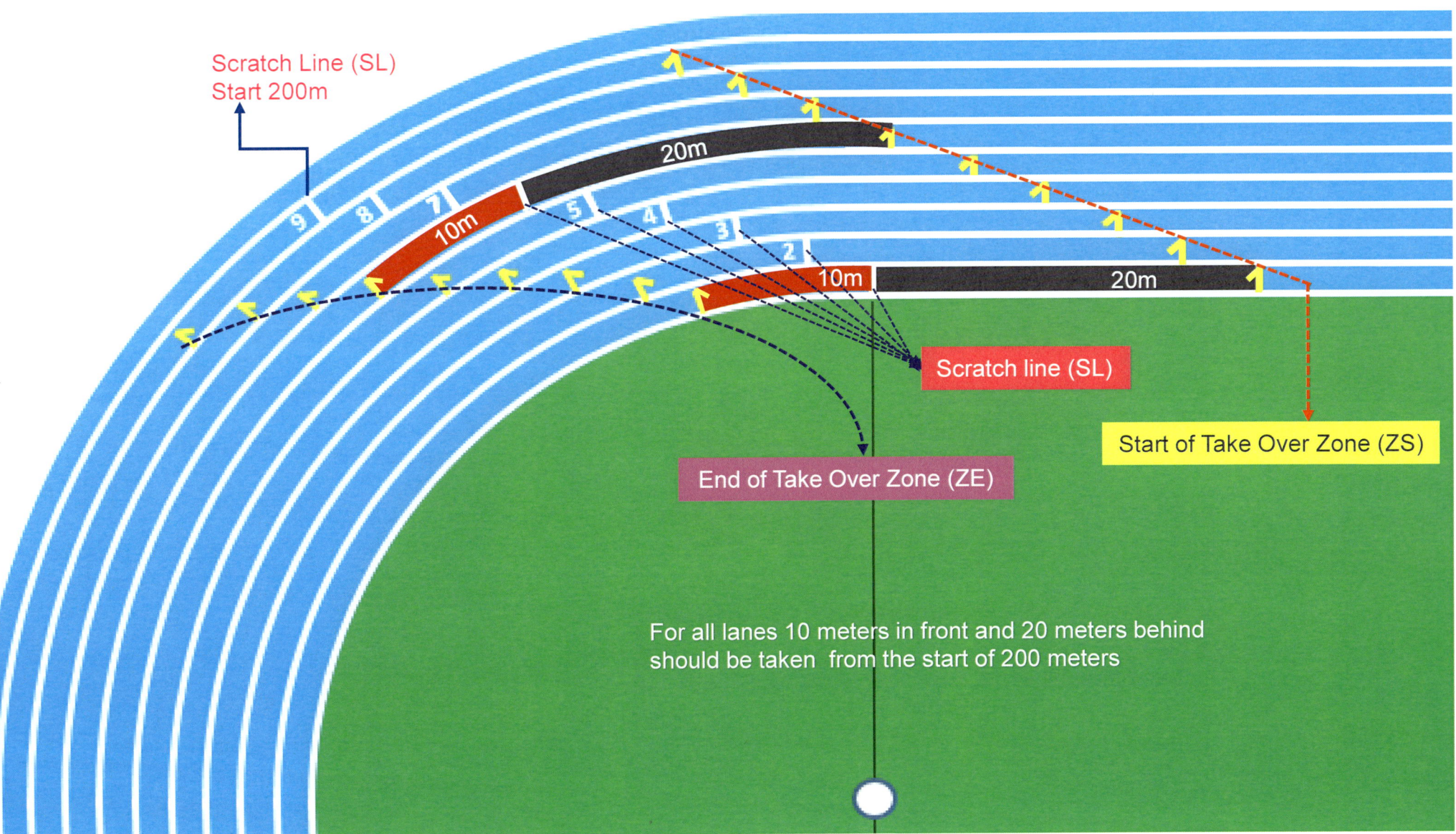

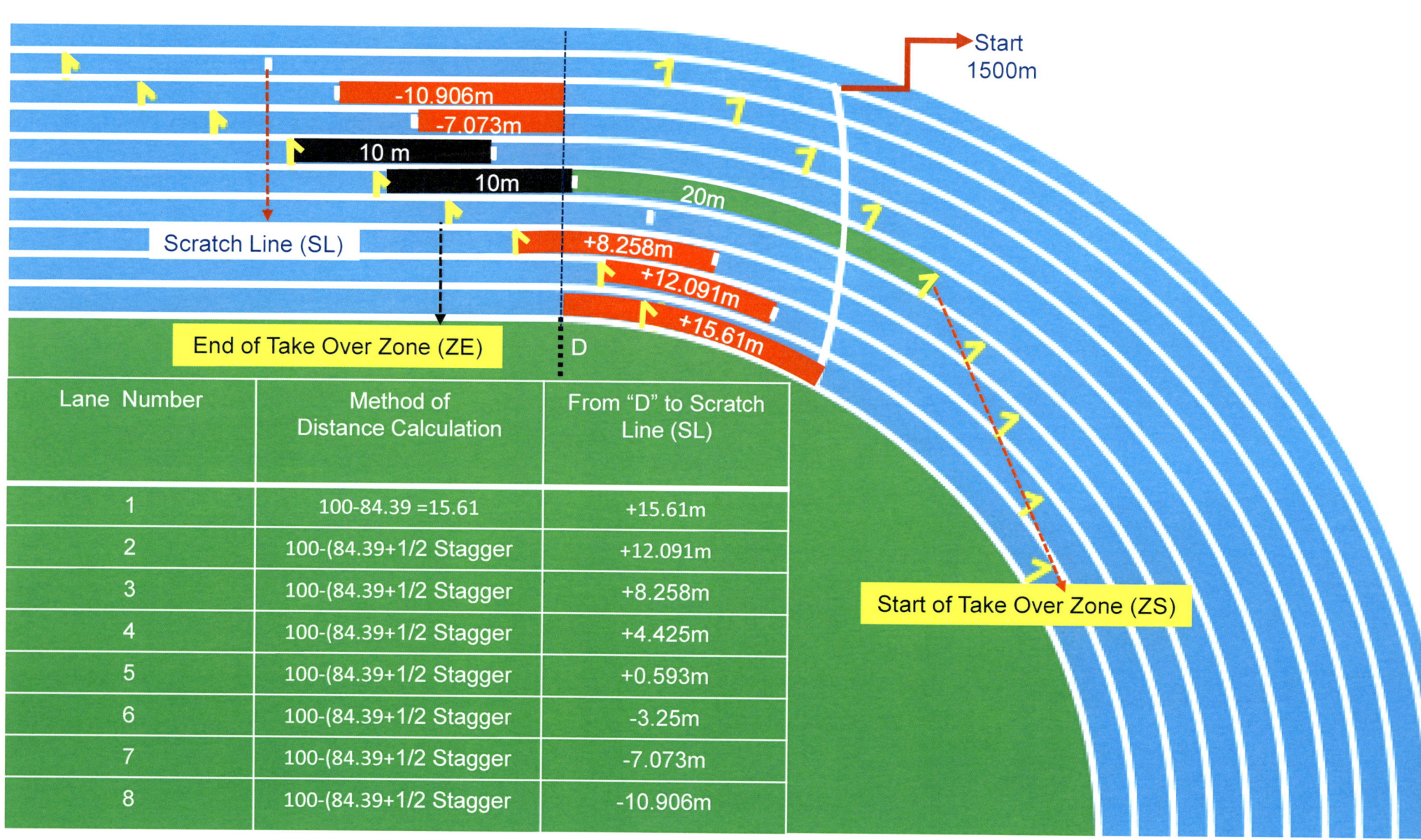

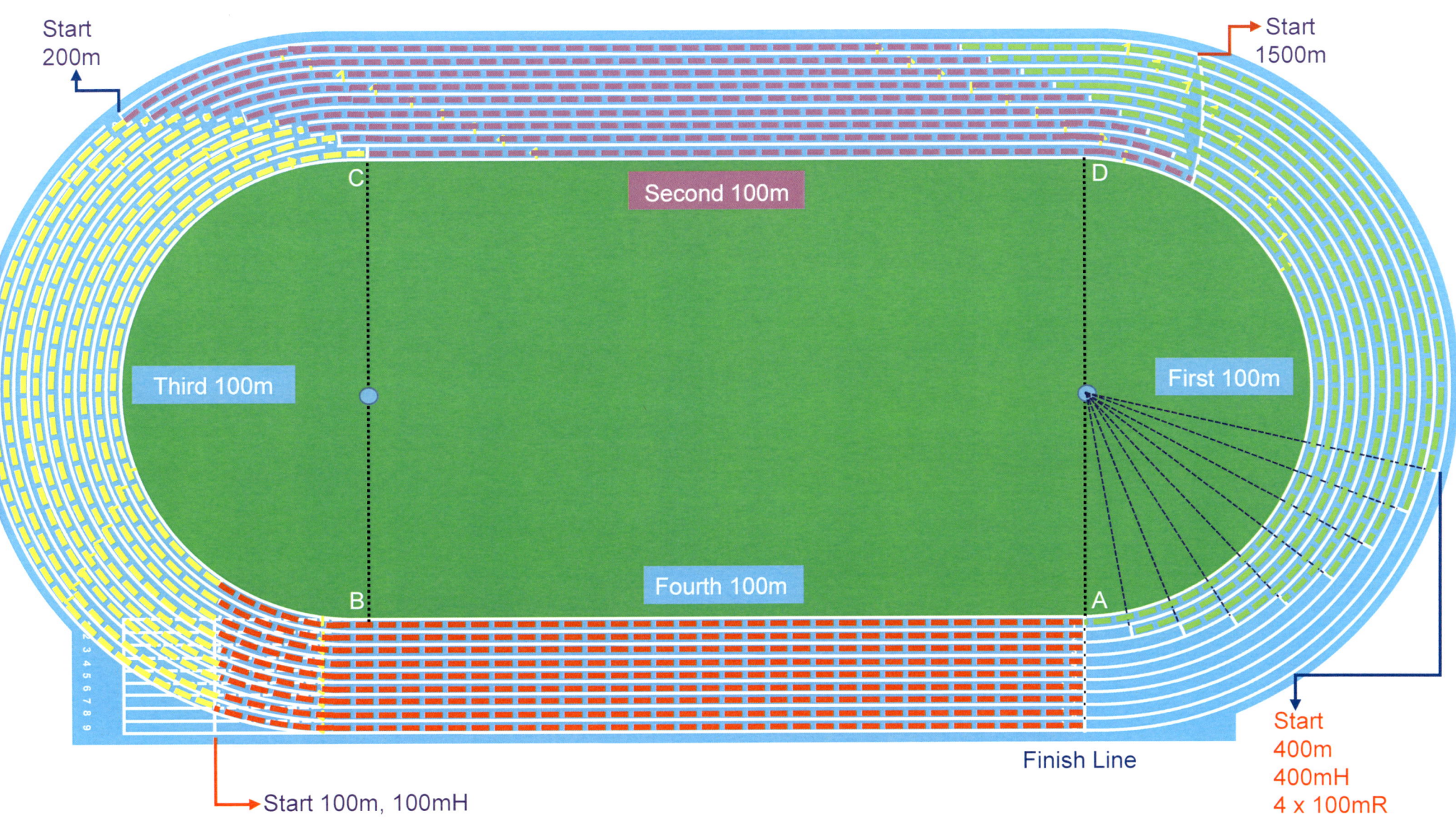

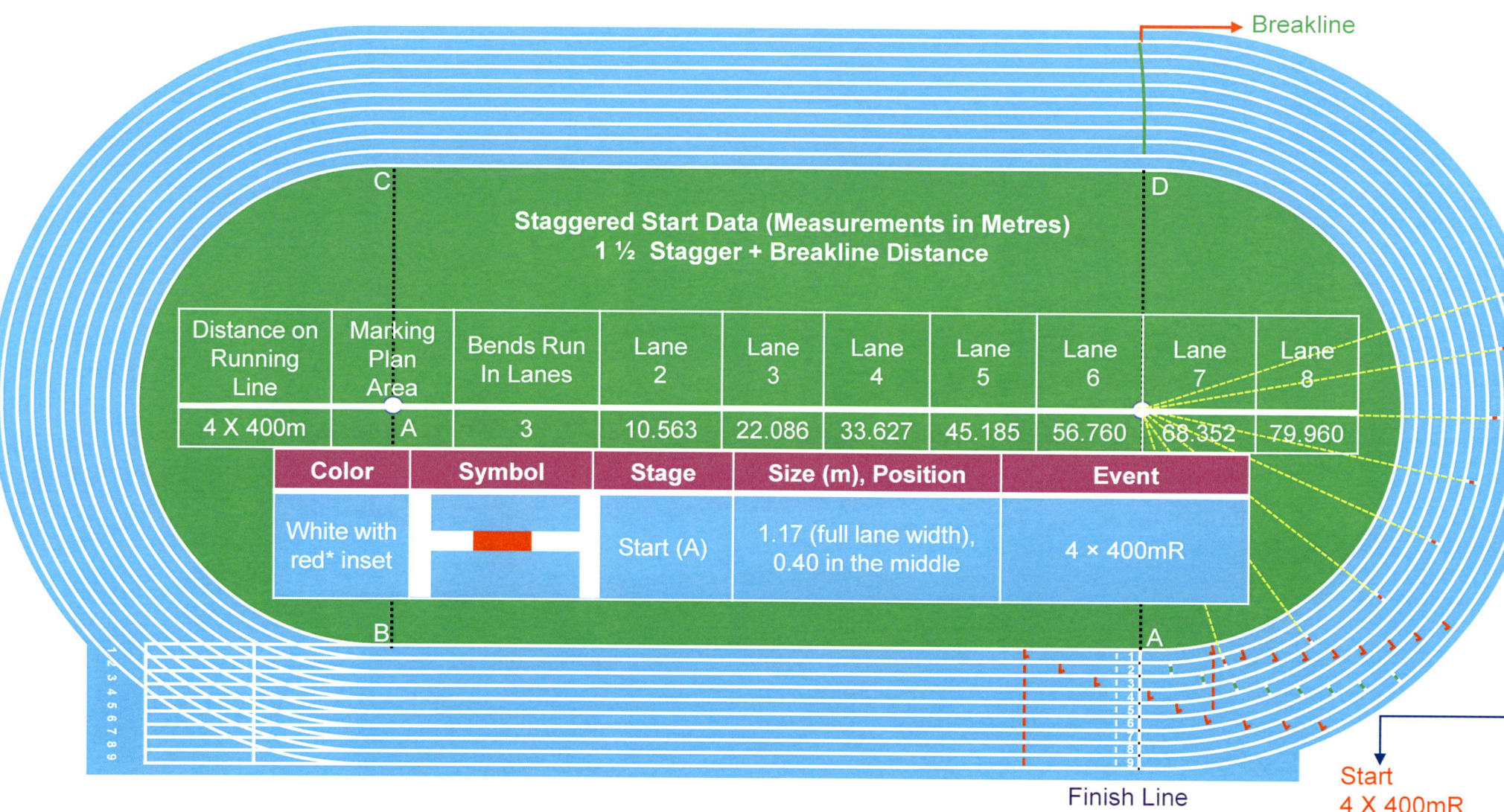

100 Metres and 110 Metres Hurdle - Height, Position and Number

Event	Height of Hurdles*	Distance from Start Line to First Hurdles**	Distance between Hurdles**	Distance from Last Hurdles to Finish Line**	Number of Hurdles
110mH Men	1.067m	13.72m	9.14m	14.02m	10
110mH U20 Men	0.991m	13.72m	9.14m	14.02m	10
110mH U18 Men	0.914m	13.72m	9.14m	14.02m	10
100mH Women / U20 Women	0.838m	13.00m	8.50m	10.50m	10
100mH U18 Women	0.762m	13.00m	8.50m	10.50m	10

*± 0.003m   **± 0.01 for 100m and 110m

Hurdle Positions

Color	Symbol	Size (m), Position	Event
Red*		0.05 x 0.10 both sides	110mH
Yellow		0.05 x 0.10 both sides	100mH
Green		0.05 x 0.10 both sides	400mH
Red*		0.125 x 0.125 inside lane 1 and outside lane 3	Steeplechase

All lines width: 0.05m.   * For red coloured tracks, blue should be used.

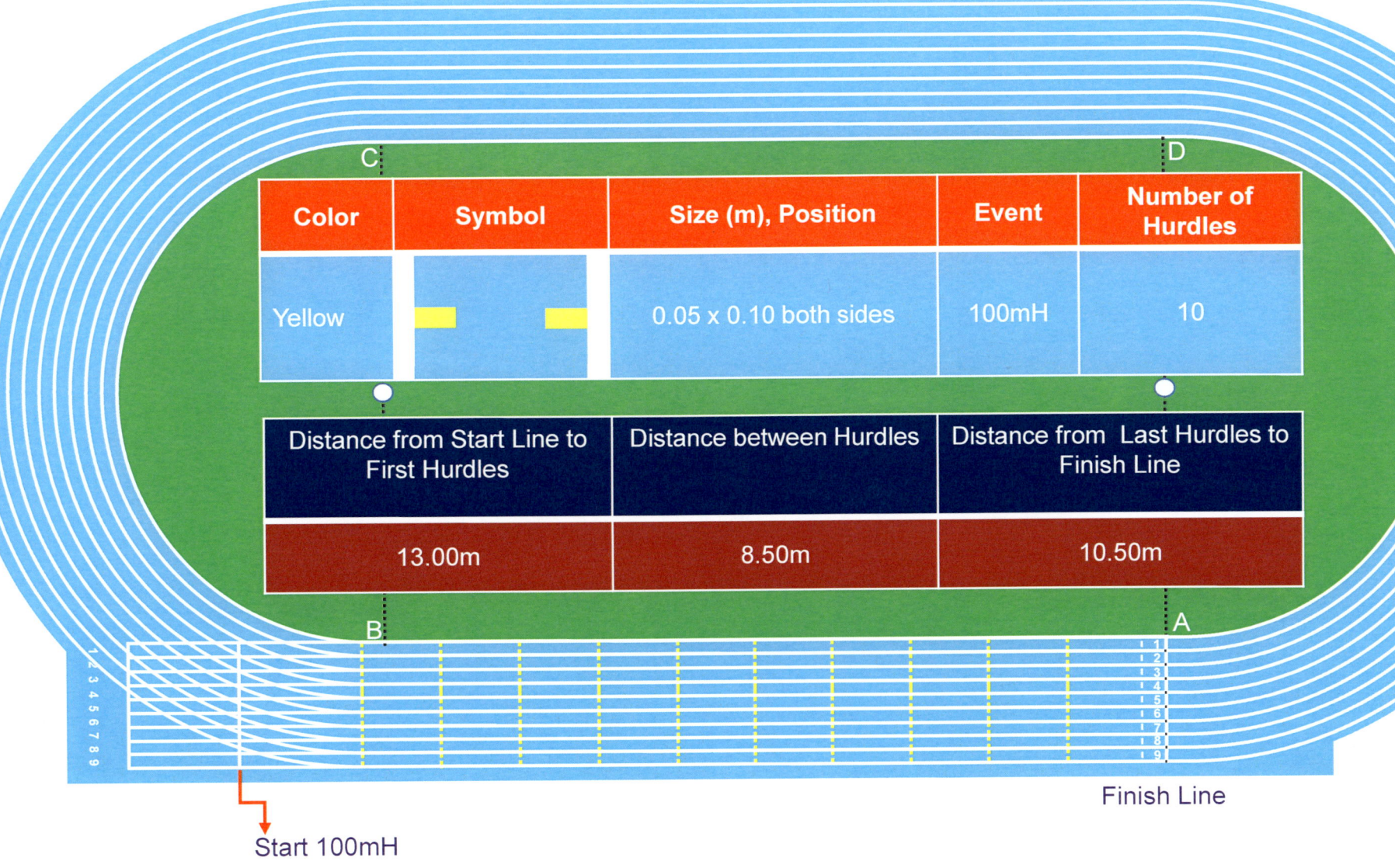

110 Metres Hurdles

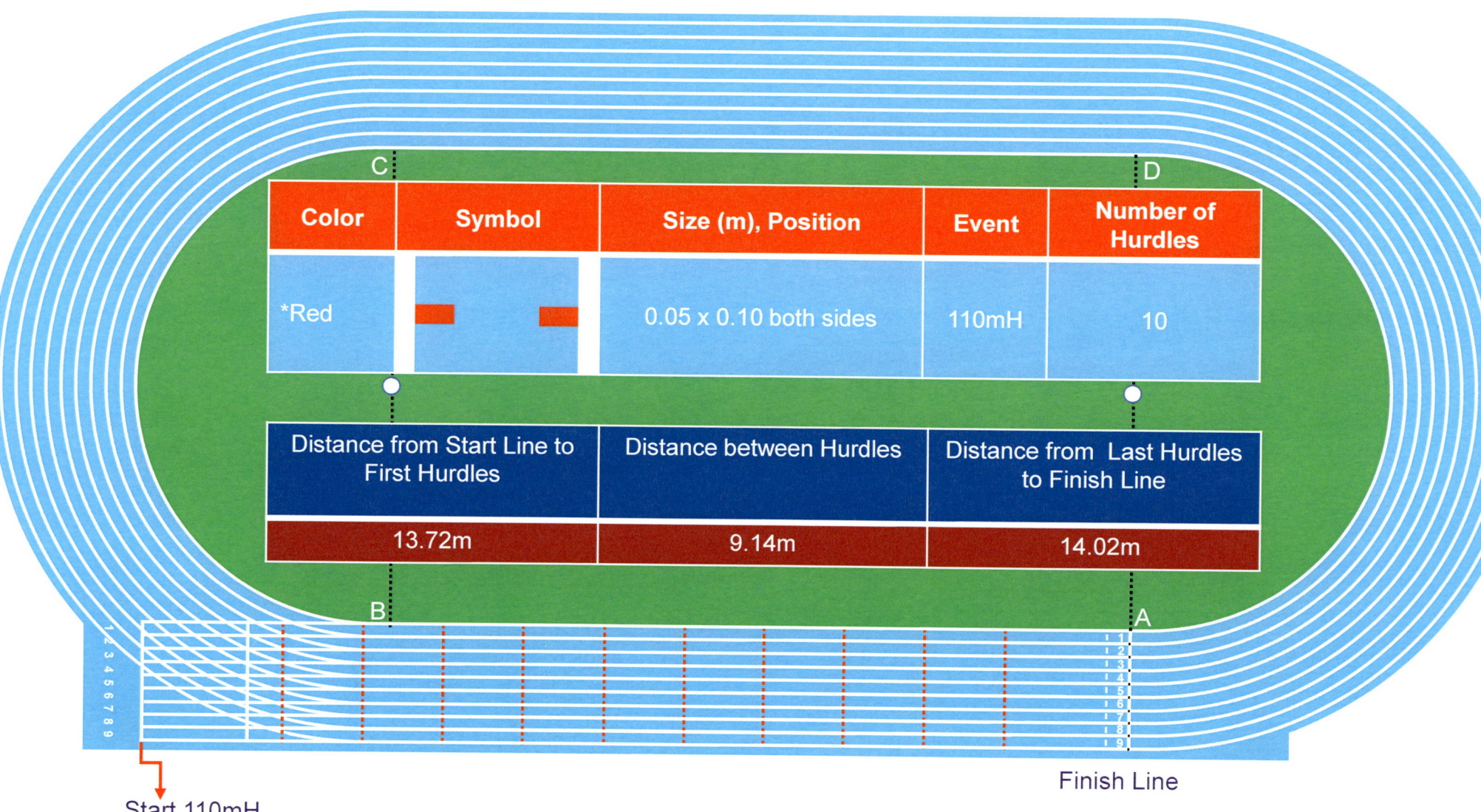

* For red coloured tracks, blue should be used.

400 Metres Hurdles – Height, Position and Number

Event	Height of Hurdles*	Distance from Start Line to First Hurdles**	Distance between Hurdles**	Distance from Last Hurdles to Finish Line**	Number of Hurdles
400mH Men / U20	0.914m	45m	35m	40m	10
400mH U18 Men	0.838m	45m	35m	40m	10
400mH Women / U20 / U18	0.762m	45m	35m	40m	10

* ± 0.03   ** ± 0.03 for 400m

80 Metres Hurdles – Height, Position and Number

Event	Height of Hurdles*	Distance from Start Line to First Hurdles**	Distance between Hurdles**	Distance from Last Hurdles to Finish Line**	Number of Hurdles
80mH Boys/ U16	0.838m	13.50m	8.60m	14.90m	7
80mH Girls/ U16	0.762m	12.00m	8.00m	12.00m	8

*± 0.03   ** ± 0.03 for 400m

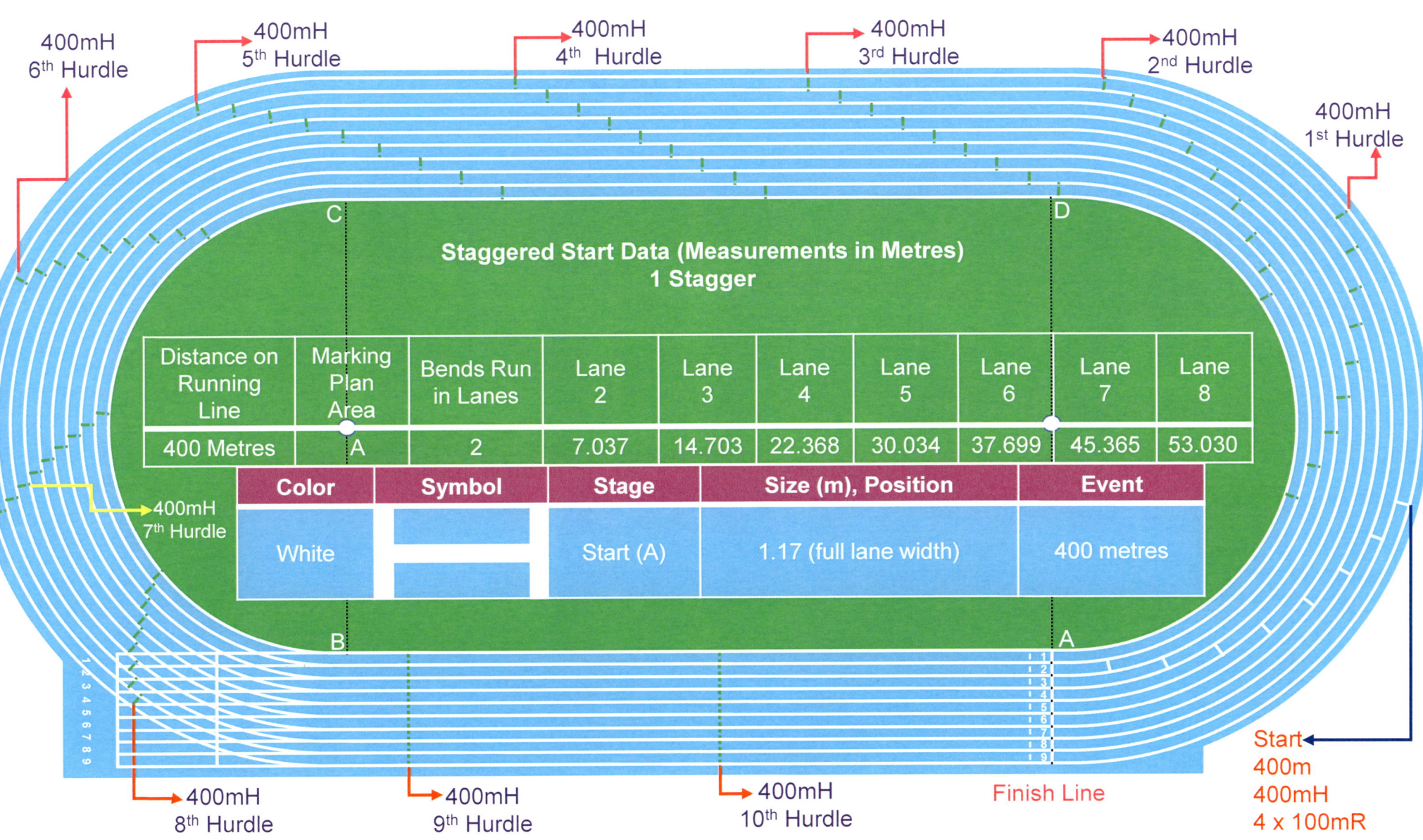

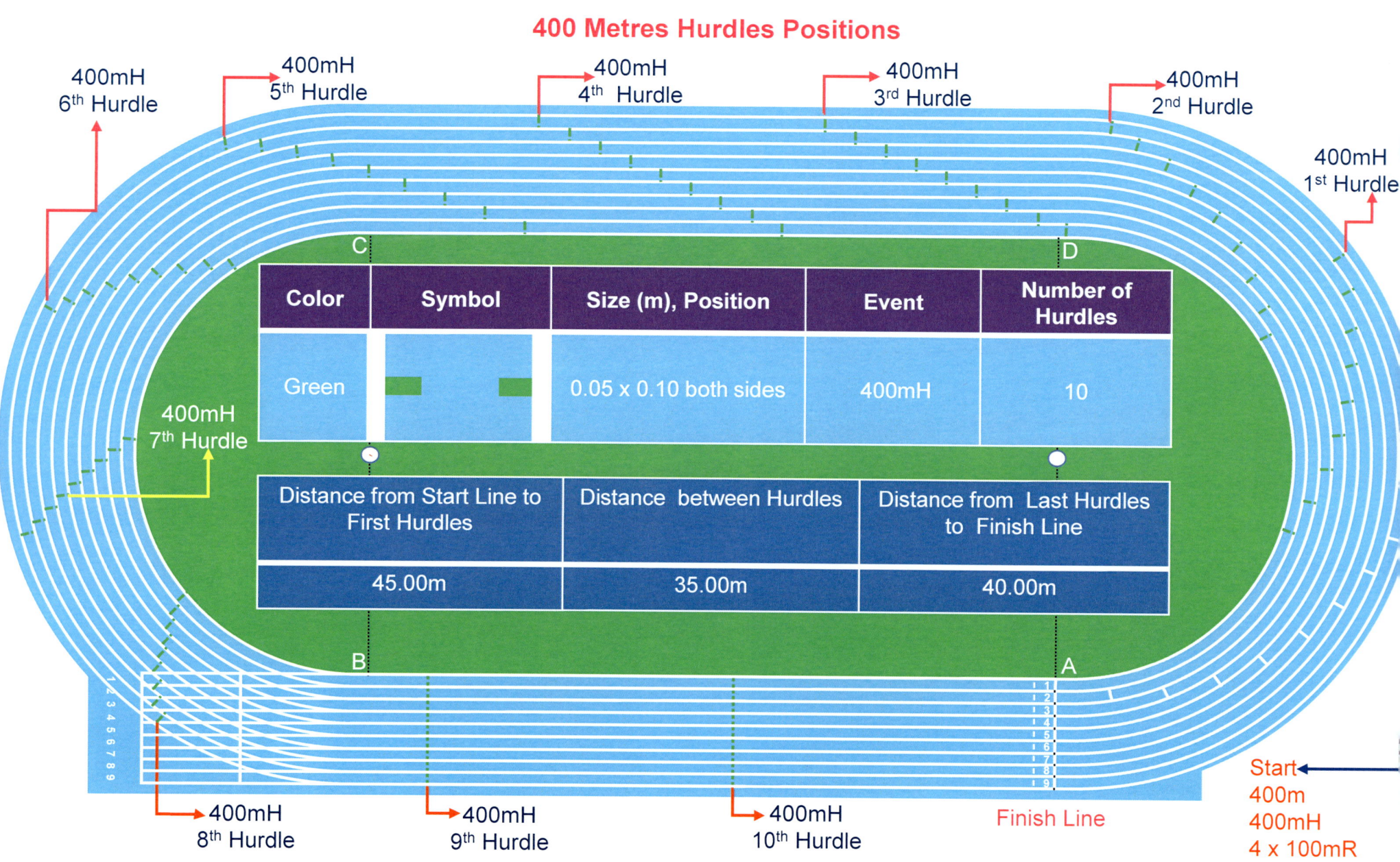

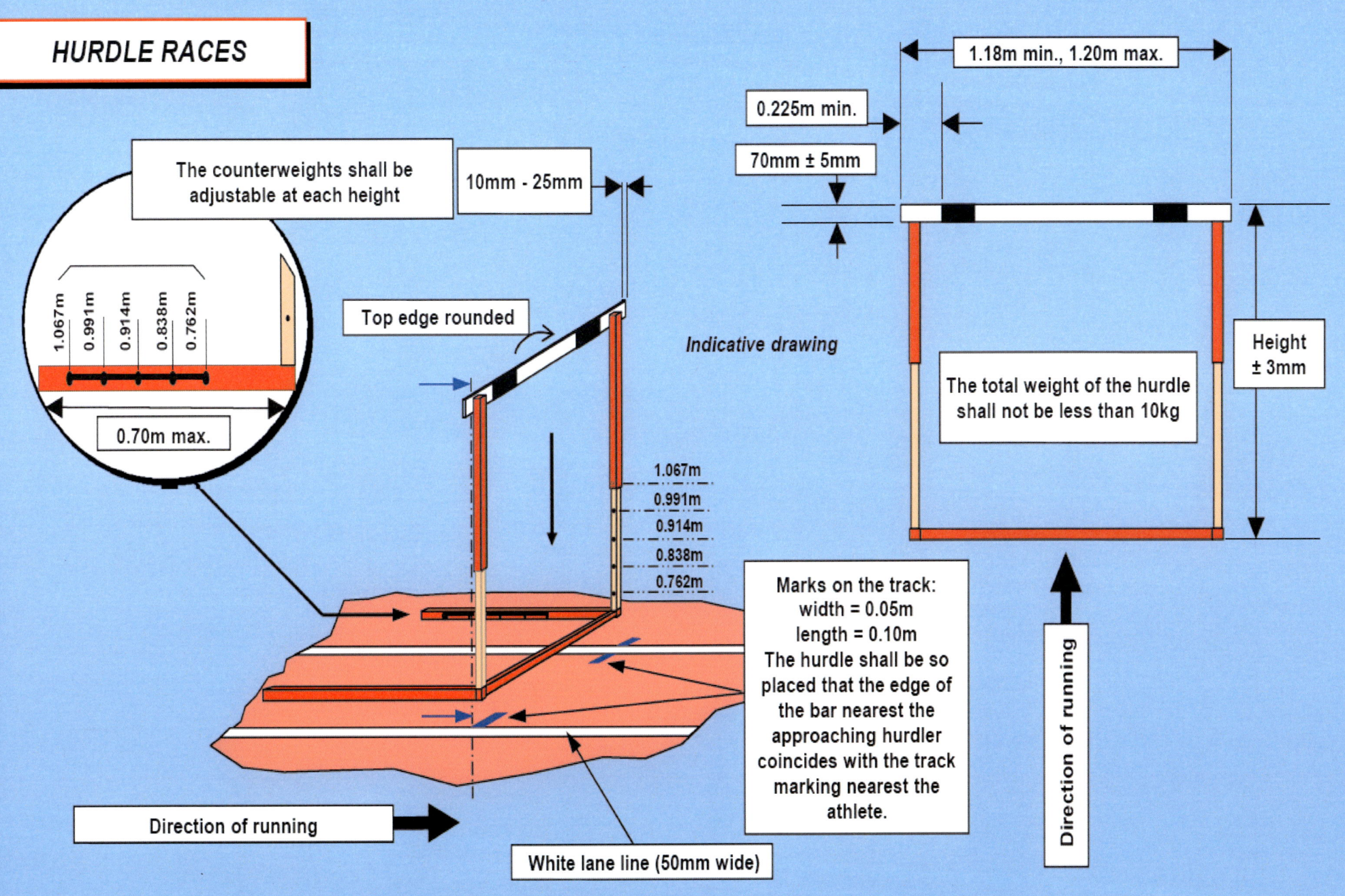

400 Metres Hurdles

Calculation for Placing the First Hurdle in Lanes 2 to 8 for the 400 Metres Hurdles

Formula = t - dh X 1 stagger ÷ t

t – Total Length of Both Bends

dh – Distance of the Hurdles in bend (Eg : Distance of hurdle in bend (First hurdle) 45m

1 Stagger - 1 Stagger Distance

Lane Number 2 = 231.22 – 45 X 7.037   ÷ 231.22 = 5.667

Lane Number 3 = 231.22 – 45 X 14.703 ÷ 231.22 = 11.841

Lane Number 4 = 231.22 – 45 X 22.368 ÷ 231.22 = 18.014

Lane Number 5 = 231.22 – 45 X 30.034 ÷ 231.22 = 24.188

Lane Number 6 = 231.22 – 45 X 37.699 ÷ 231.22 = 30.362

Lane Number 7 = 231.22 – 45 X 45.365 ÷ 231.22 = 36.536

Lane Number 8 = 231.22 – 45 X 53.030 ÷ 231.22 = 43.709

400 Metres Hurdles

Calculation for Placing the Fourth and Fifth Hurdles in Lanes 2 to 8 for the 400 Metres Hurdles

Formula = t - dh X full stagger ÷ t

t – Total Length of Both Bends

dh – Distance of the Hurdles in bend (Eg : Distance of hurdle in bend (Fourth and Fifth Hurdle) 45+35+35+0.61

Stagger - 1 Stagger Distance

Lane Number 2 = 231.22 – 115 X 7.037 ÷ 231.22 = 3.518

Lane Number 3 = 231.22 – 115 X 14.703 ÷ 231.22 = 7.351

Lane Number 4 = 231.22 – 115 X 22.368 ÷ 231.22 = 11.184

Lane Number 5 = 231.22 – 115 X 30.034 ÷ 231.22 = 15.017

Lane Number 6 = 231.22 – 115 X 37.699 ÷ 231.22 = 18.849

Lane Number 7 = 231.22 – 115 X 45.365 ÷ 231.22 = 22.682

Lane Number 8 = 231.22 – 115 X 53.030 ÷ 231.22 = 26.515

Hurdles Position Table

Hurdles Position	Distance of the Hurdles	Distance run on Bends	Lane Numbers							
			1	2	3	4	5	6	7	8
1	45	45	-	5.667	11.841	18.014	24.188	30.362	36.536	43.709
2	80	80	-	4.602	9.657	14.628	19.642	24.655	29.669	34.682
3	115	115	-	3.537	7.390	11.243	15.096	18.948	22.802	26.654
4	150	115.61	-	3.518	7.351	11.184	15.017	18.849	22.682	26.515
5	185	115.61	-	3.518	7.351	11.184	15.017	18.849	22.682	26.515
6	220	135.61	-	2.909	6.079	9.249	12.419	15.588	18.758	21.928
7	255	170.61	-	1.844	3.854	5.863	7.872	9.882	11.891	13.900
8	290	205.61	-	0.779	1.628	2.477	3.326	4.175	5.024	5.873
9	325	231.22	-	-	-	-	-	-	-	-
10	360	231.22	-	-	-	-	-	-	-	-

Measurements in Metres.

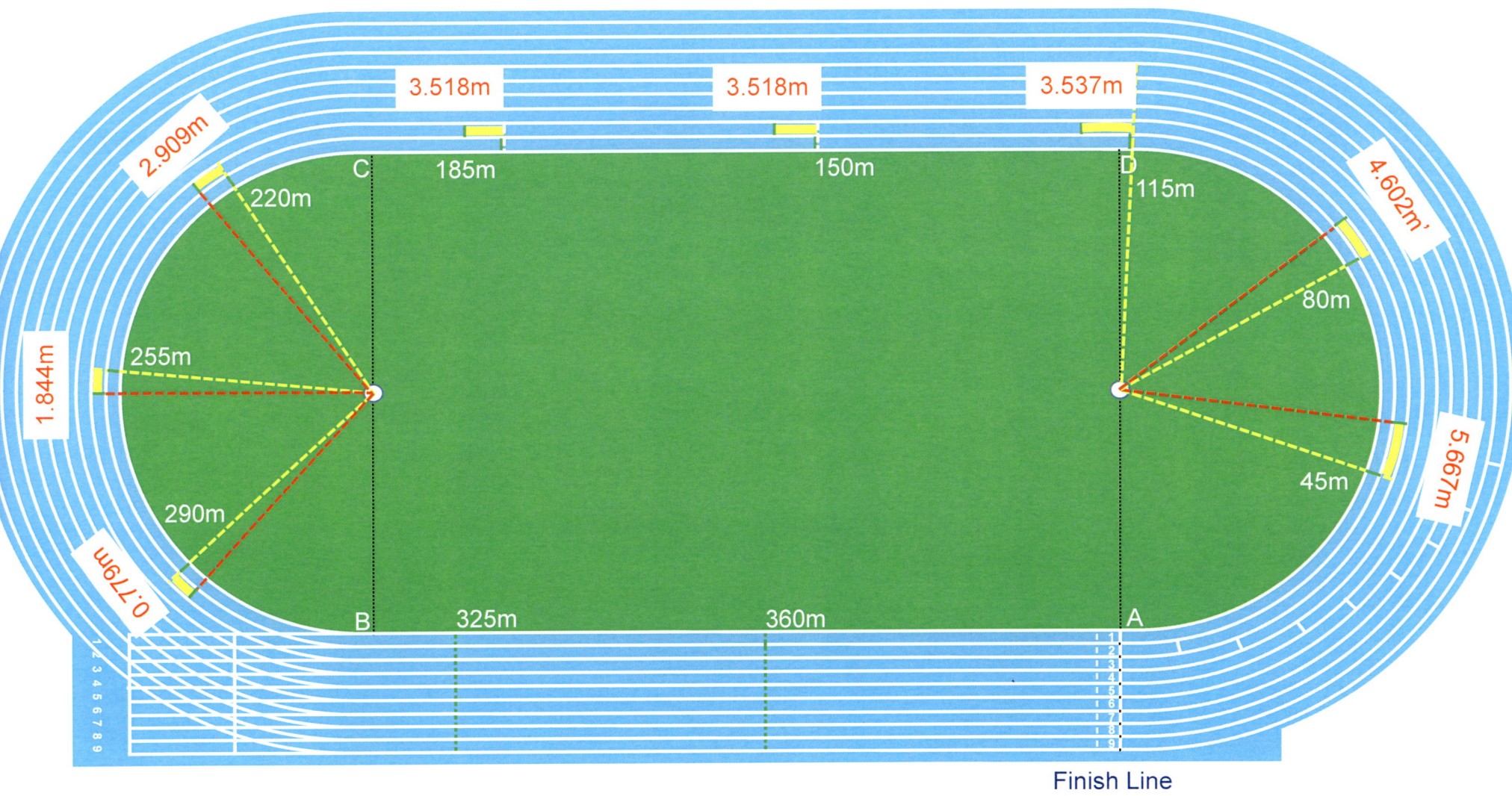

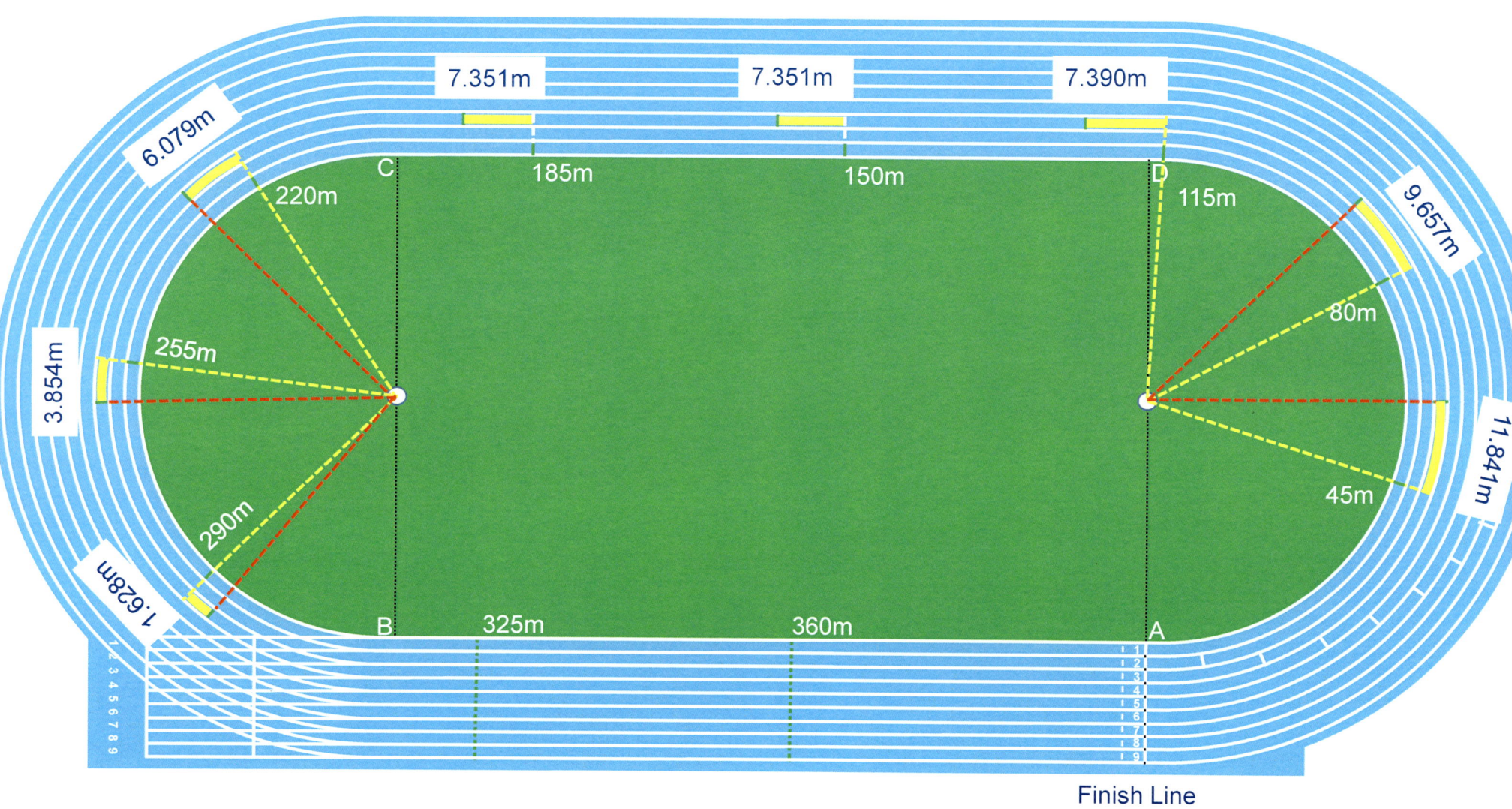

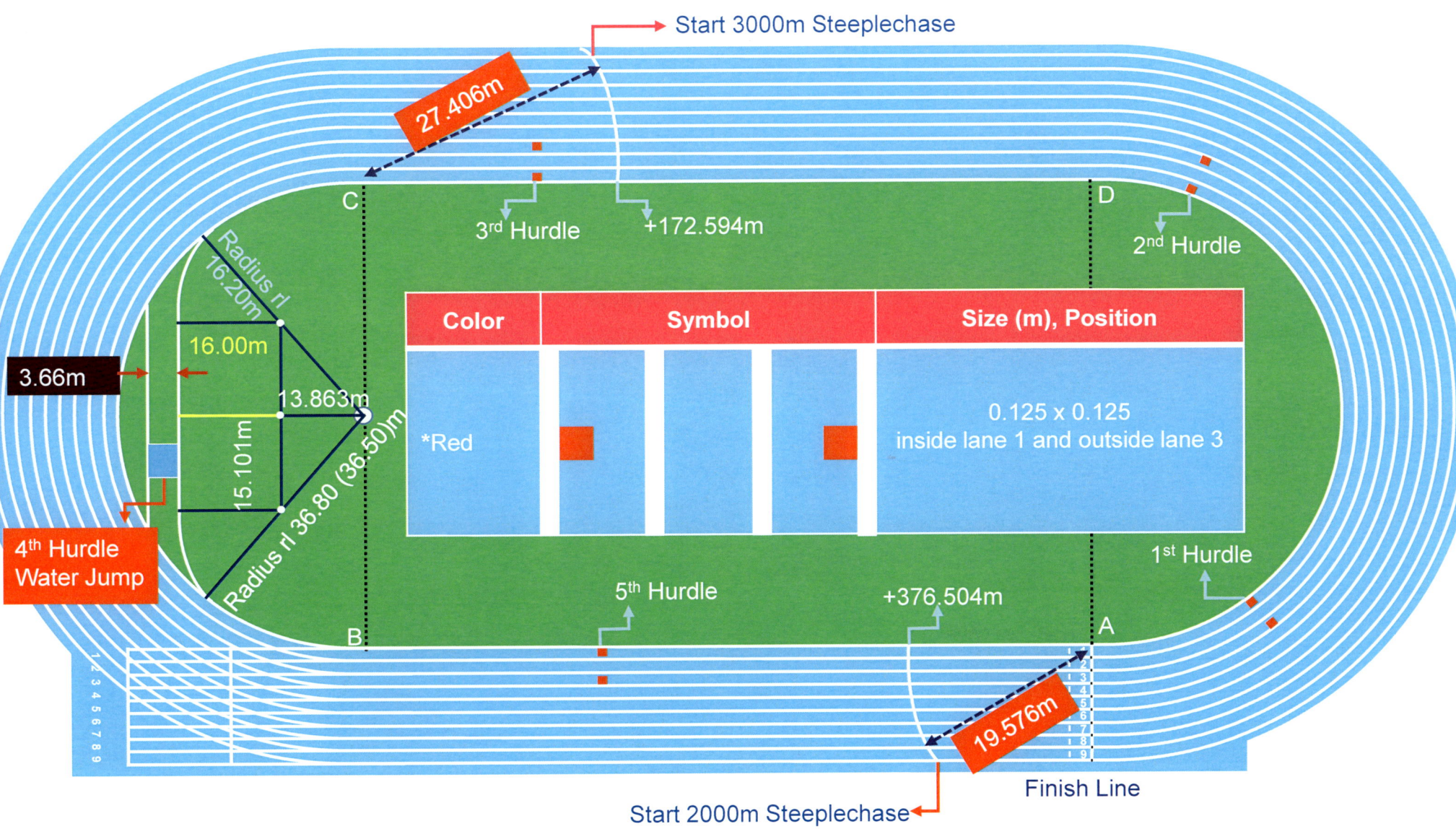

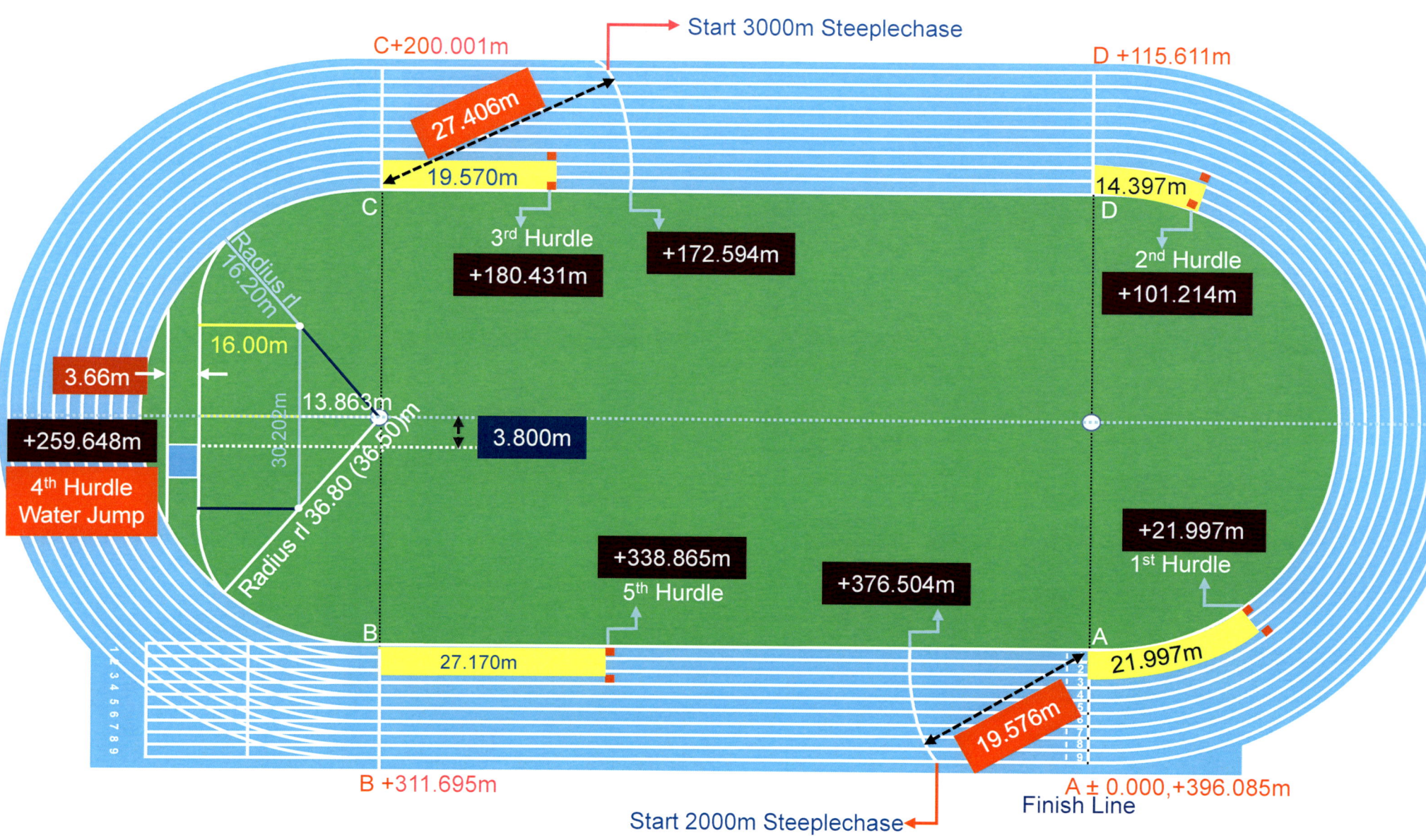

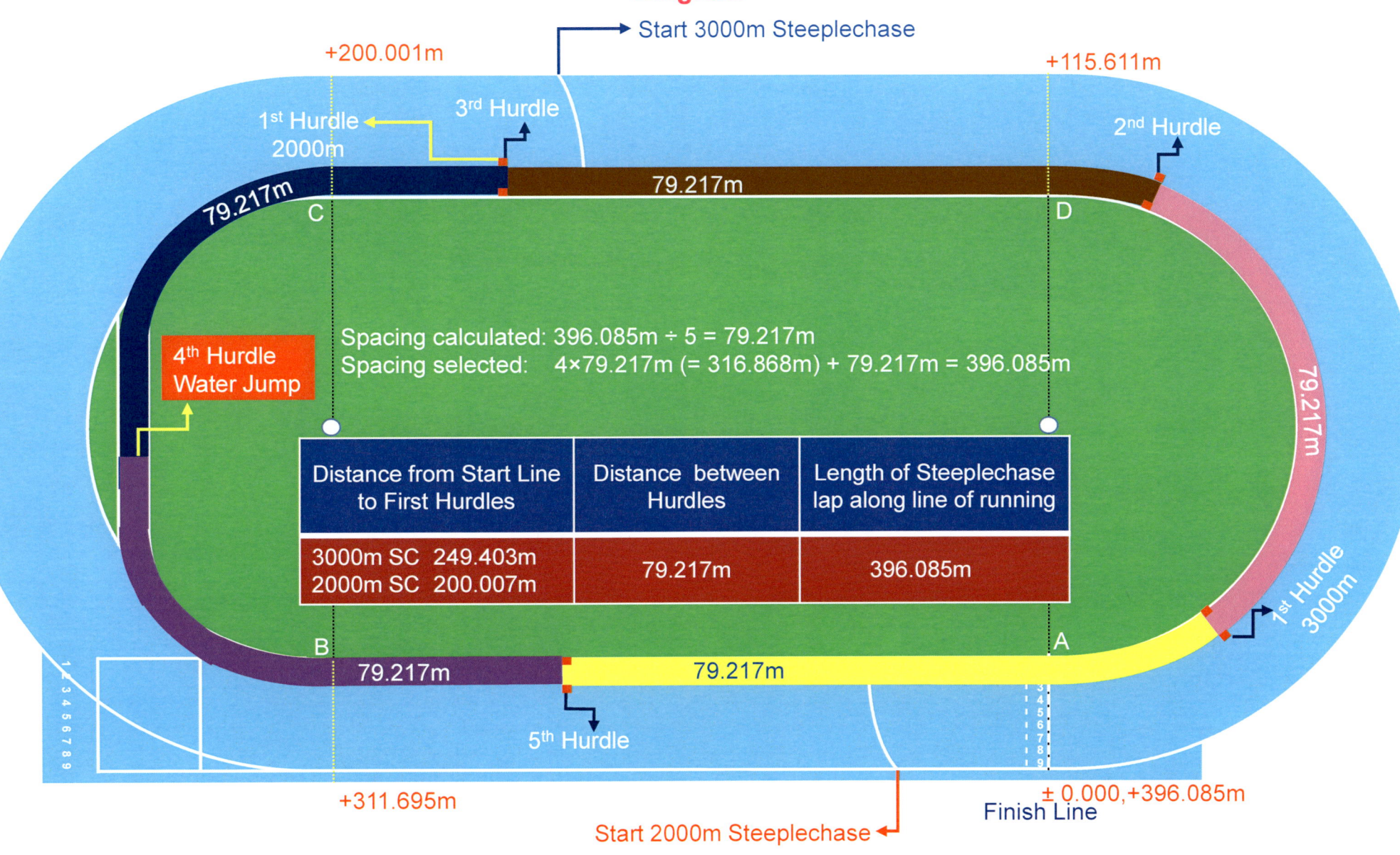

Steeplechase Track with Water Jump Inside the Bend Integrated Into the 400 Metre Standard Oval Track
(dimensions in m)
Calculation of the Length of Running (Lr)

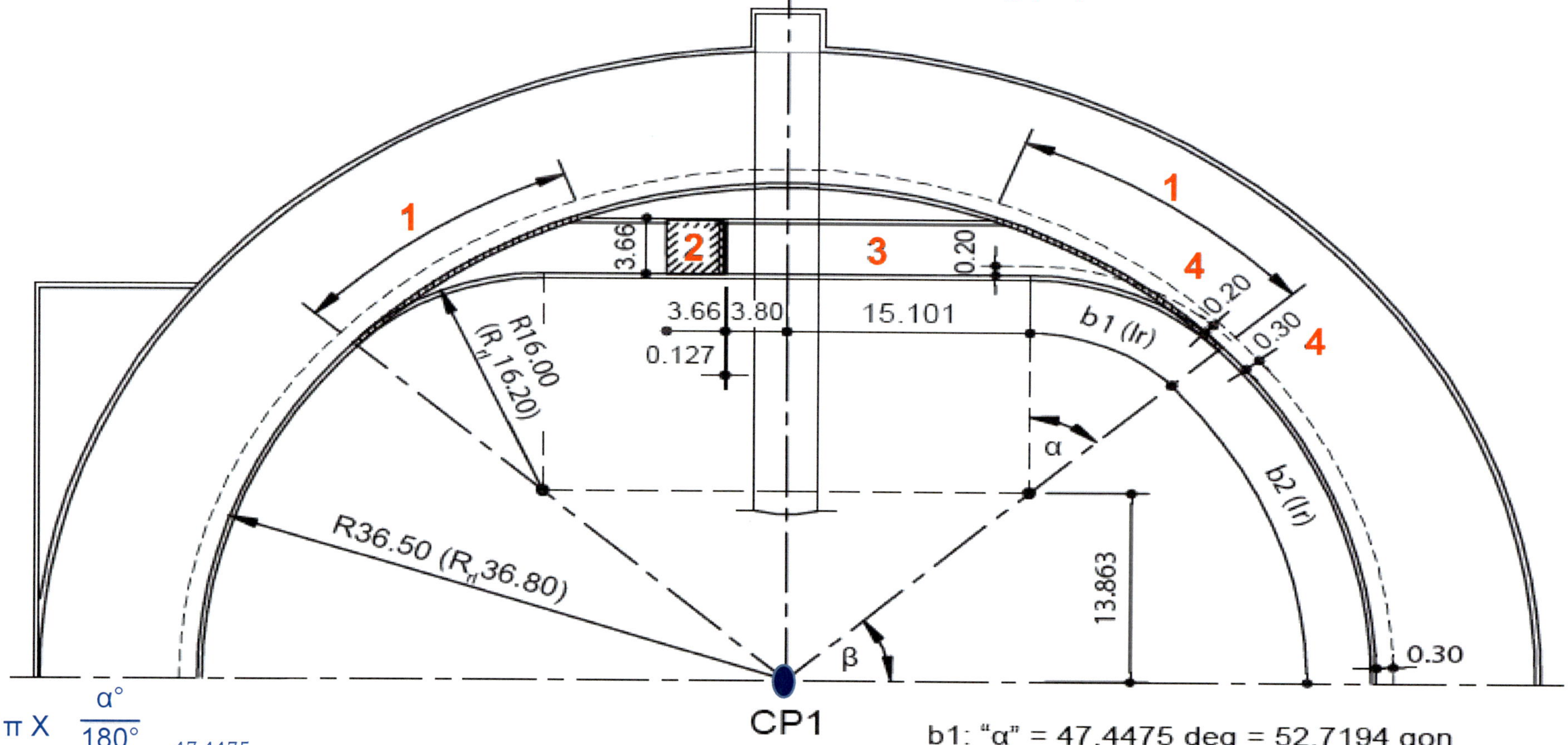

$b = r \times \pi \times \dfrac{\alpha°}{180°}$

$b1\ lr = 16.20 \times \pi \times \dfrac{47.4475}{180°} = 13.4155m$

$b2\ lr = 36.80 \times \pi \times \dfrac{42.5525}{180°} = 27.3307m$

Length of running of water jump bend:
2 X 13.41545 + 2 X 27.3307 + 2 X 15.101 = 111.6943m

Length of running of the water jump bend is 3.916m shorter than the semicircle bend of the StandardTrack (36.80m X π = 115.6106m)

b1: "α" = 47.4475 deg = 52.7194 gon
b2: "β" = 42.5525 deg = 47.2806 gon
1. Removable track border
2. Water jump
3. Straight
4. Distance between running line and track inside edge

Steeplechase Track with Water Jump Inside the Bend Integrated Into the 400 Metre Standard Oval Track
Calculation of The Length of Running (Lr)

Length of steeplechase lap measured along the running line (from A to A) over the water jump on the inside bend:

Semicircle bend (R = 36.80m)	= 115.6106m
Straights of 84.3900m each	= 168.7800m
Water jump bend: : 2 X 13.41545 + 2 X 27.3307 + 2 X 15.101	= 111.6943m

(2 Transition bends b1 of 13.41545m each = 26.8309m
2 Semicircle bend sections b2 of 27.3307m each = 54.6614m
Middle straight 2x 15.101m = 30.2020m)

Total = 396.0849m

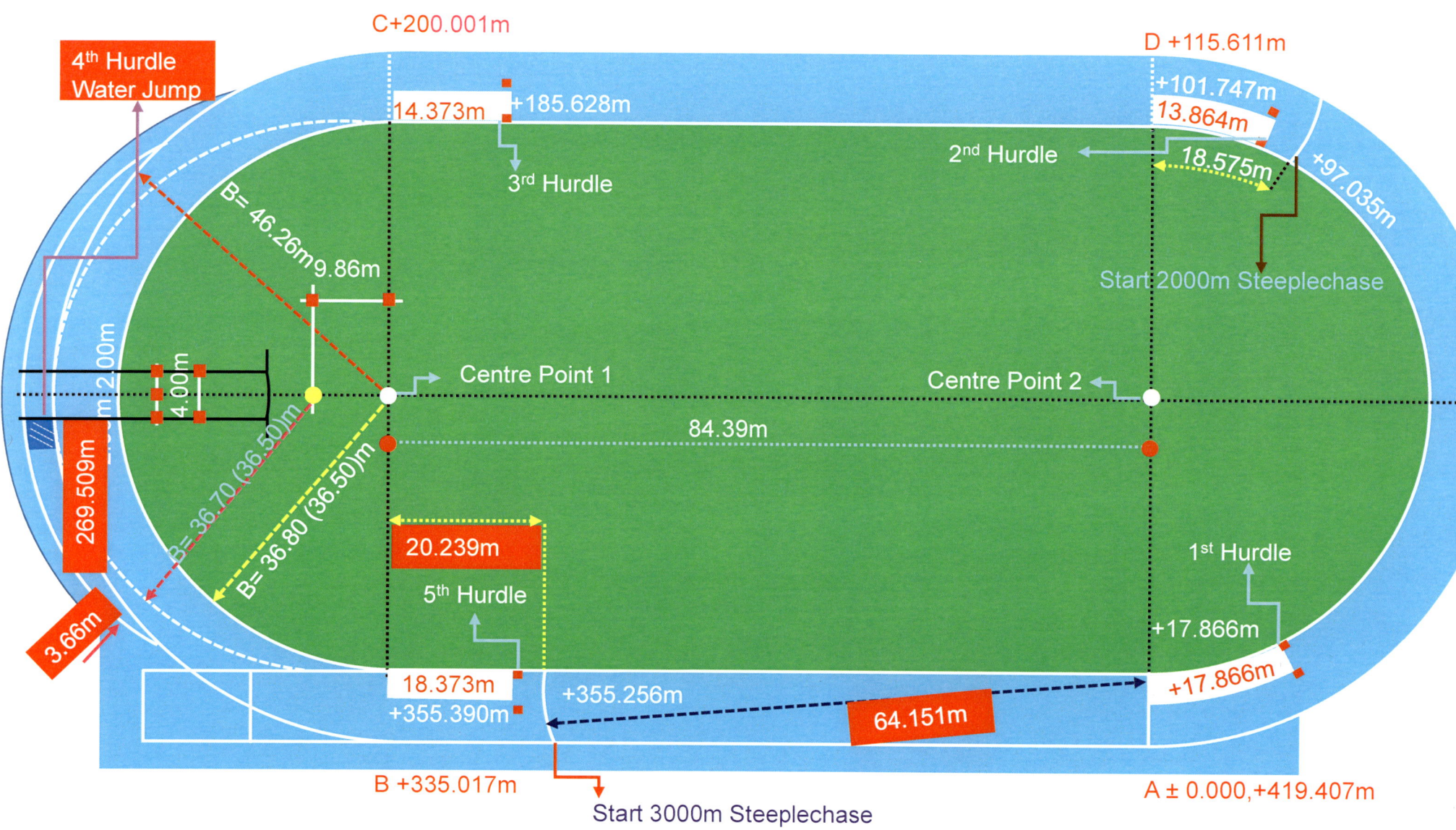

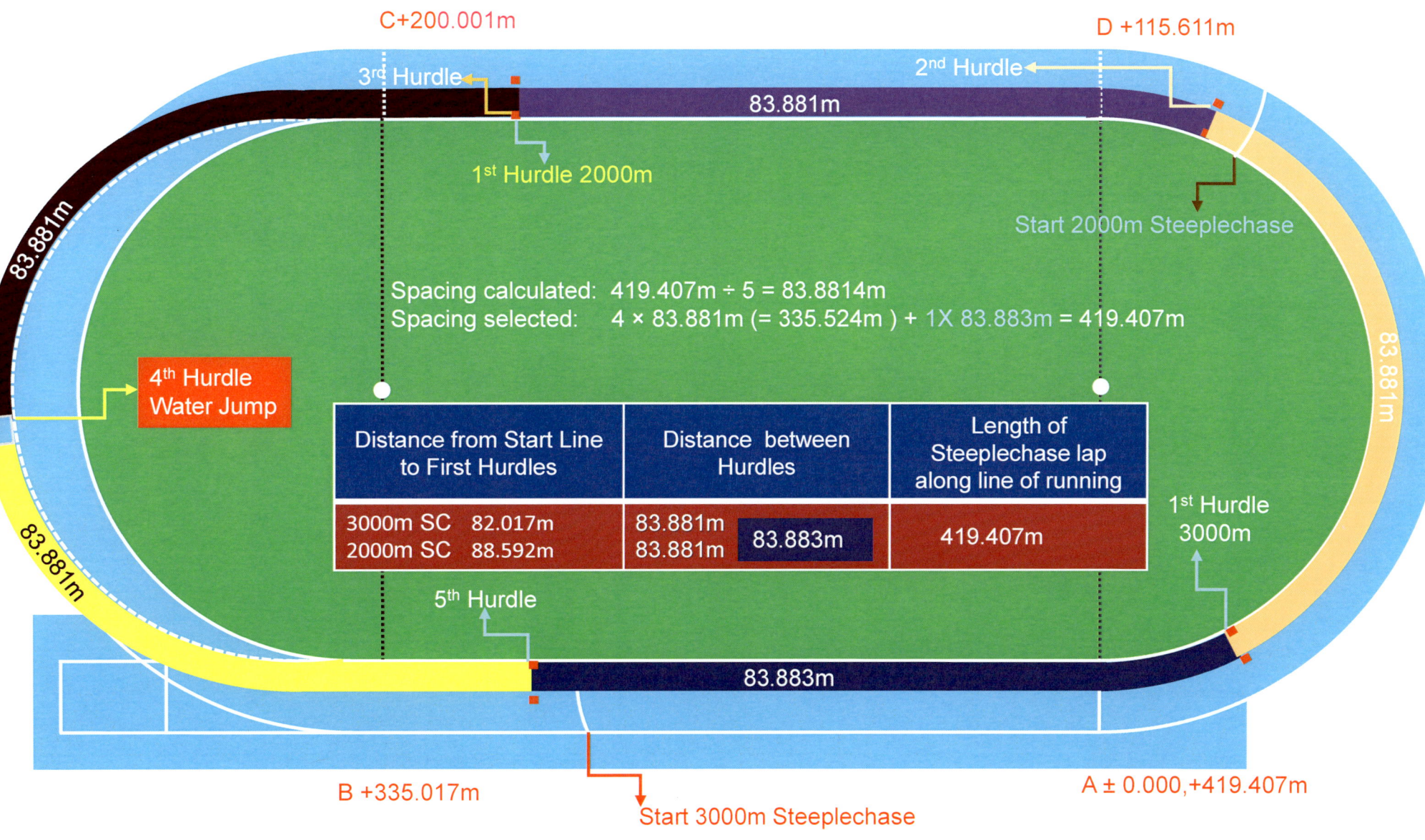

Steeplechase Track with Water Jump outside the Bend Integrated Into the 400 Metre Standard Oval Track
(dimensions in m)
Calculation of the Length Of Running (Lr)

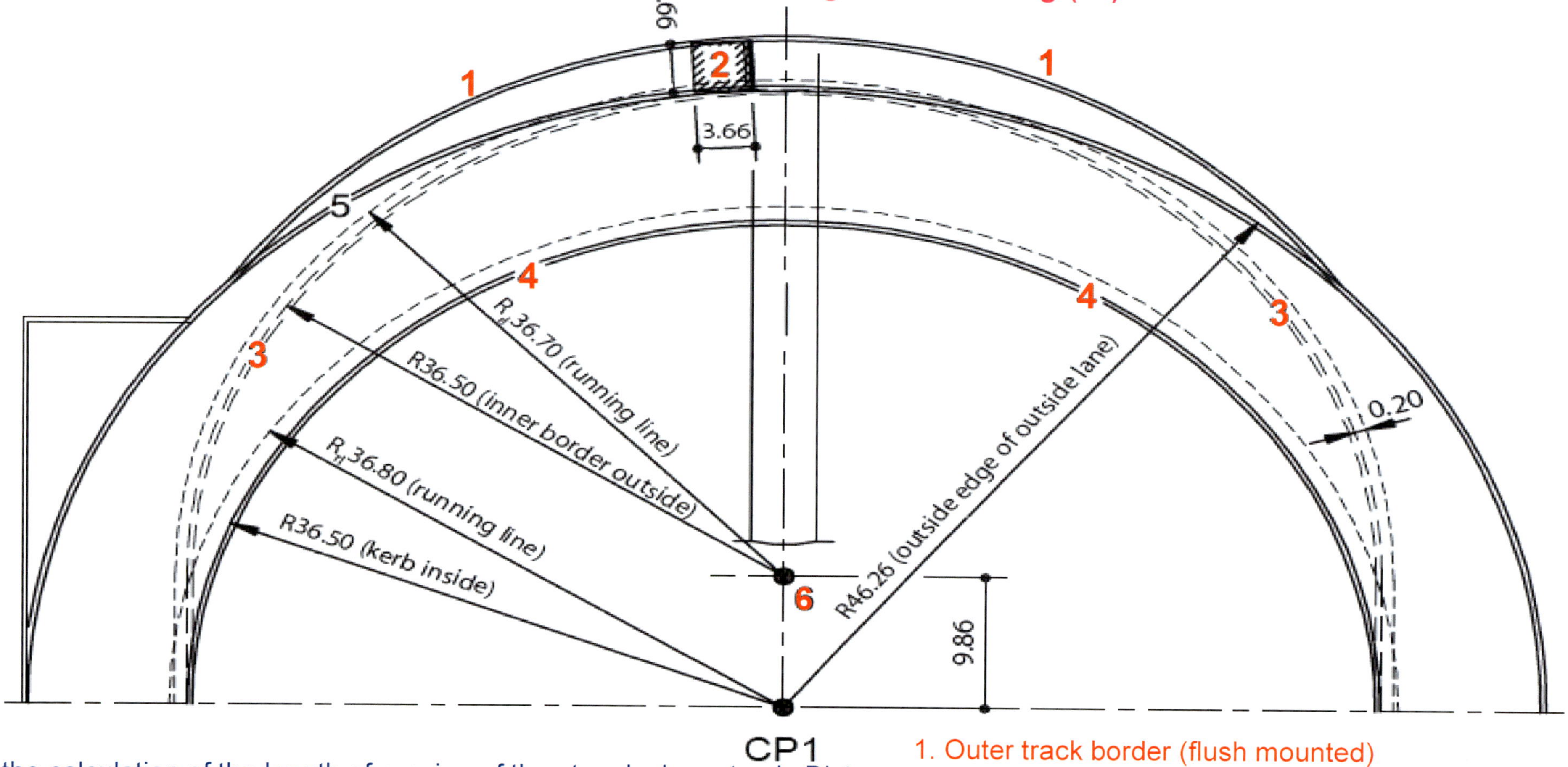

For the calculation of the length of running of the steeplechase track: Distance of running line (rl) and the marking: 0.20m.

Length of running of water jump bend: $9.86 \times 2 + 36.70 \times \pi = 135.0165$ m.

Length of running of the water jump bend 19.406m longer than the semicircle bend of the Standard Track ($36.80\text{m} \times \pi = 115.6106$m).

1. Outer track border (flush mounted)
2. Water jump
3. R=36.50 (Inner border outside edge of steeplechase track)
4. Inner track border (0.05m high)
5. Outer track border (flush mounted)
6. Centre point of additional circle

Steeplechase Track with Water Jump Outside The Bend Integrated Into the 400 Metre Standard Track
Calculation of The Length of Running (Lr)

Length of steeplechase lap measured along the running line (from A to A) over the water jump on the outside bend

Semicircle bend (R = 36.80m)	= 115.6106m
Straights of 84.3900m each	= 168.7800m
Water jump bend	= 135.0165m

(2 transition straights of 9.8600m each = 19.7200m

Curved section (R = 36.70m) = 115.2965m)

Total = 419.4071m

Height and Number of Hurdles for Steeplechase Track with Water Jump Inside and Outside the Bend Integrated Into the 400 Metre Standard Oval Track

Event	Height of Hurdles*	Number of Hurdles
3000m Steeplechase Senior Men and U20 Men	0.914m*	35 (28 hurdle jumps (3.94m) and 7 water jumps (3.66m)
2000m Steeplechase U18 Men	0.838m*	23 (18 hurdle jumps (3.94m) and 5 water jumps (3.66m)
3000m Steeplechase Senior Women and U20 Women	0.762m*	35 (28 hurdle jumps (3.94m) and 7 water jumps (3.66m)
2000m Steeplechase U18 Women	0.762m*	23 (18 hurdle jumps (3.94m) and 5 water jumps (3.66m)

* ± 0.003m

STEEPLECHASE RACES

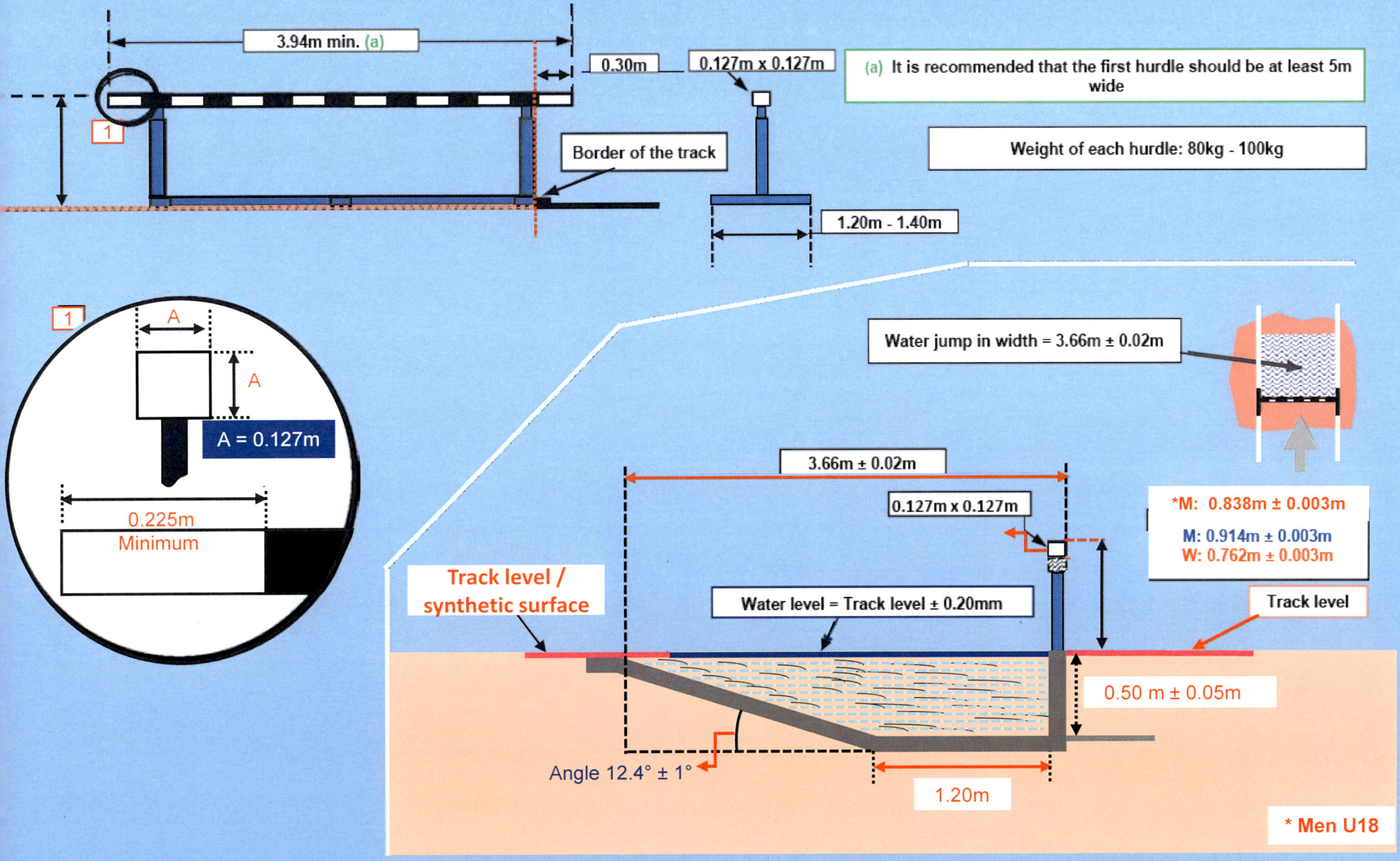

- 3.94m min. (a)
- 0.30m
- 0.127m x 0.127m
- Border of the track
- 1.20m - 1.40m

(a) It is recommended that the first hurdle should be at least 5m wide

Weight of each hurdle: 80kg - 100kg

1
- A
- A = 0.127m
- 0.225m Minimum

Water jump in width = 3.66m ± 0.02m

- 3.66m ± 0.02m
- 0.127m x 0.127m
- *M: 0.838m ± 0.003m
- M: 0.914m ± 0.003m
- W: 0.762m ± 0.003m

Track level / synthetic surface

Water level = Track level ± 0.20mm

Track level

- 0.50 m ± 0.05m
- Angle 12.4° ± 1°
- 1.20m

* Men U18

FIELD EVENTS

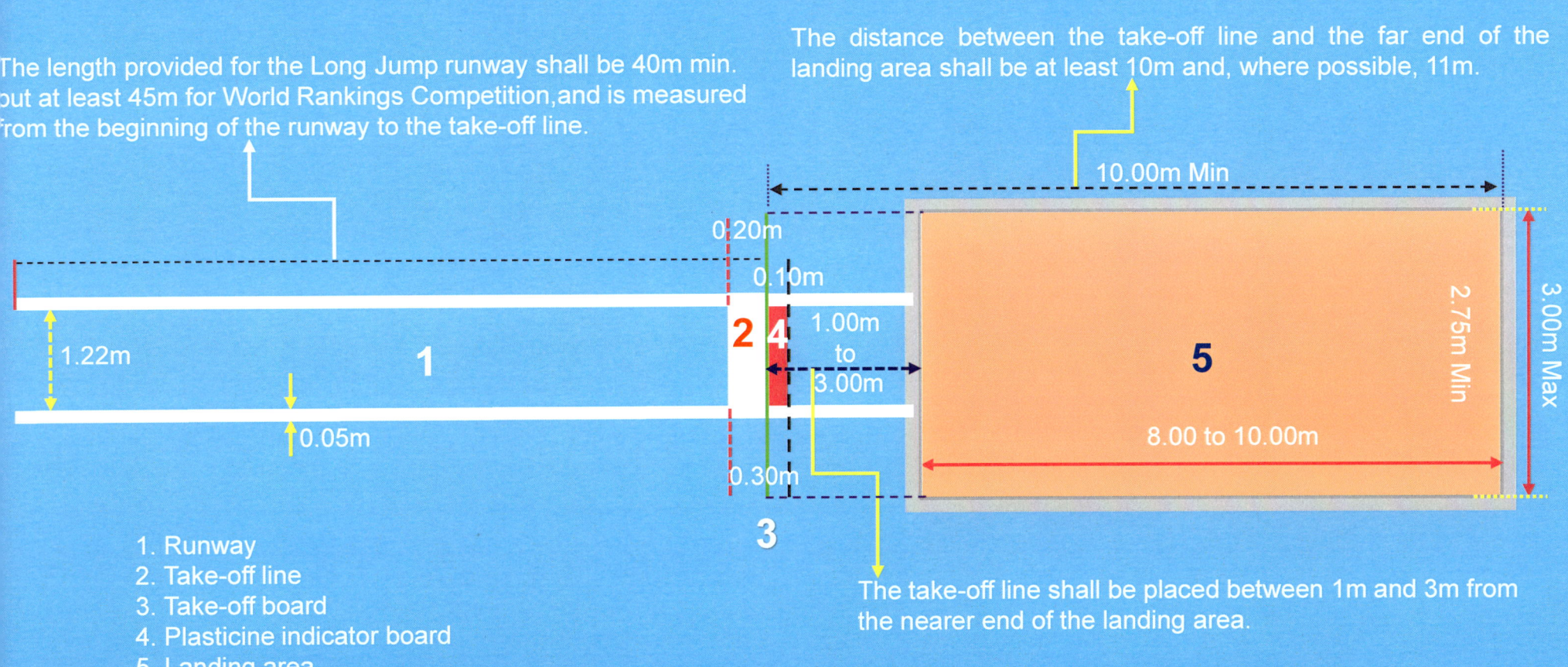

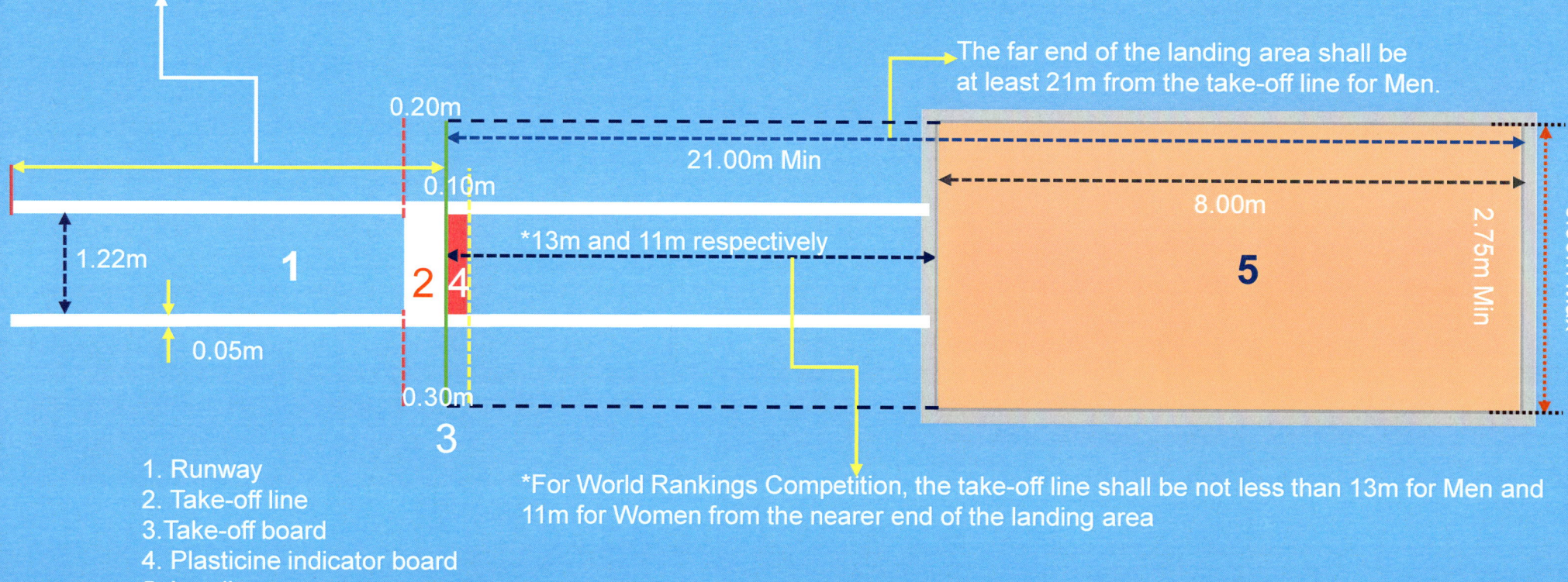

High Jump Runway and Landing Area

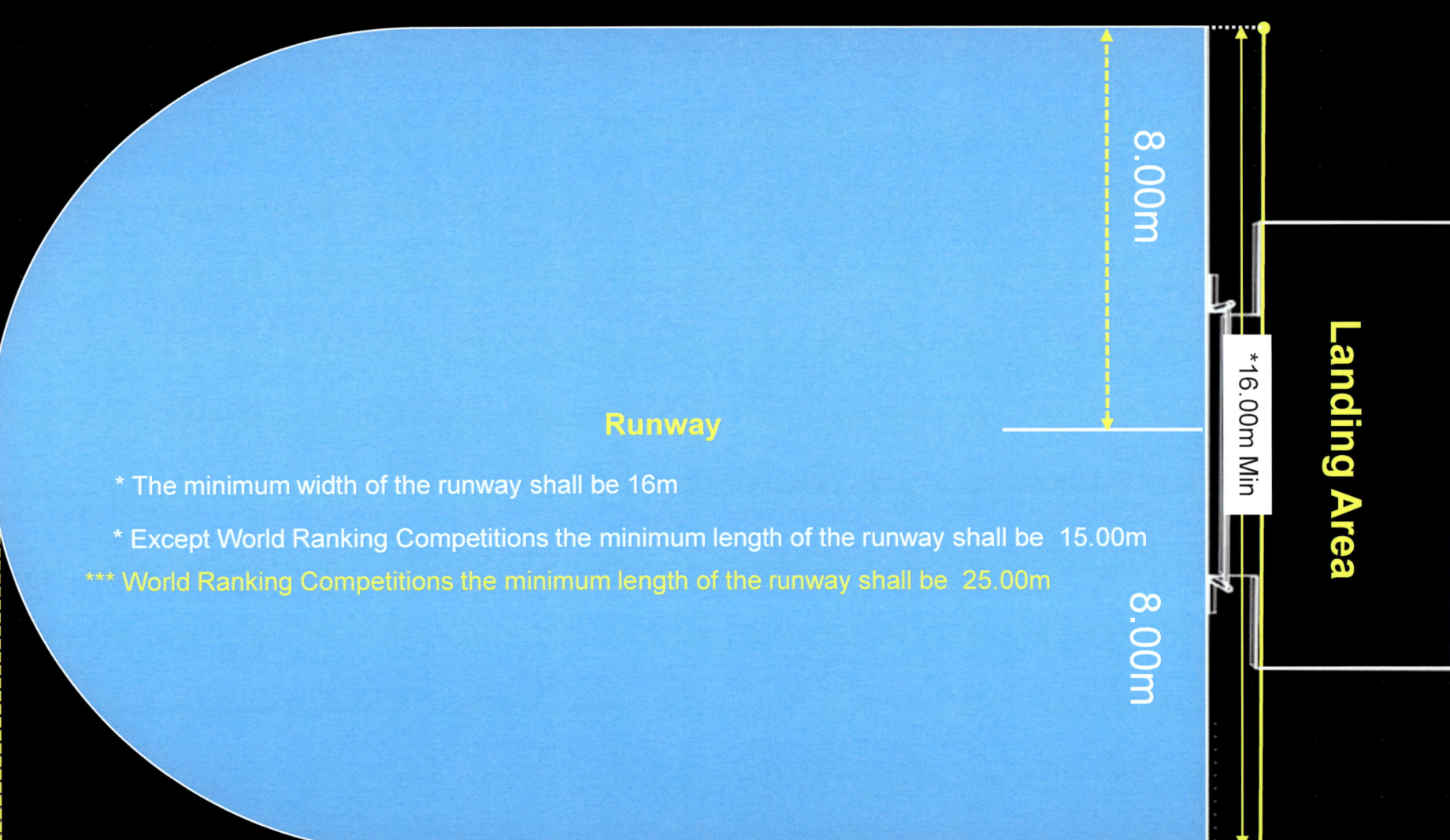

High Jump Runway and Landing Area

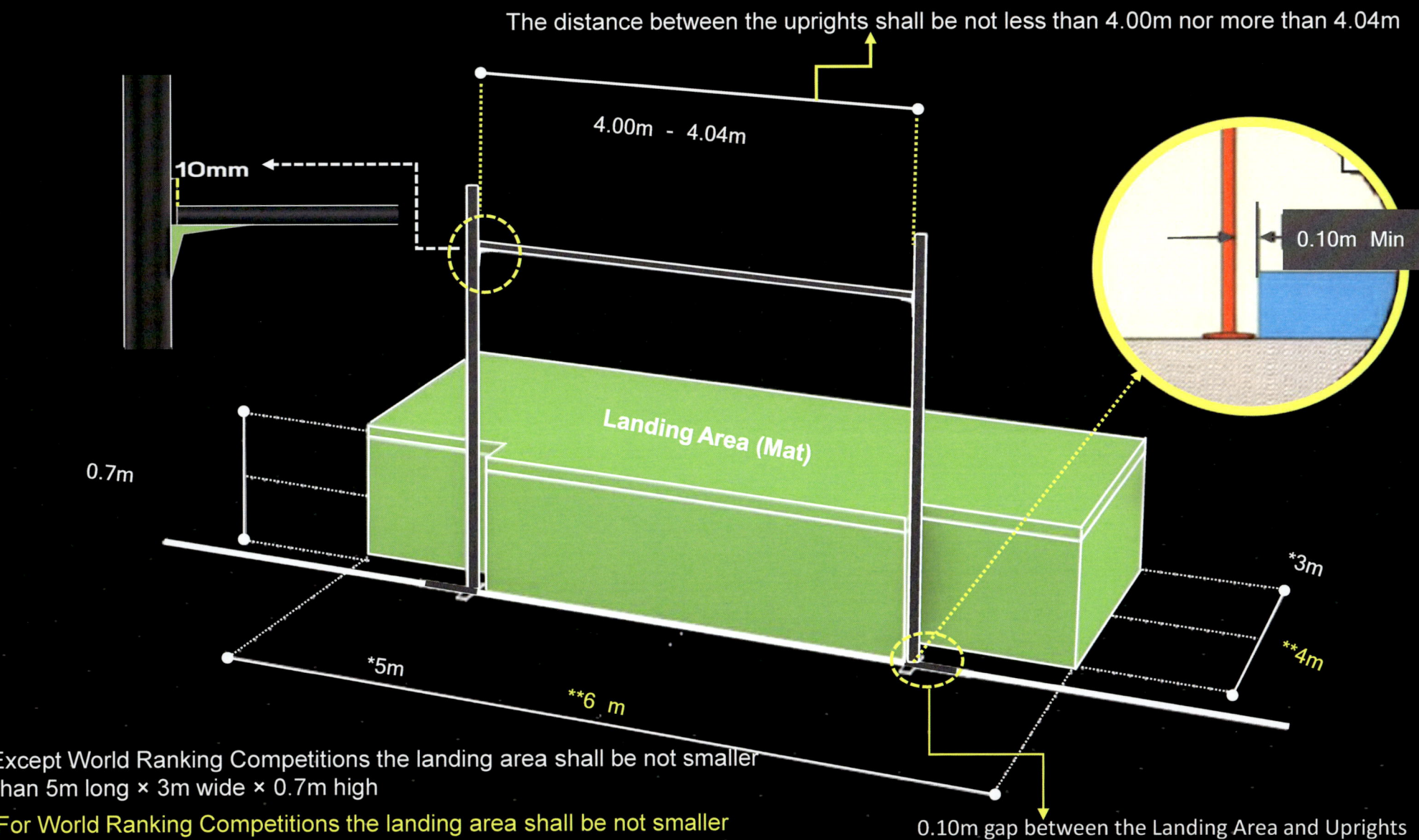

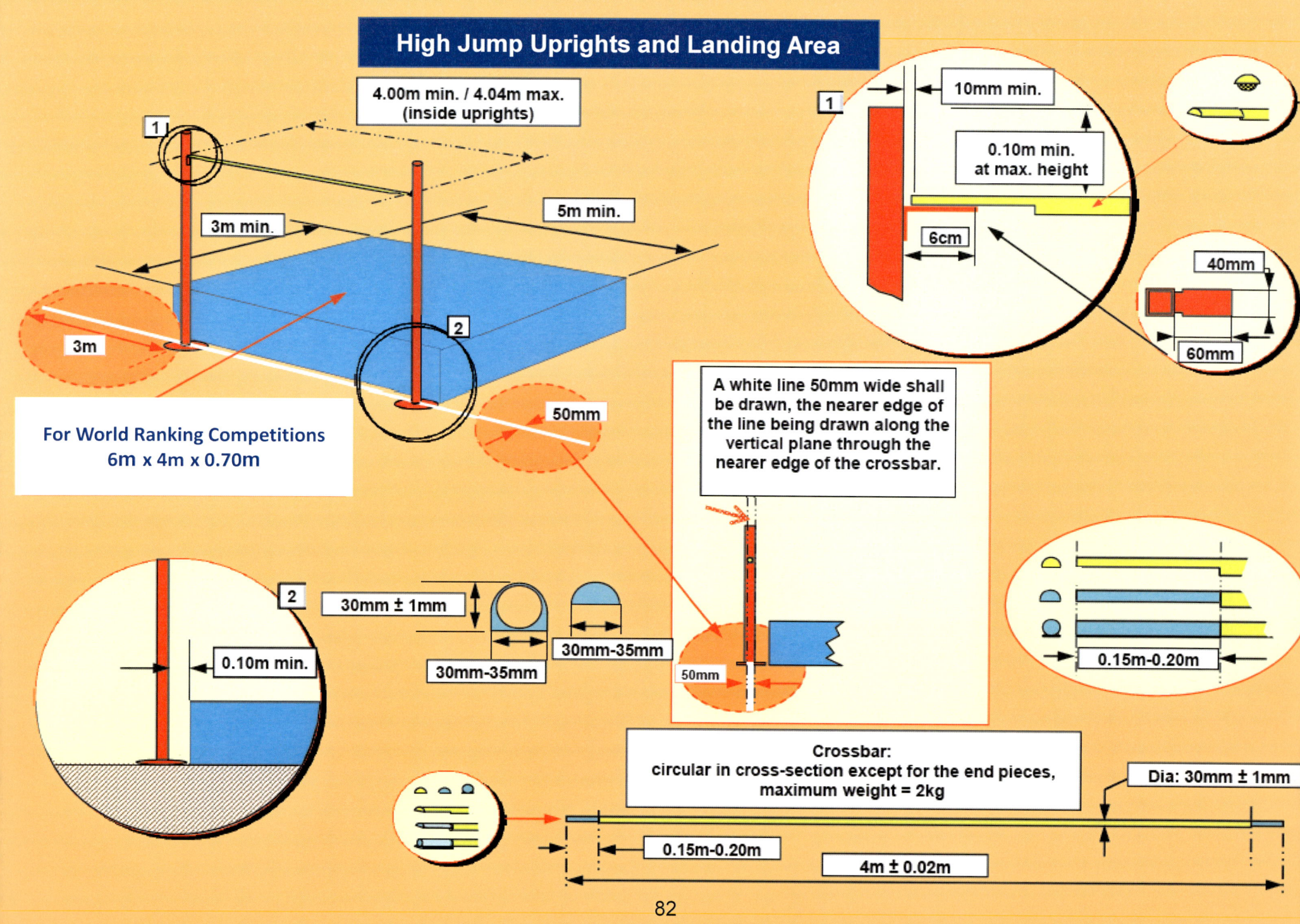

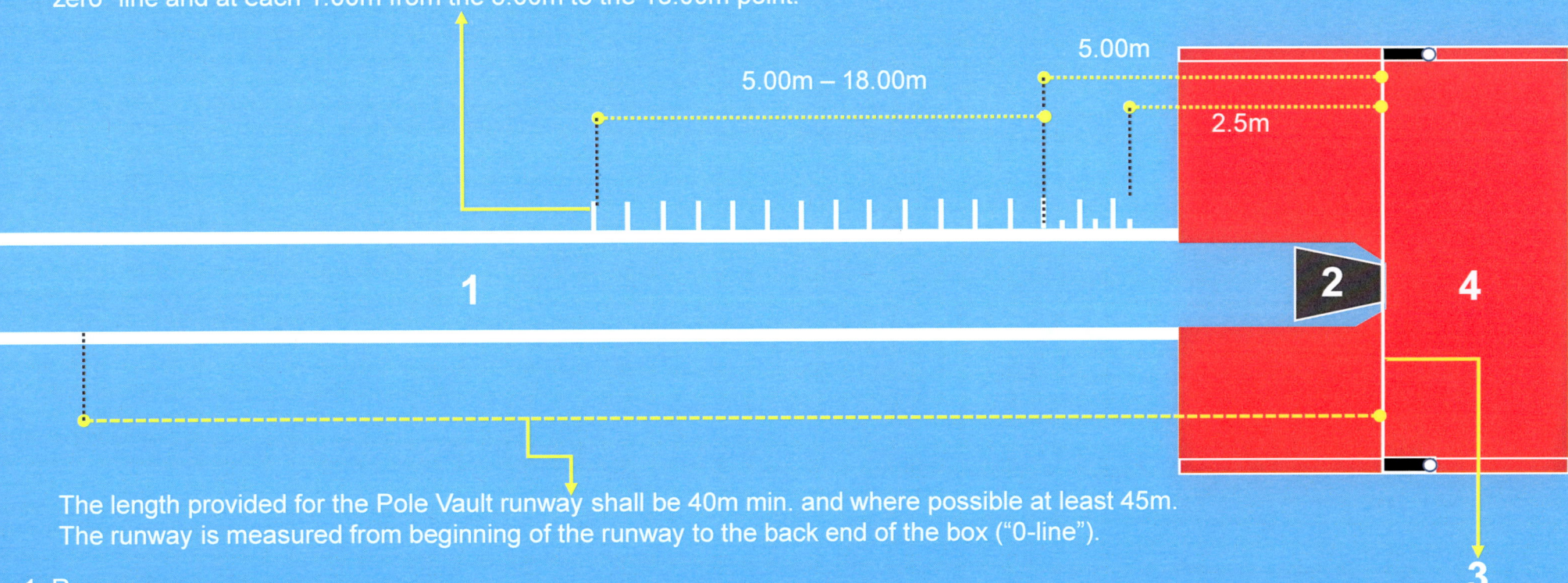

Pole Vault Uprights and Landing Area

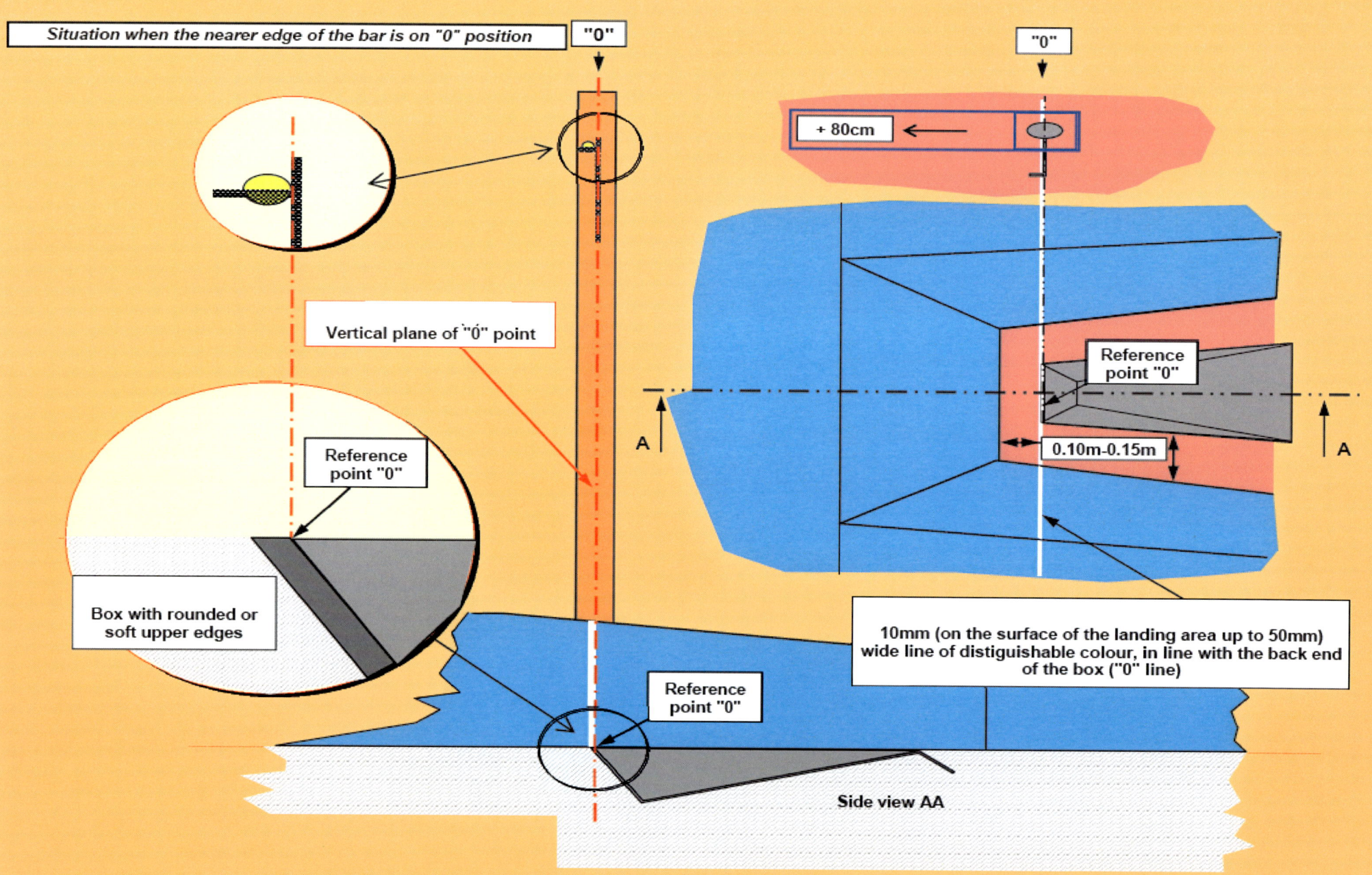

Pole Vault Landing Area

Landing Area
World Ranking Competitions 6m X 6m X 0.80m
Other Competitions 5m X 5m X 0.80m

- 6m min.
- 5m min.
- 5m min.
- 6m min.
- Protective pad (uprights)
- Moving uprights or supports
- 0cm–80cm
- "0"
- Not smaller than 2m
- 1.22m ±0.01m
- 50mm
- 0.20m
- 1.080m
- Level of Runway
- 30°
- 105°
- 0.20m
- 1.00m
- 0.224m
- Rigid material
- 1.084m
- 0.60m
- 0.408m
- 0.15m
- Angle 120°

Length of the runway 40m min. and where possible at least 45m

(A) - Additional surface for the athlete's safety

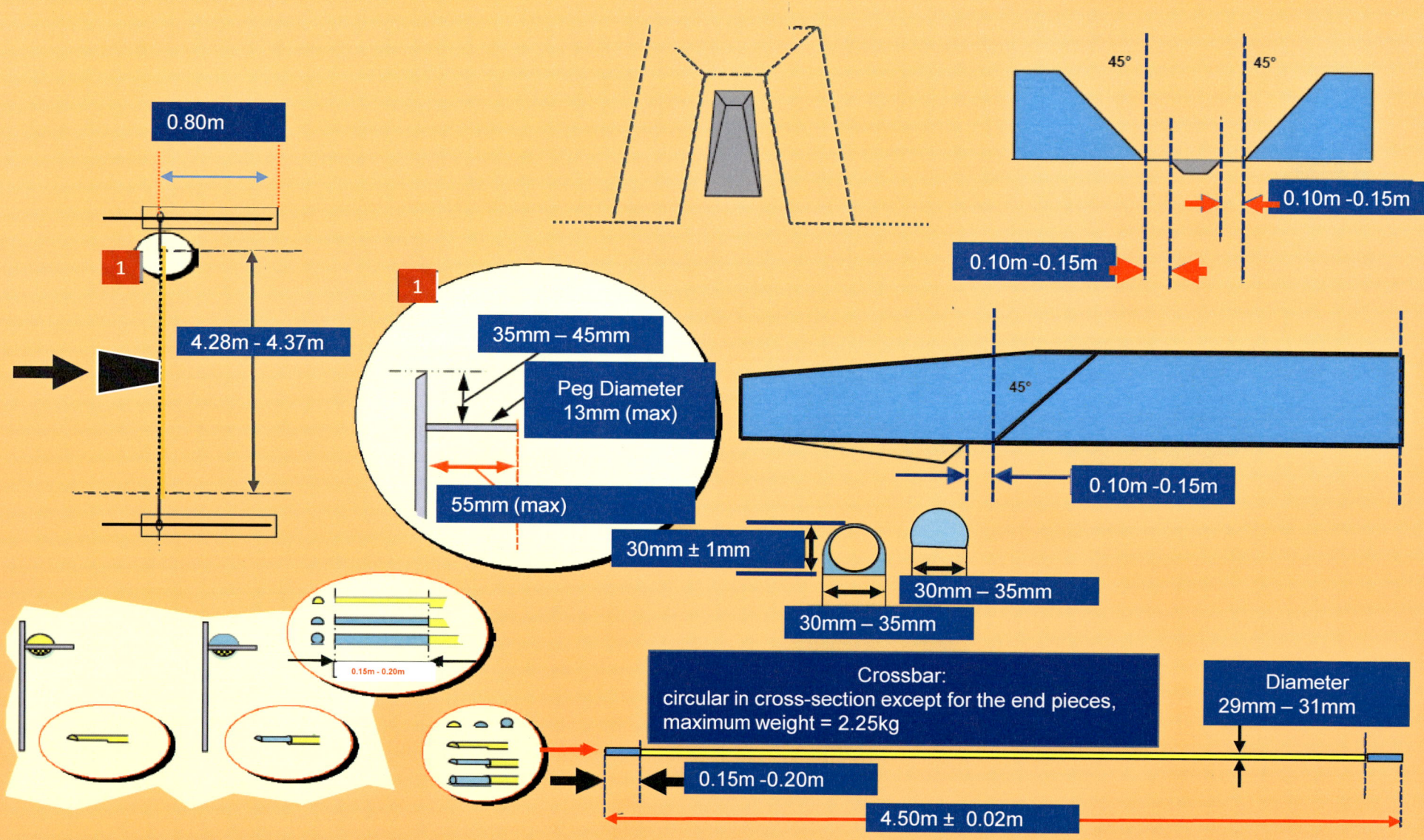

Throwing Events Official Implements

Implement	Women U18	Women U20 / Senior	Men U18	Men U20	Men Senior
Shot	3.000kg	4.000kg	5.000kg	6.000kg	7.260kg
Discus	1.000kg	1.000kg	1.500kg	1.750kg	2.00kg
Hammer	3.000kg	4.000kg	5.000kg	6.000kg	7.260kg
Javelin	500g	600g	700g	800g	800g

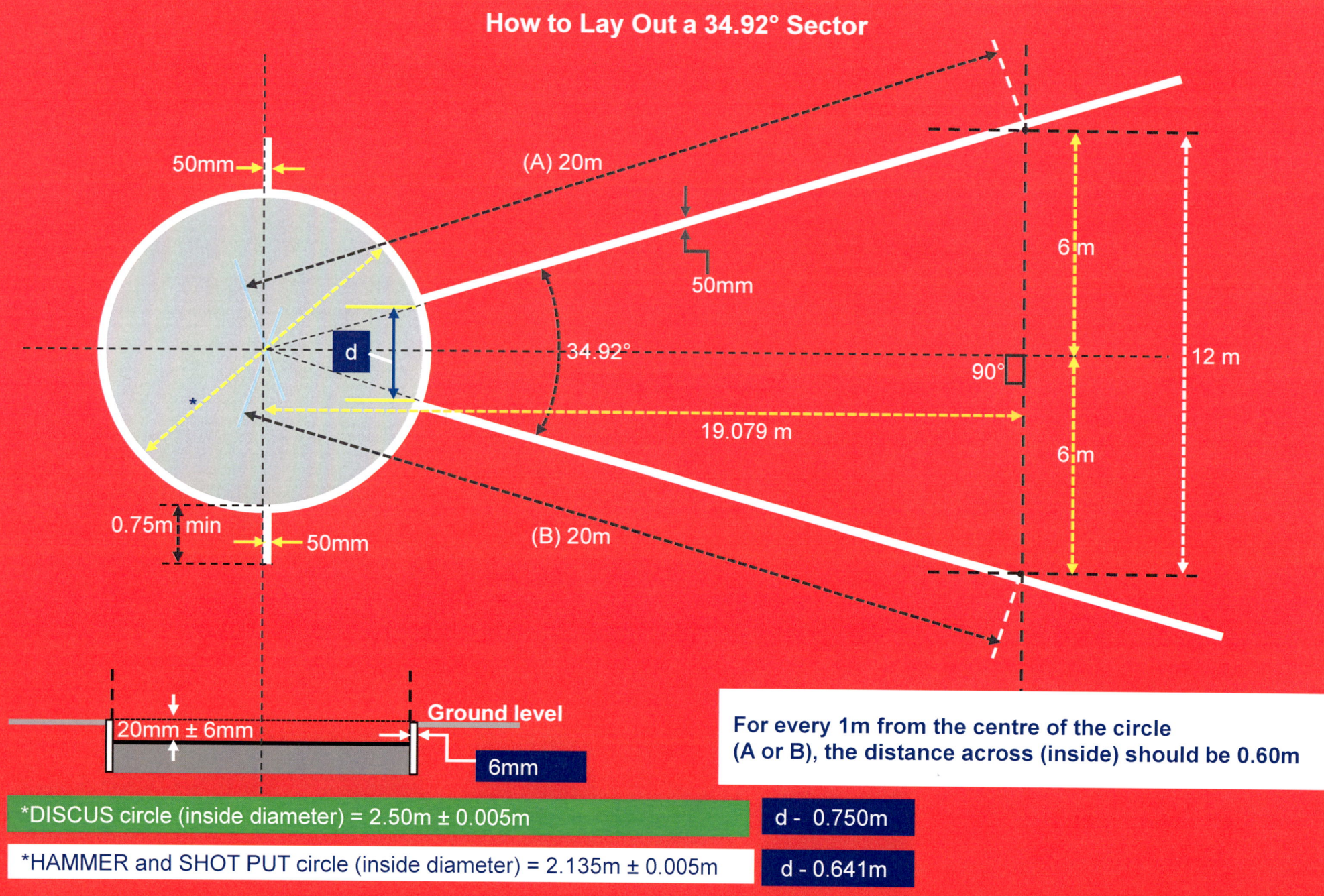

Shot Put Circle and Landing Sector

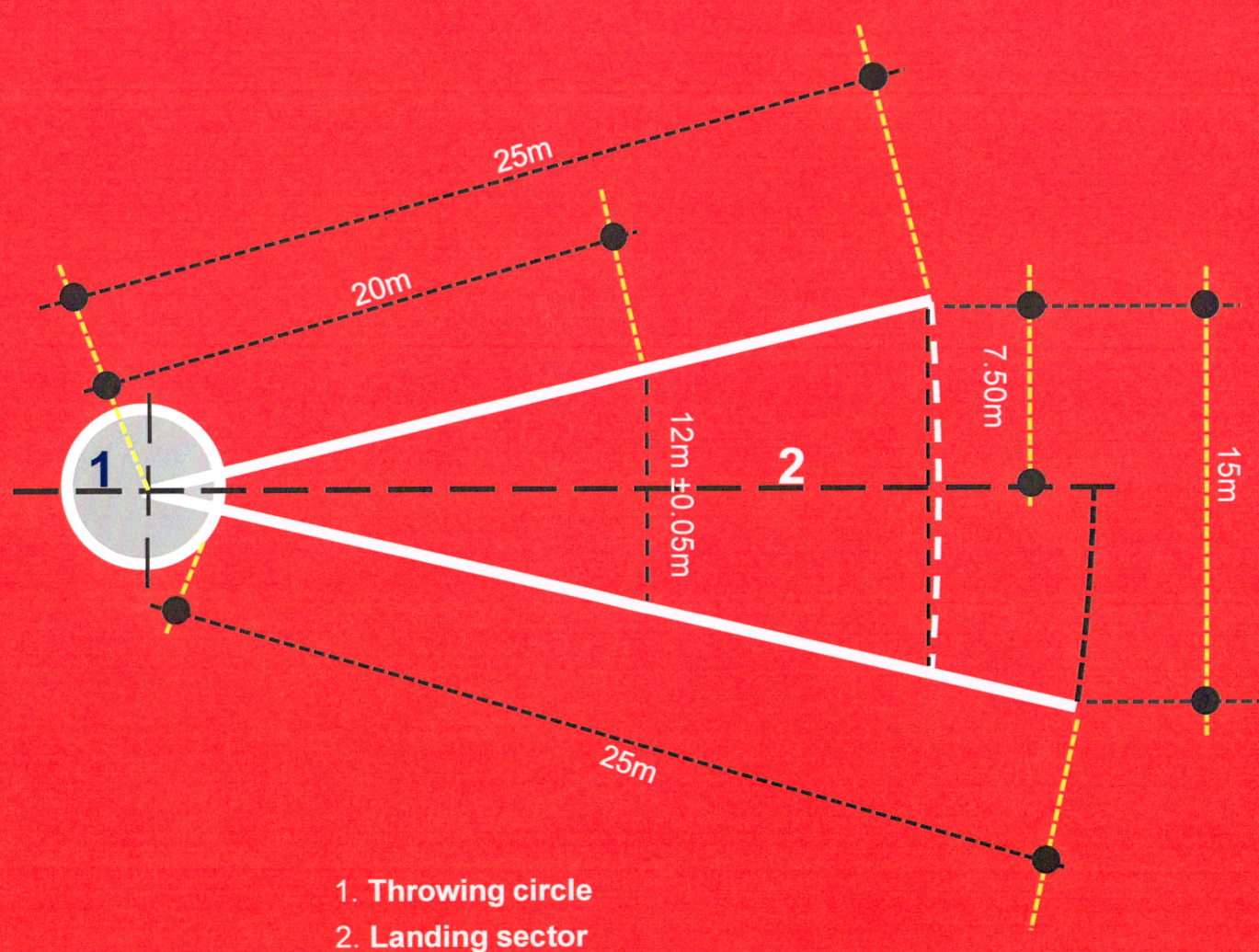

1. **Throwing circle**
2. **Landing sector**

Shot Put Circle and Stop Board

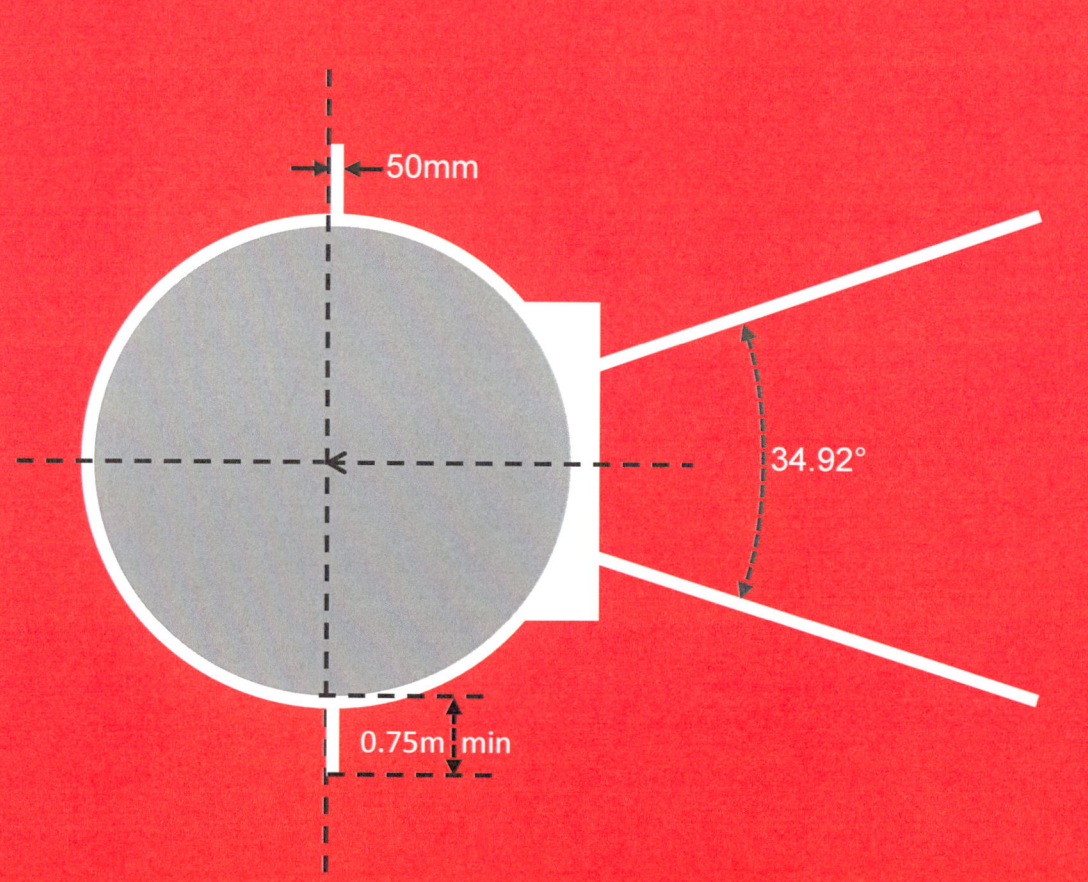
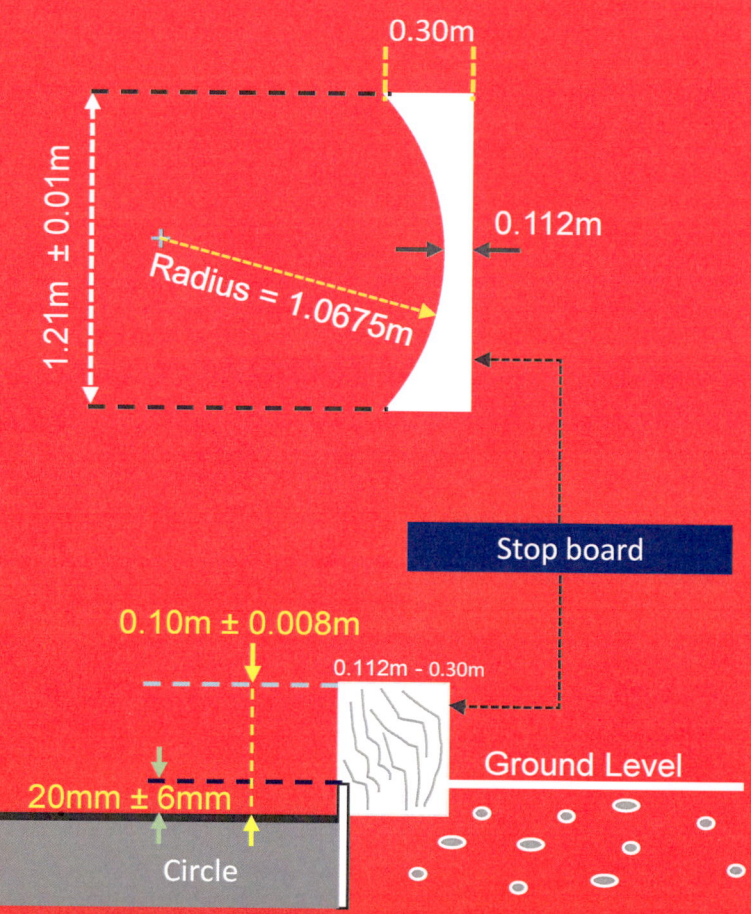

SHOT PUT circle (inside diameter) = 2.135m ± 0.005m

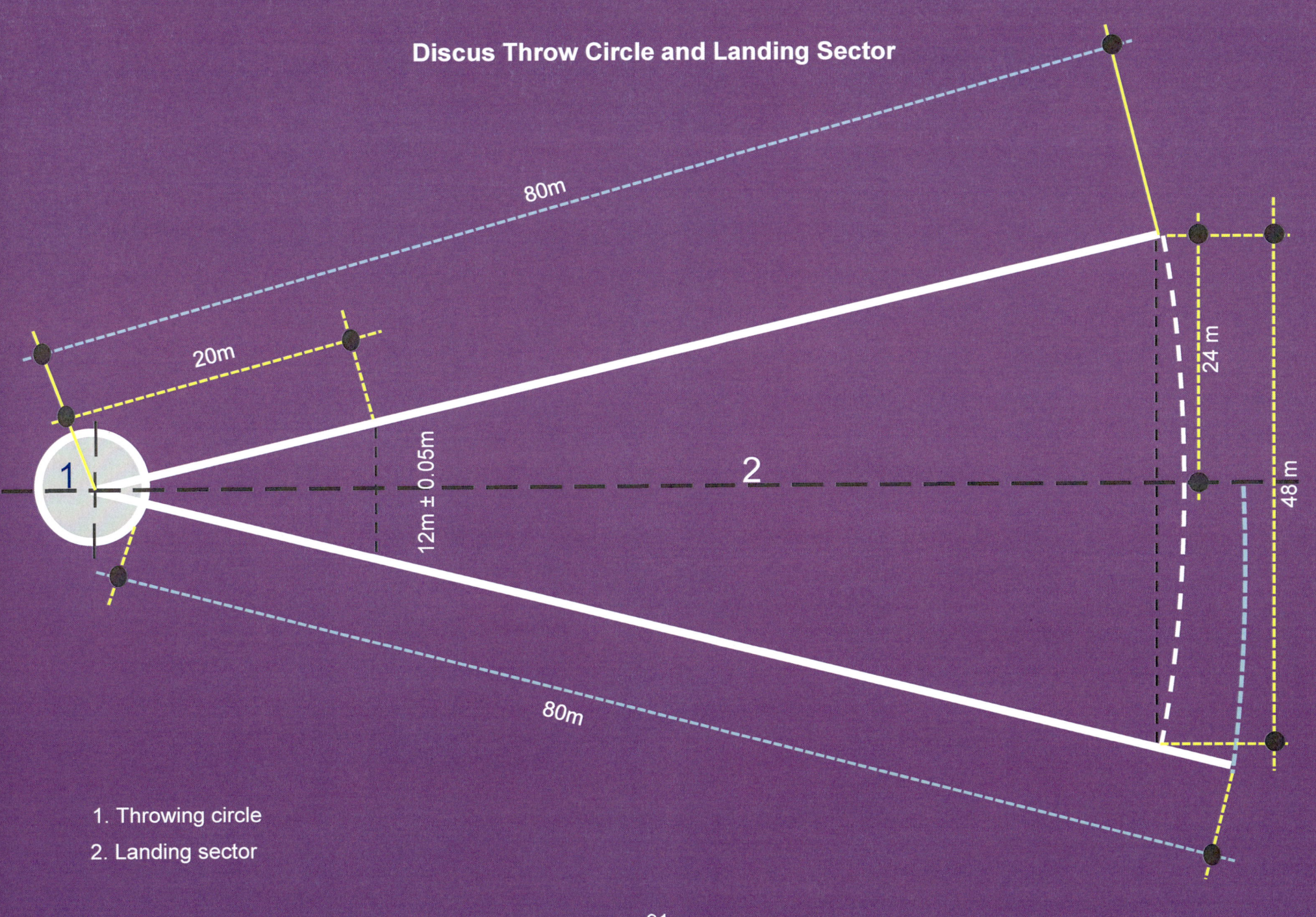

Cage for Discus Throw Only (with cage dimensions to netting)

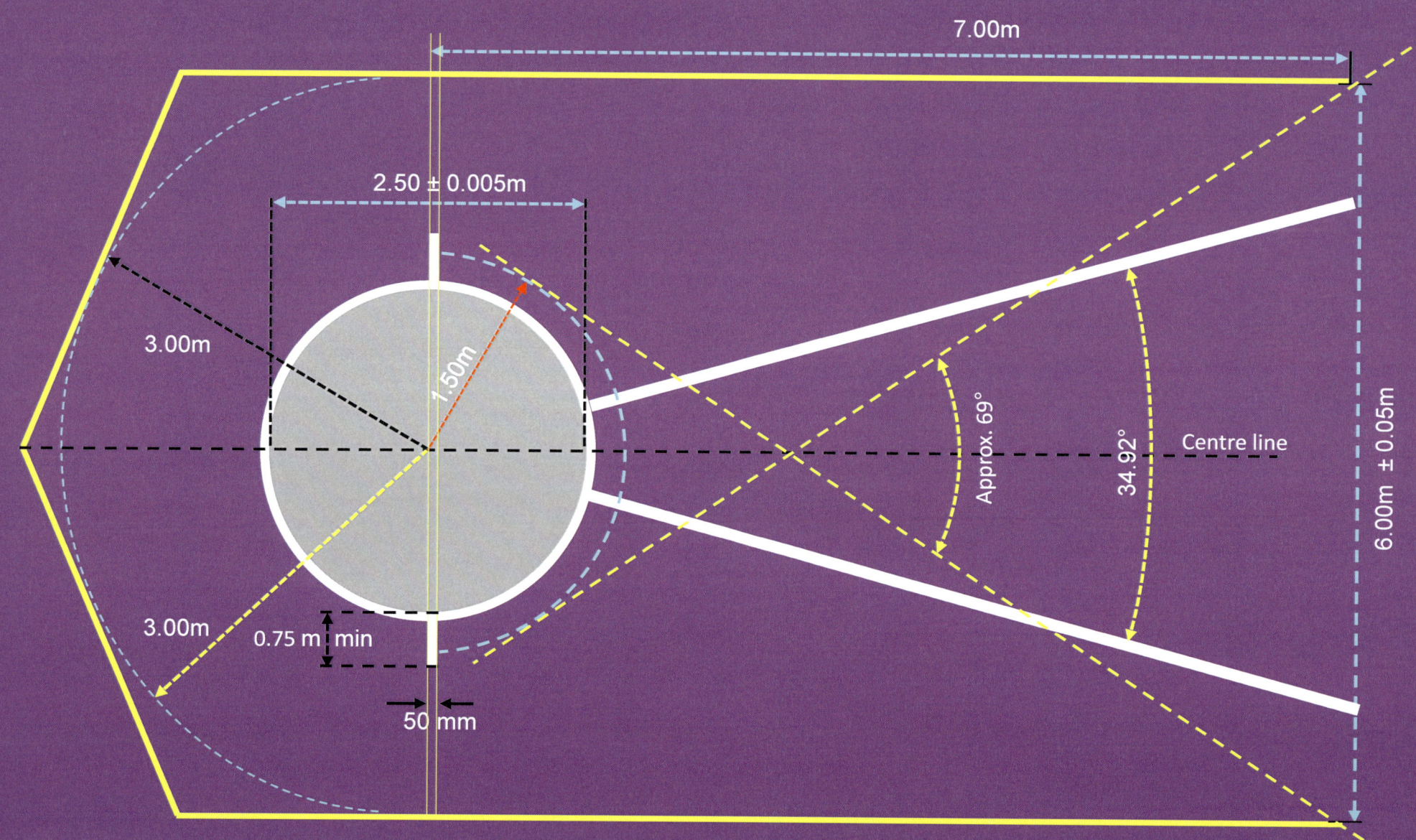

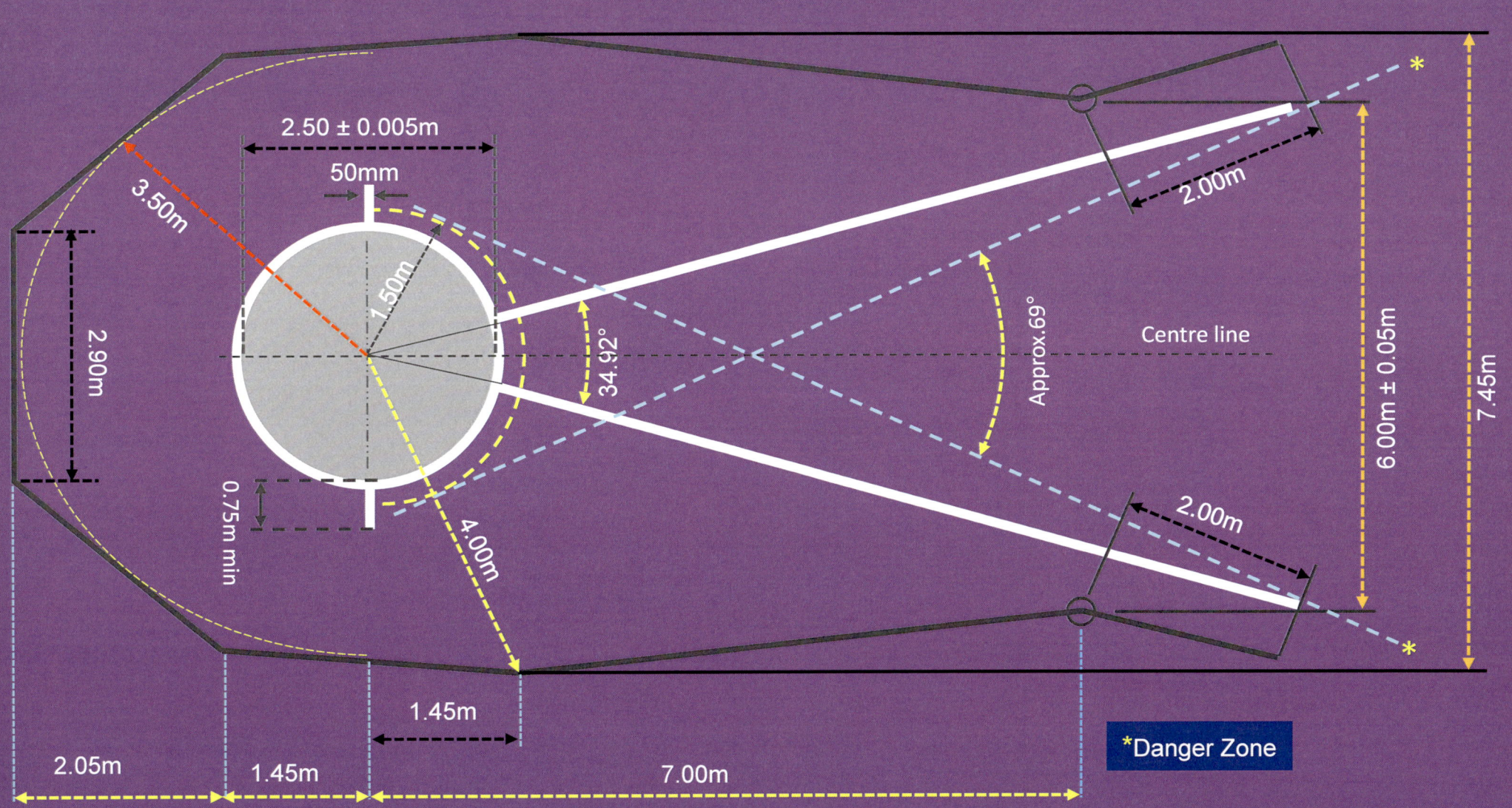

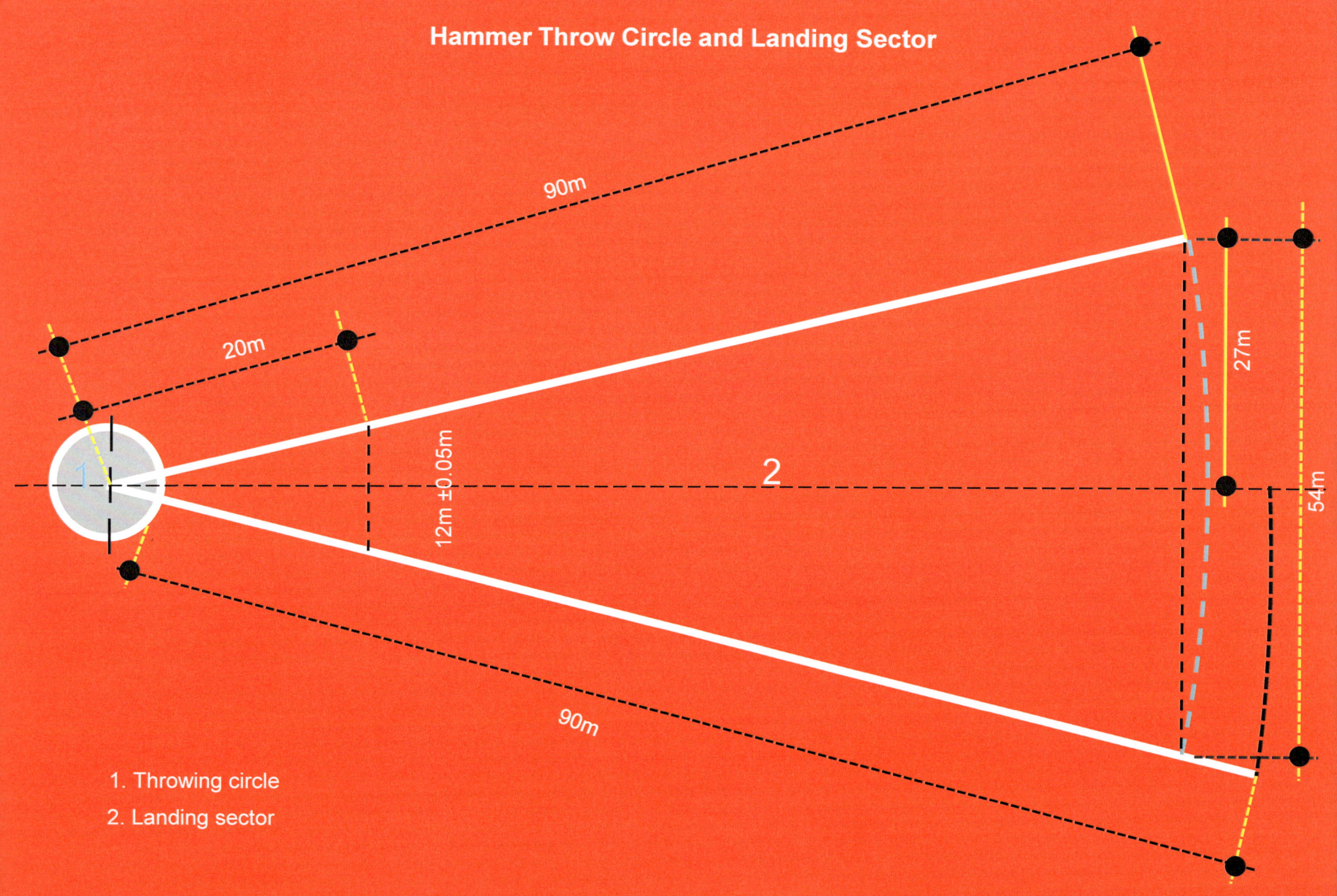

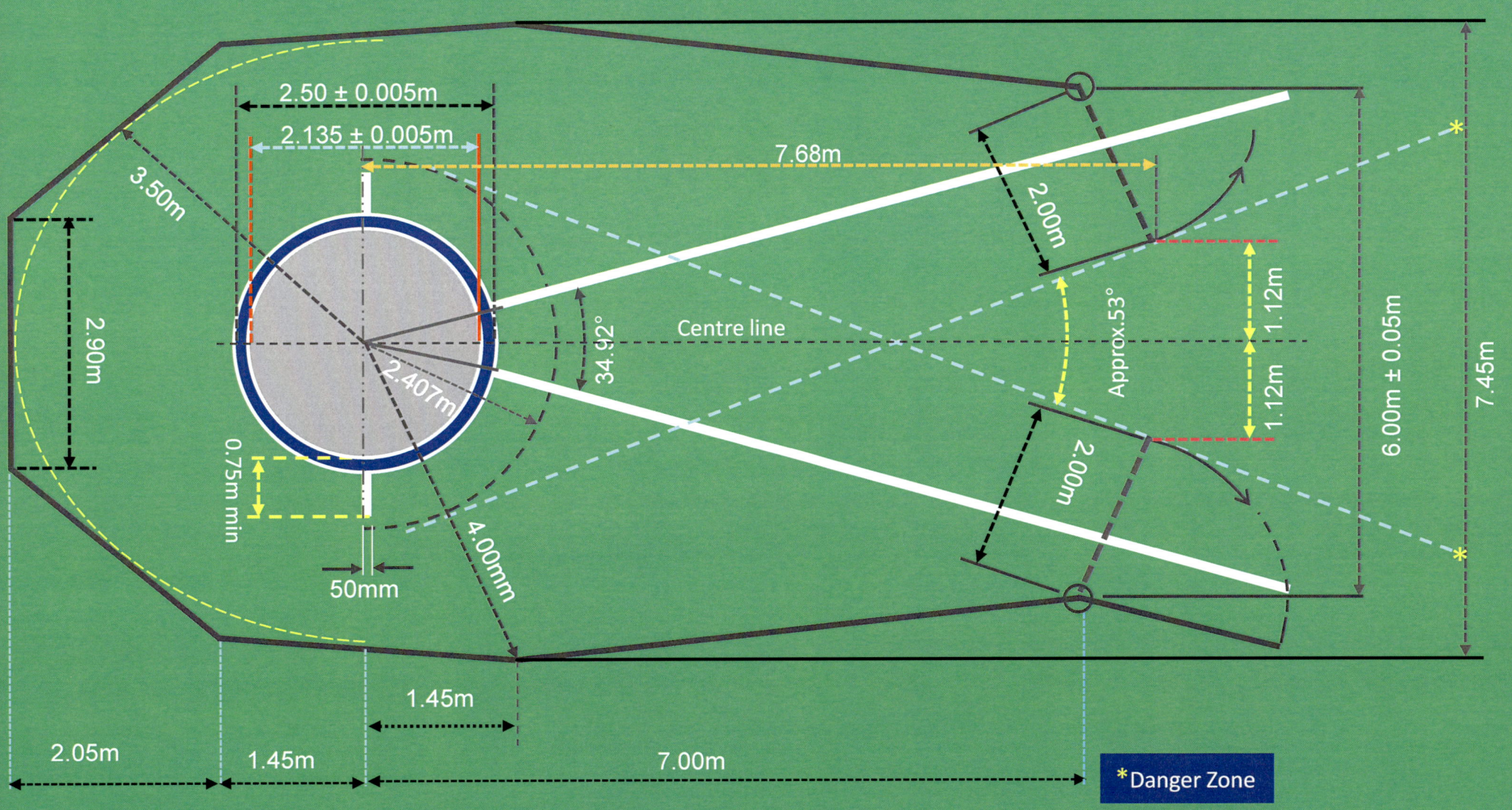

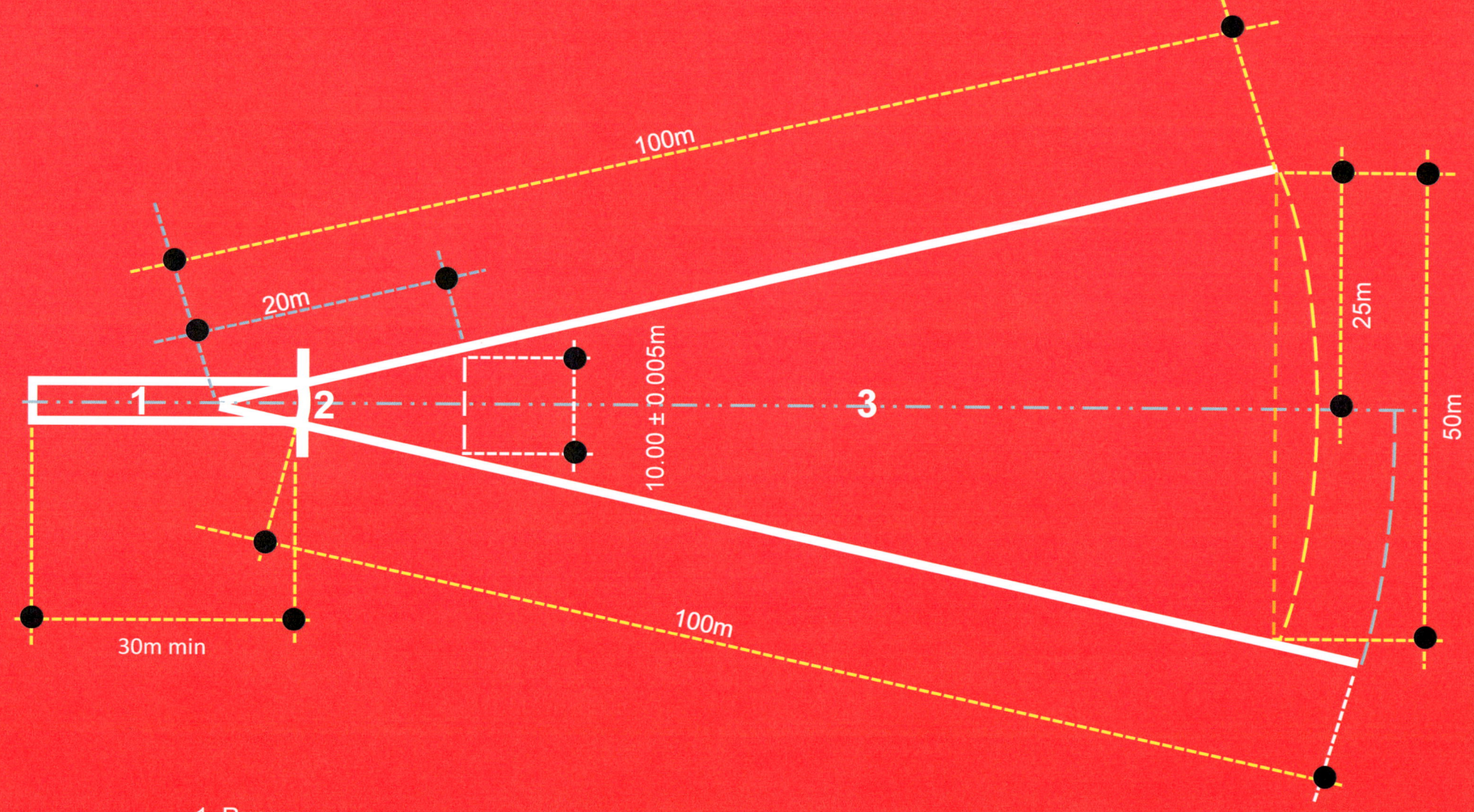

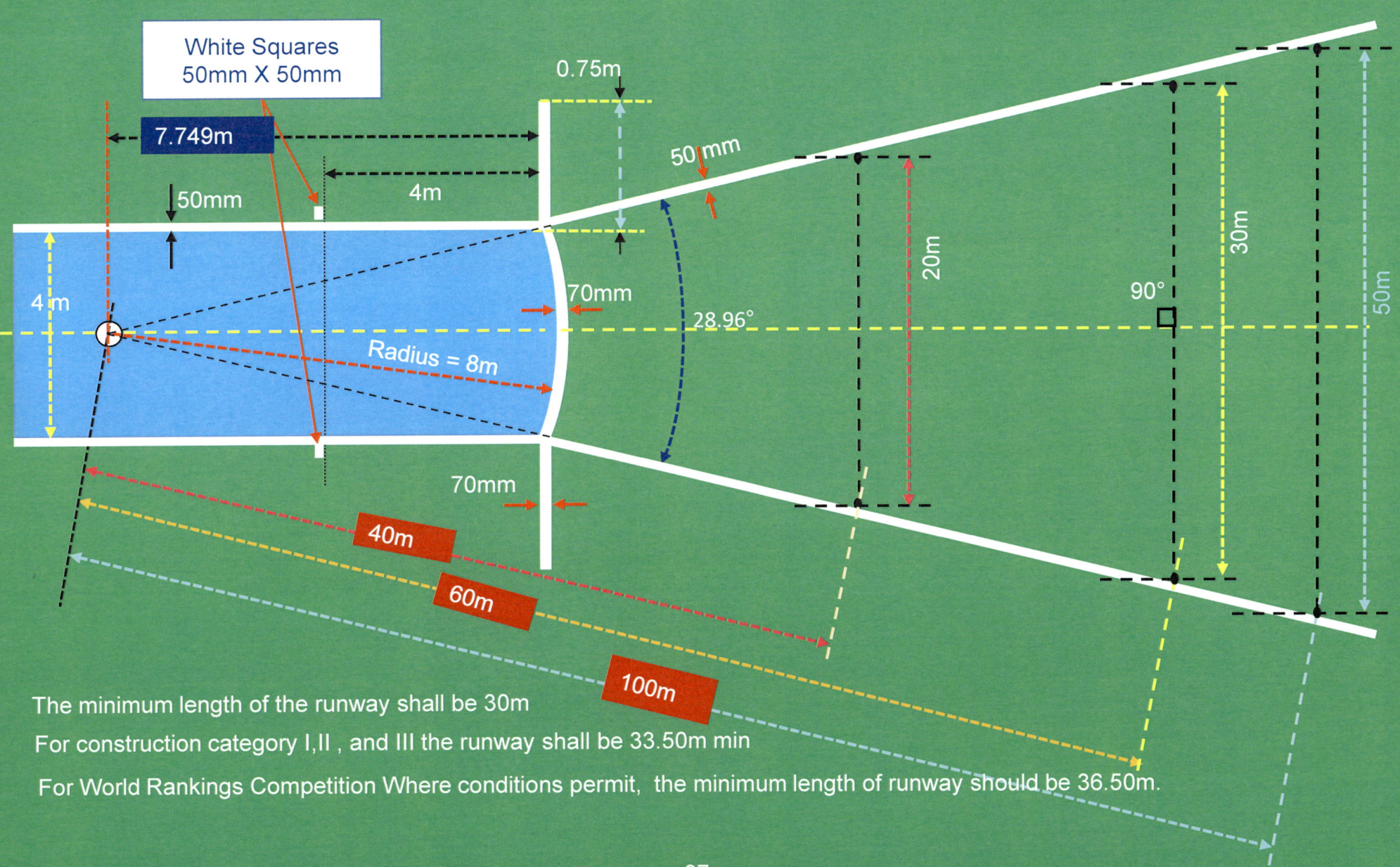

200 METRE OVAL TRACK

TRACK EVENTS

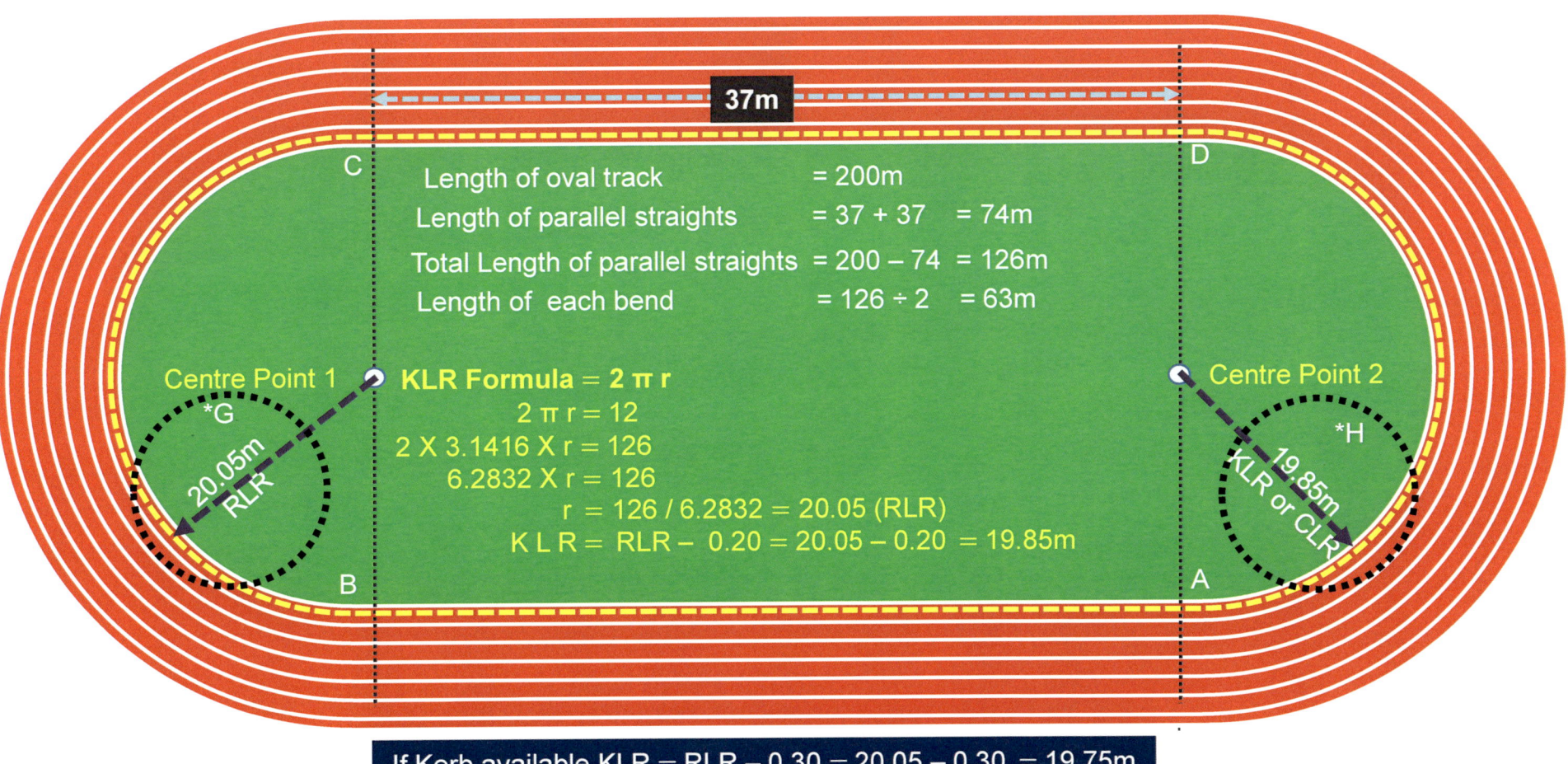

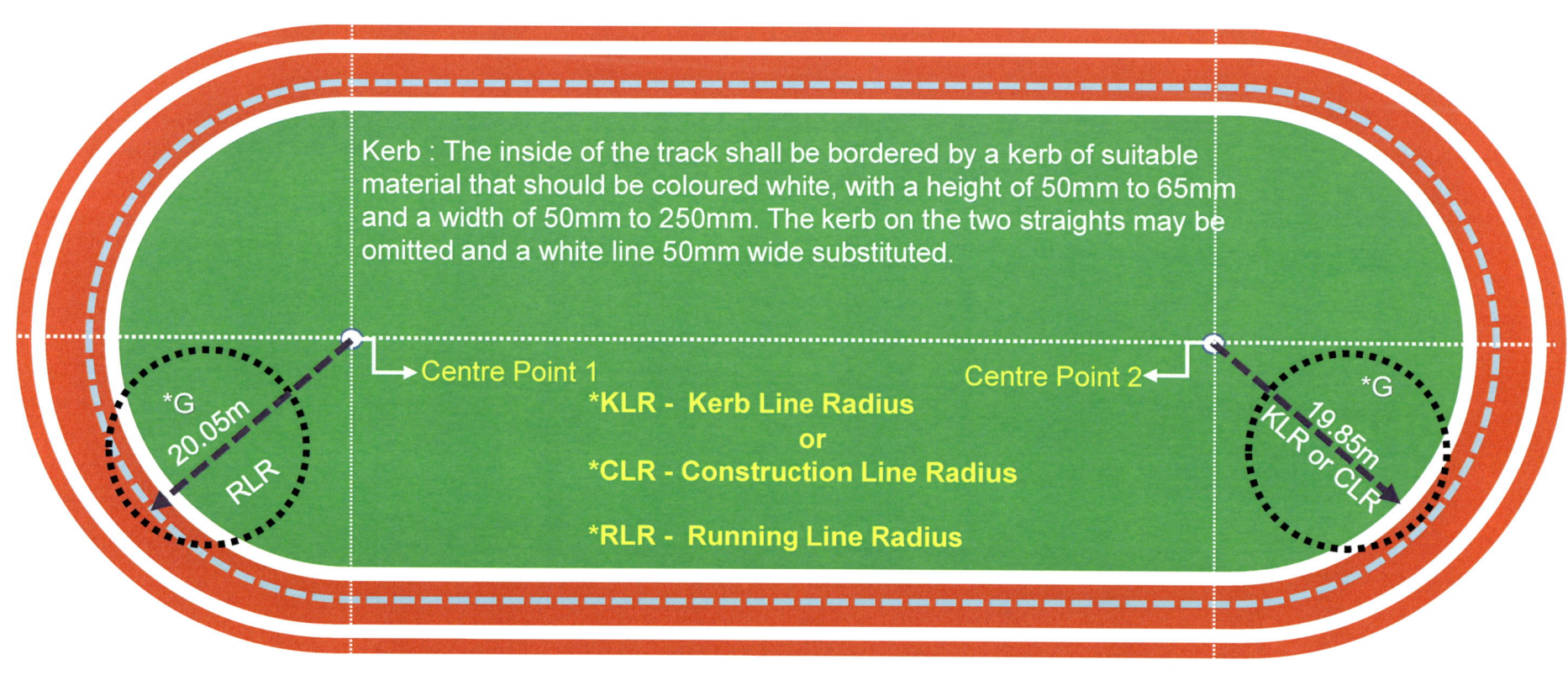

200 Metre Oval Track Set Out Measurement

Set Out Measurement	Metres
Length of parallel straights	37.000
Kerb radius of semicircle bend	19.850
Radius of measurement line (running line) in lane 1 (0.20m outside kerb)	20.053
Length of each bend on kerb line	62.360
Length of each bend along running line	62.999
Length of oval track on kerb line	198.721
Length of oval track along of running line	200.000
Width of the lane including the 0.05m line on the outside	1.22m ± 0.01

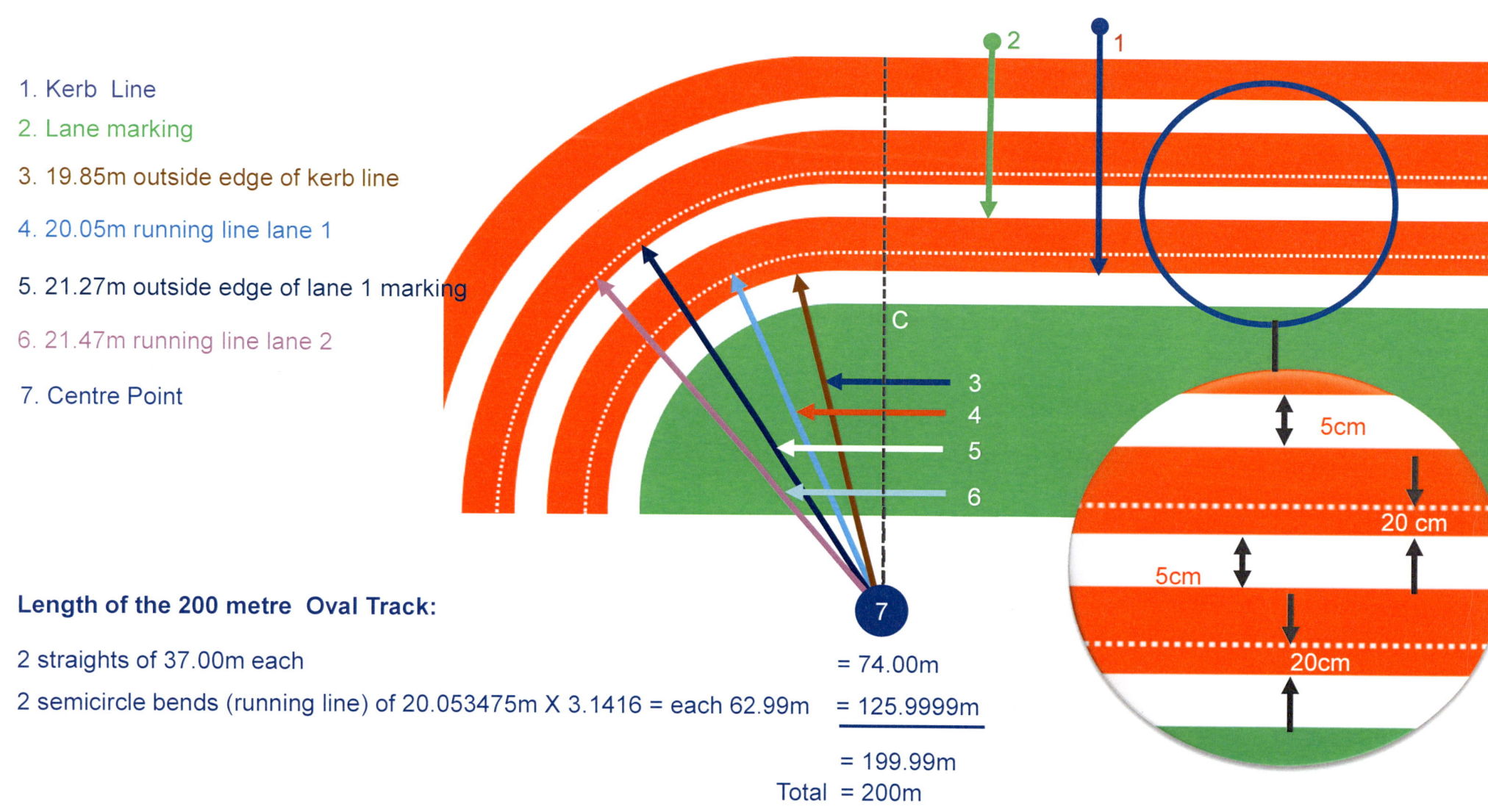

Setting Out Plan and Dimensions of the 200 Metre Oval Track

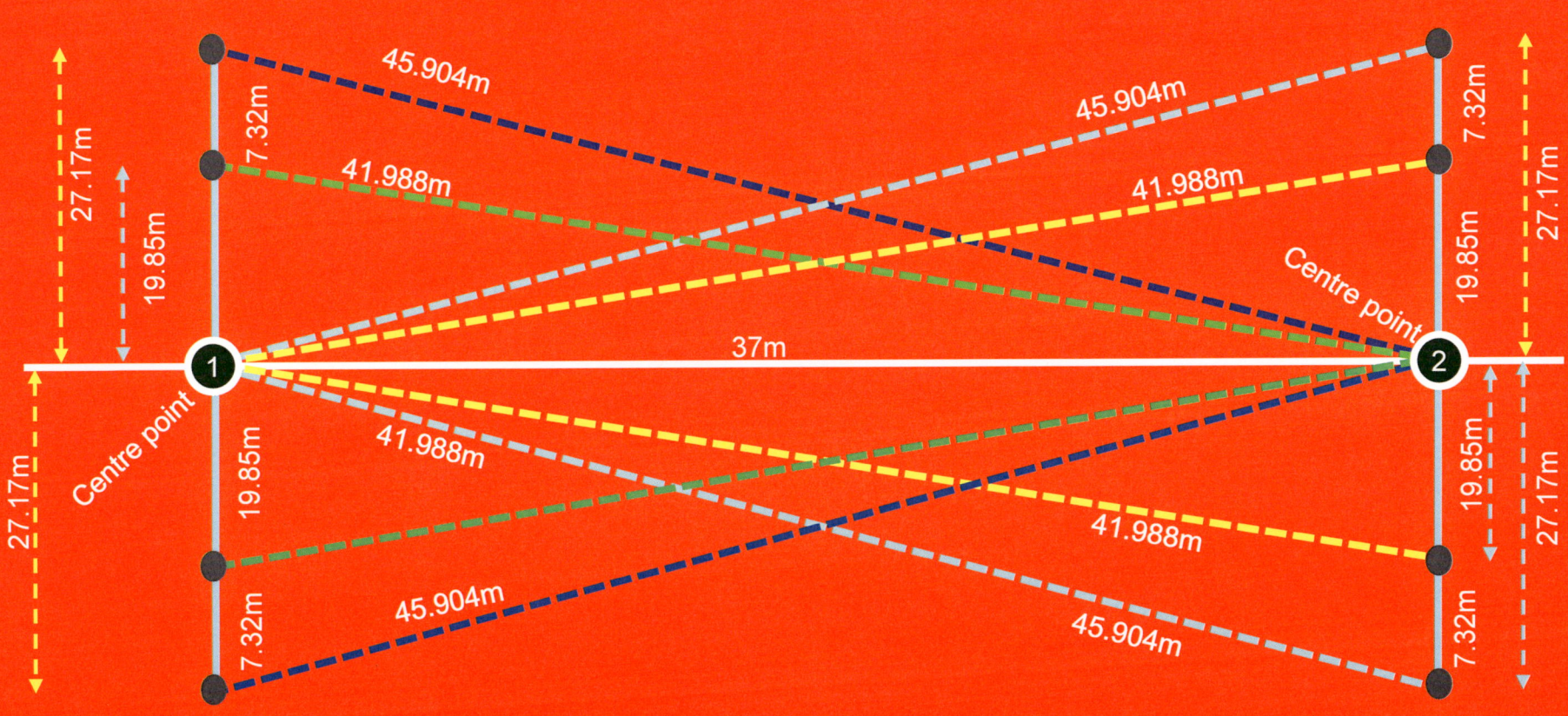

105

Setting Out Plan and Dimensions of the 200 Metre Oval Track

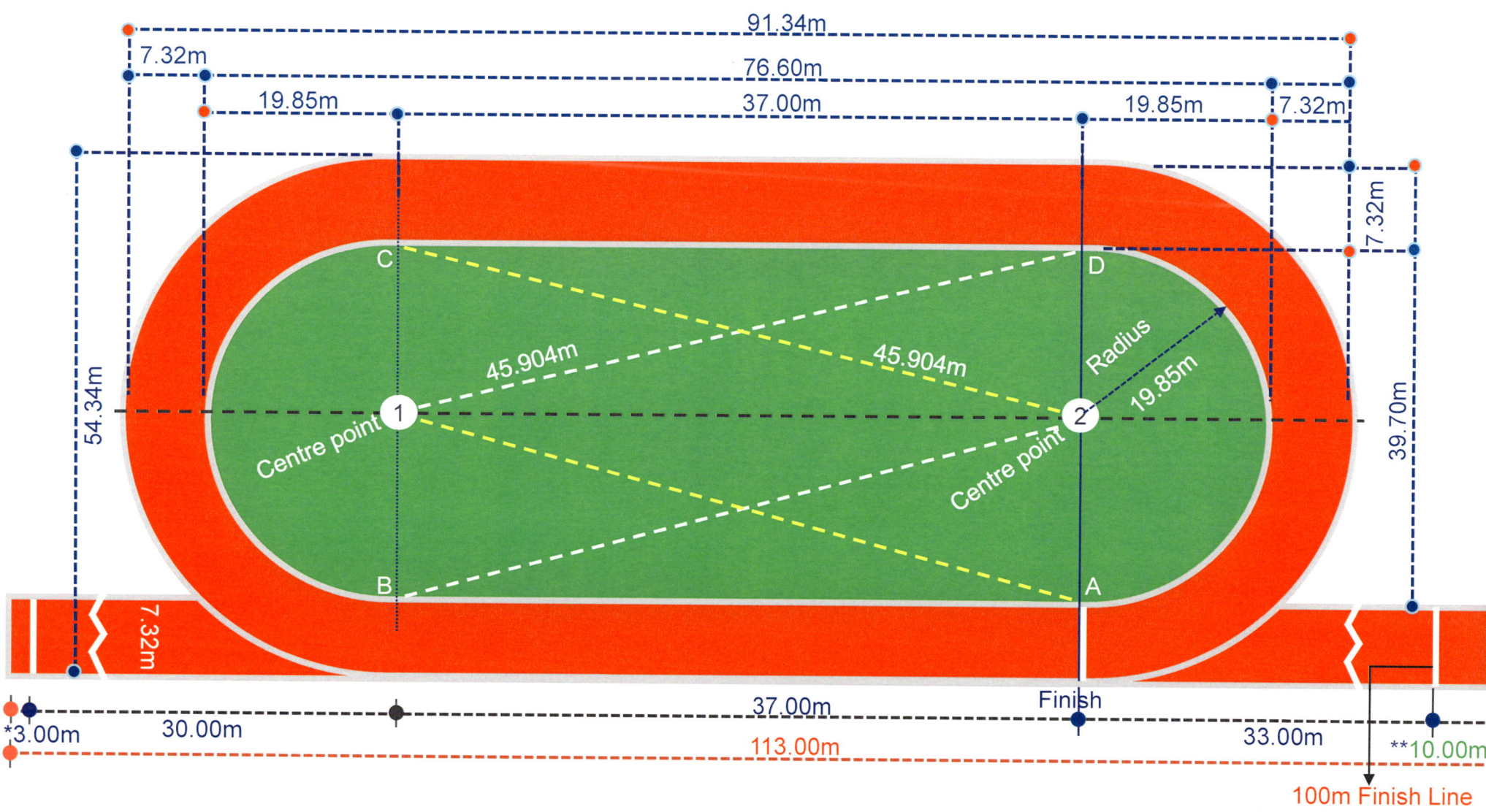

*The straight shall incorporate a starting area, *3.00m minimum., and run-out, **10.00m minimum

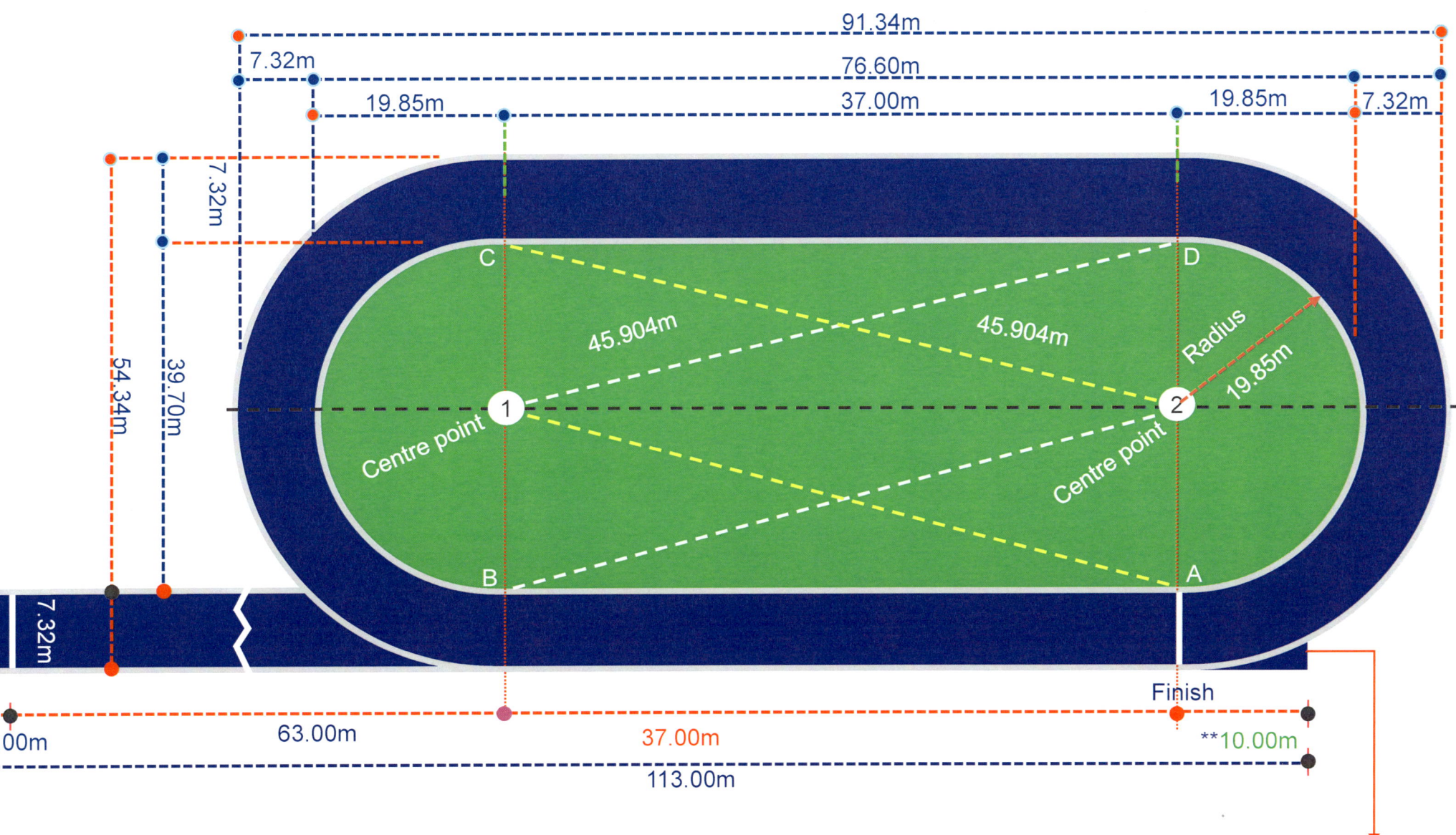

Setting Out Plan and Dimensions of the 200 Metre Oval Track

The straight shall incorporate a starting area, *3.00m minimum., and run-out, **10.00m minimum

Calculation of Staggers
(For the track without raised kerb)

Stagger Formula W (n–1) X 2 π

W – Width of the lane

n – Number of the lane

π - Value 3.141

Example : Lane number 2 = 1.22 (2–1) X 2 X 3.1416 = 7.66

1 Stagger = 7.66

1/2 Stagger = 7.66 ÷ 2 = 3.83

1 1/2 Stagger = 7.66 + 3.83 = 11.49

Stagger	Lane Number 1	Lane Number 2	Lane Number 3	Lane Number 4	Lane Number 5	Lane Number 6
1/2	----	3.83	7.66	11.49	15.33	19.16
1	----	7.66	15.33	22.99	30.66	38.32
1 1/2	----	11.49	22.99	34.48	45.99	57.48

As per World Athletics suggestion, the π Value is 3.1416

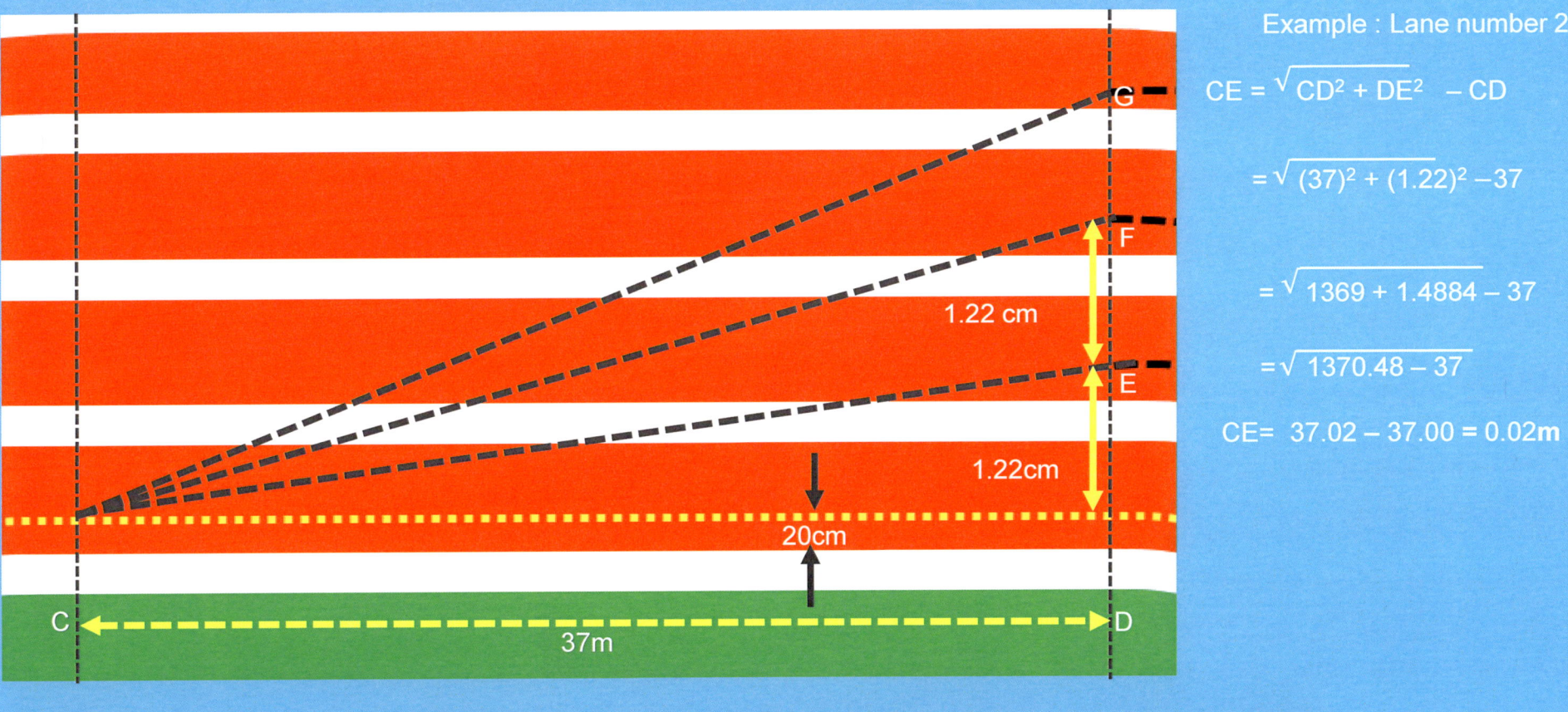

Breakline Marking
(For the track without raised kerb)

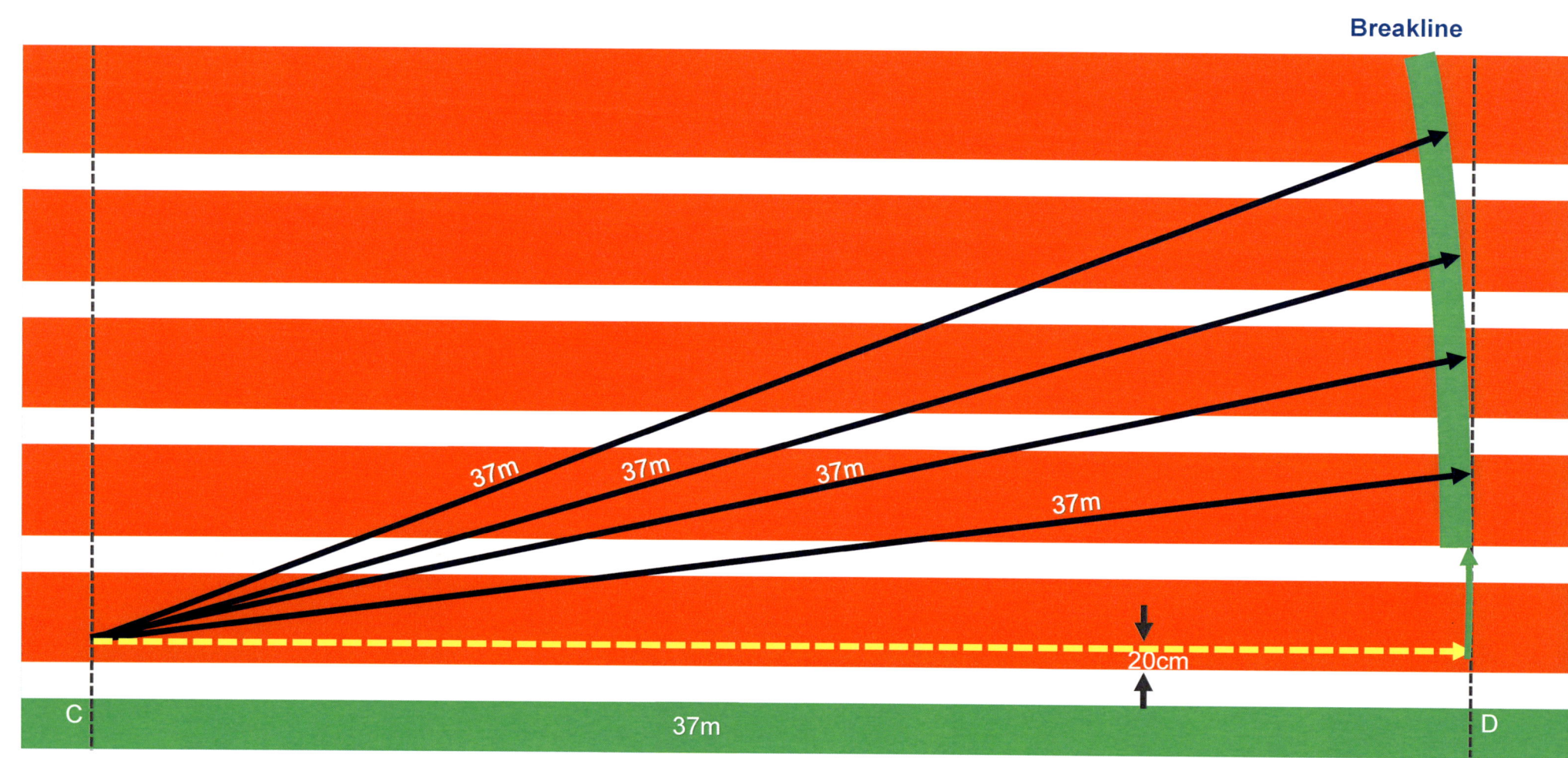

100 Metres

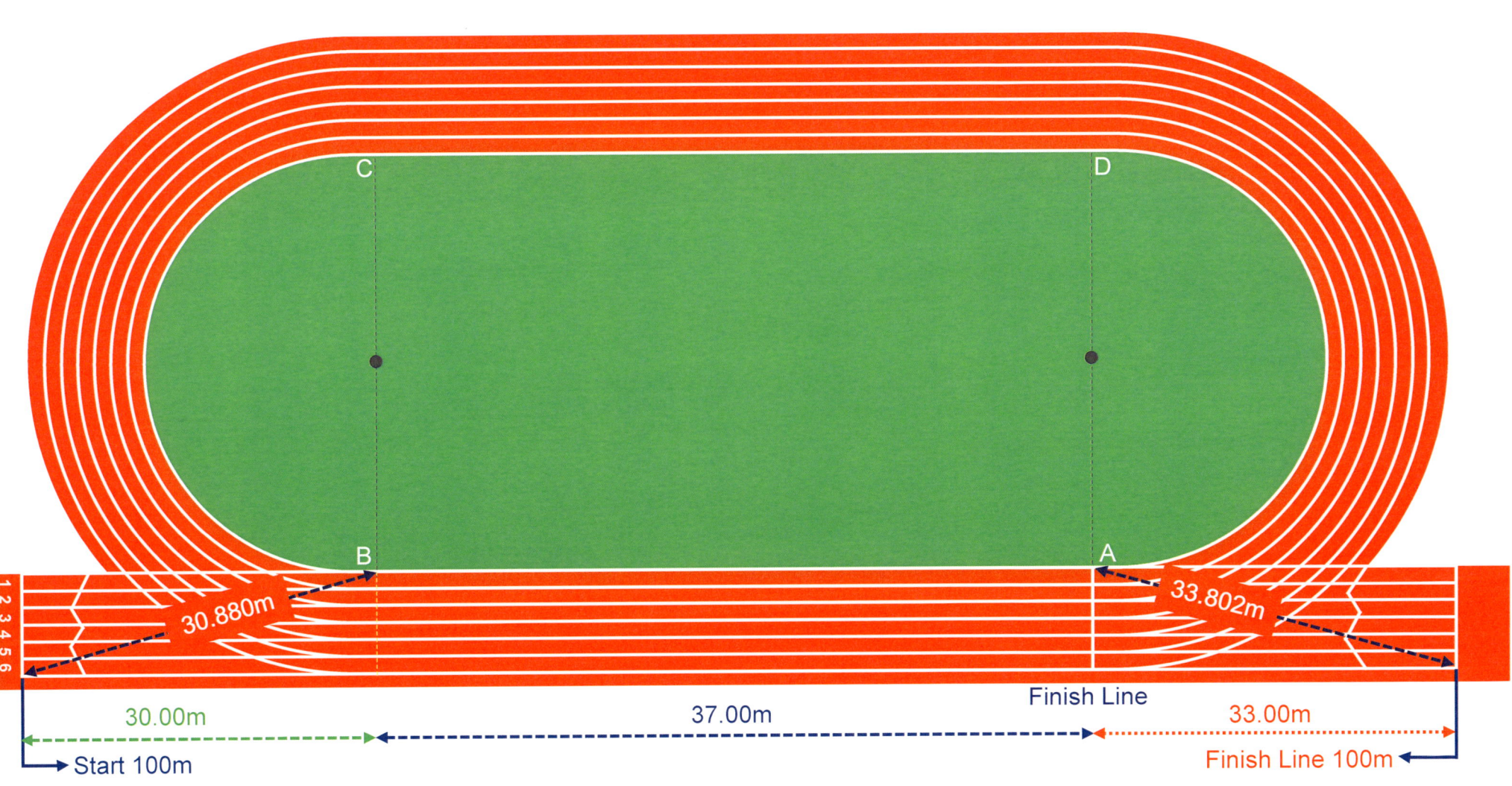

200 Metres

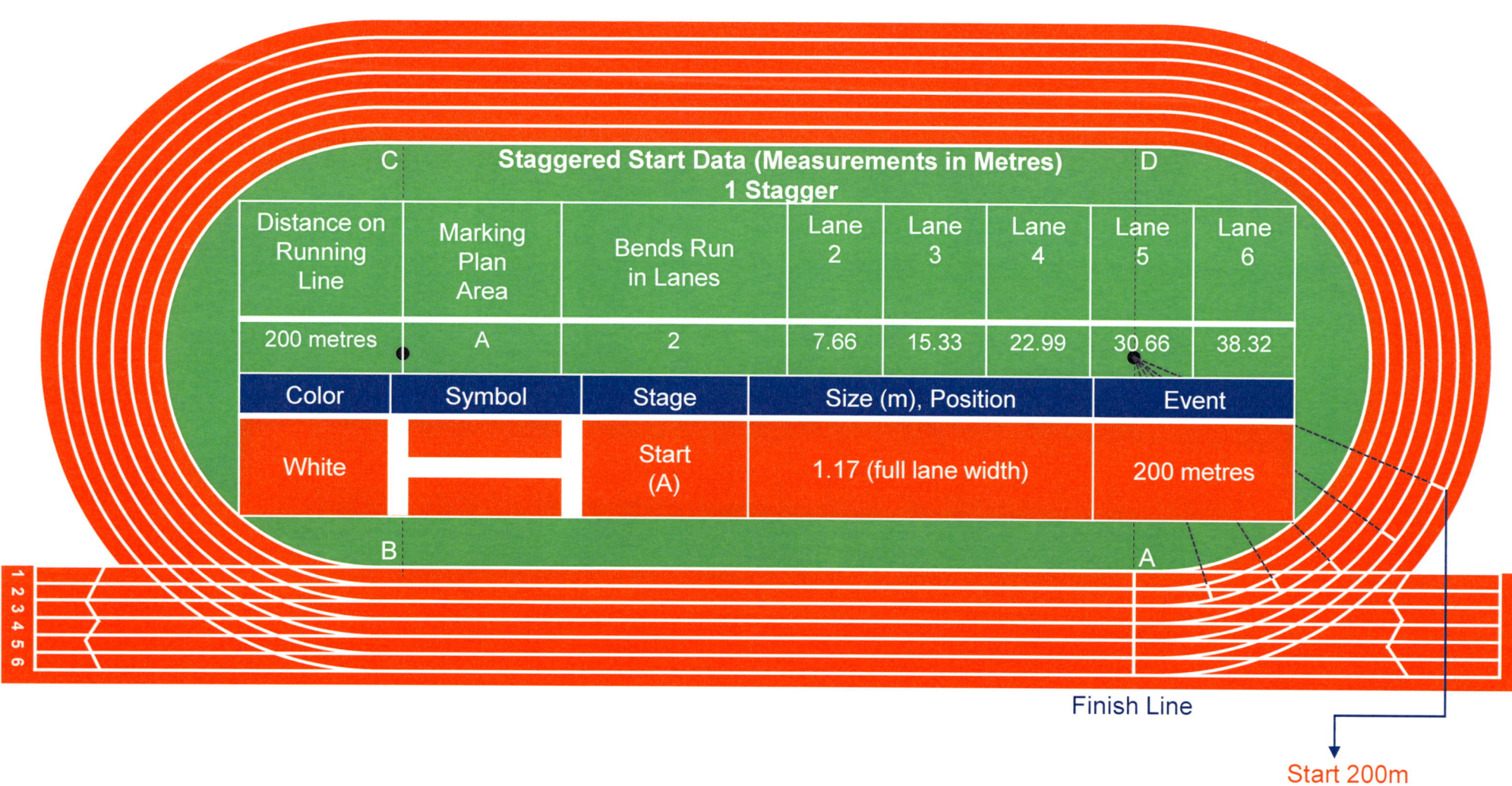

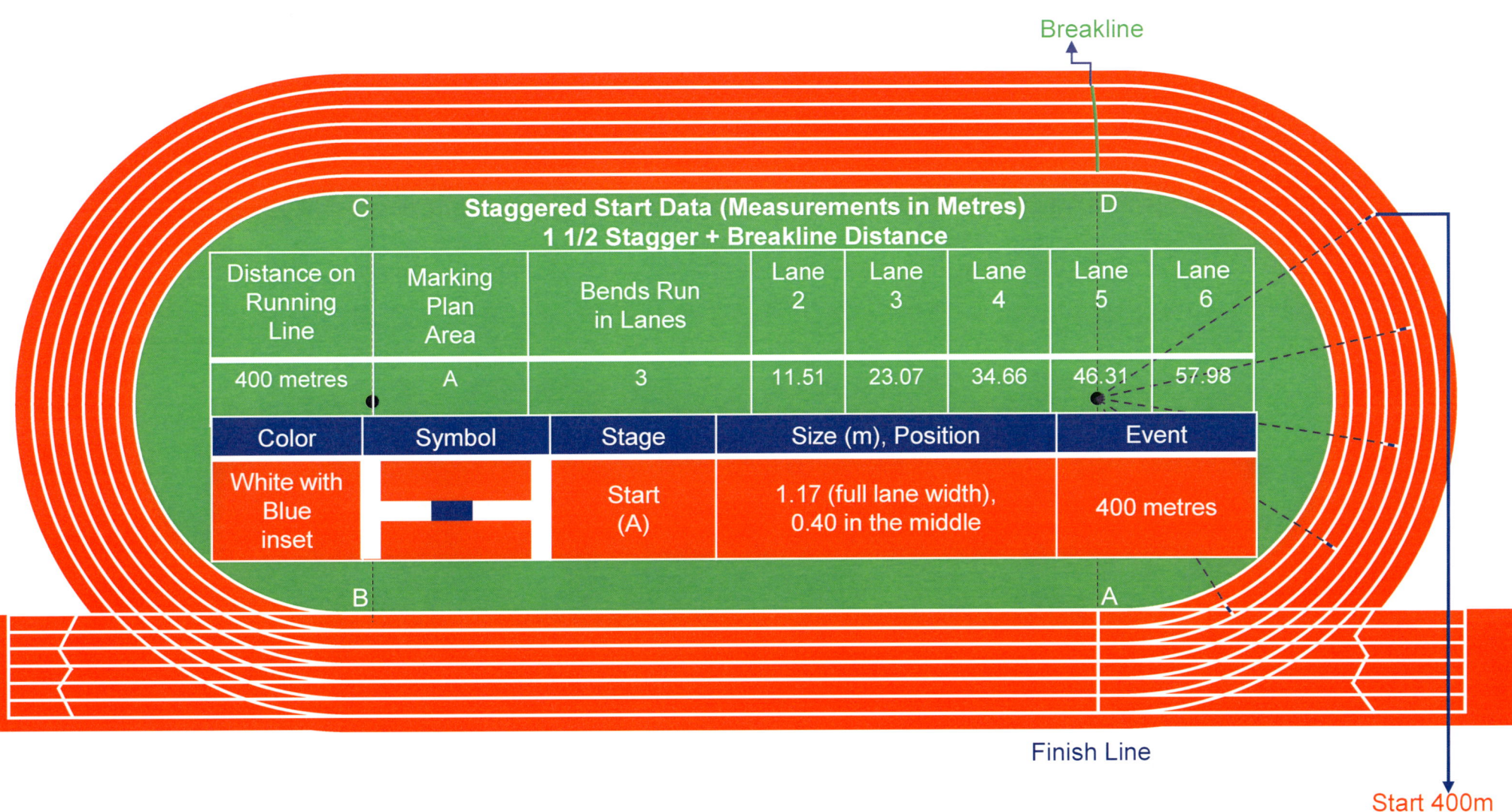

800 Metres

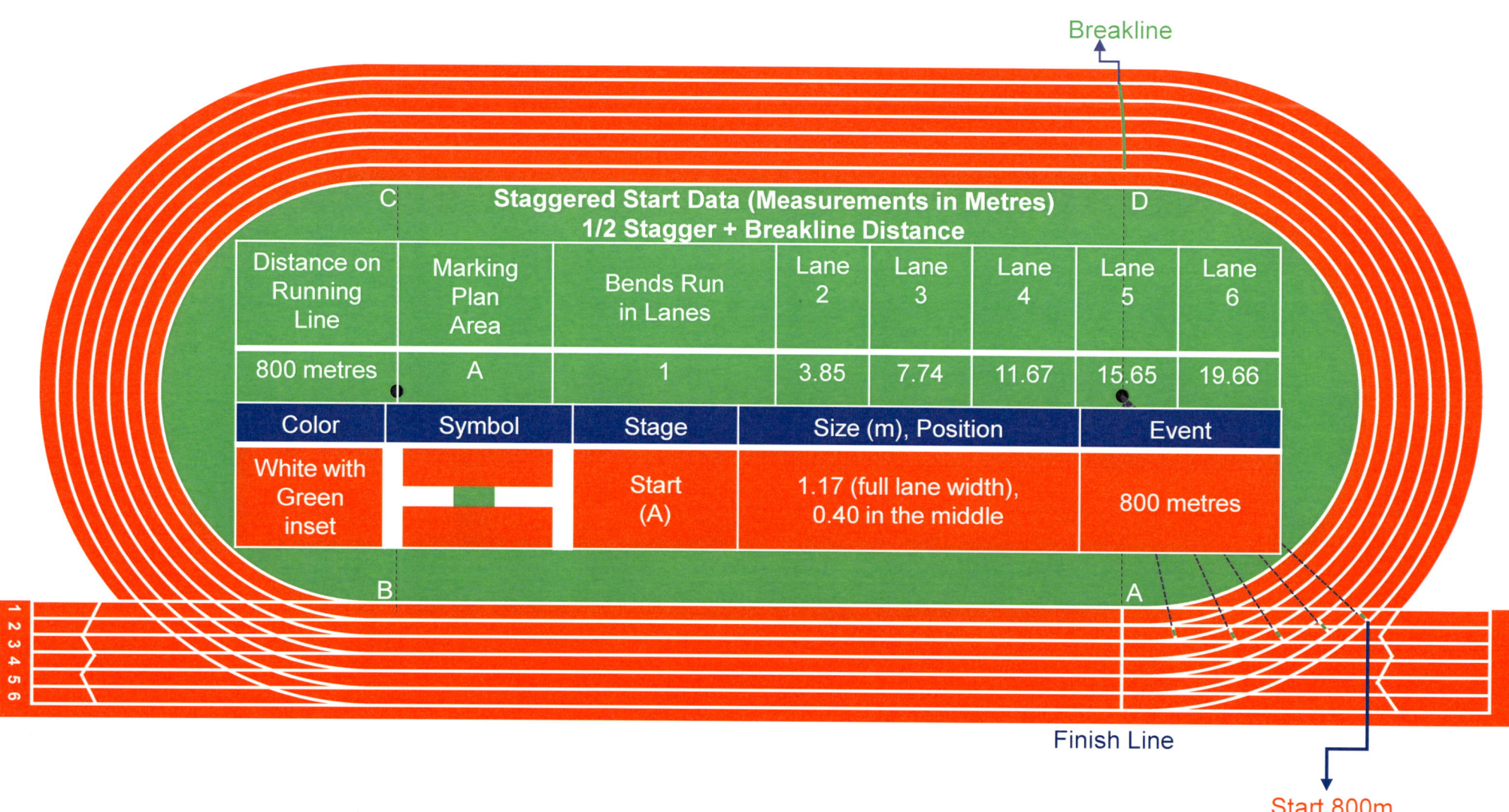

1500 Metres

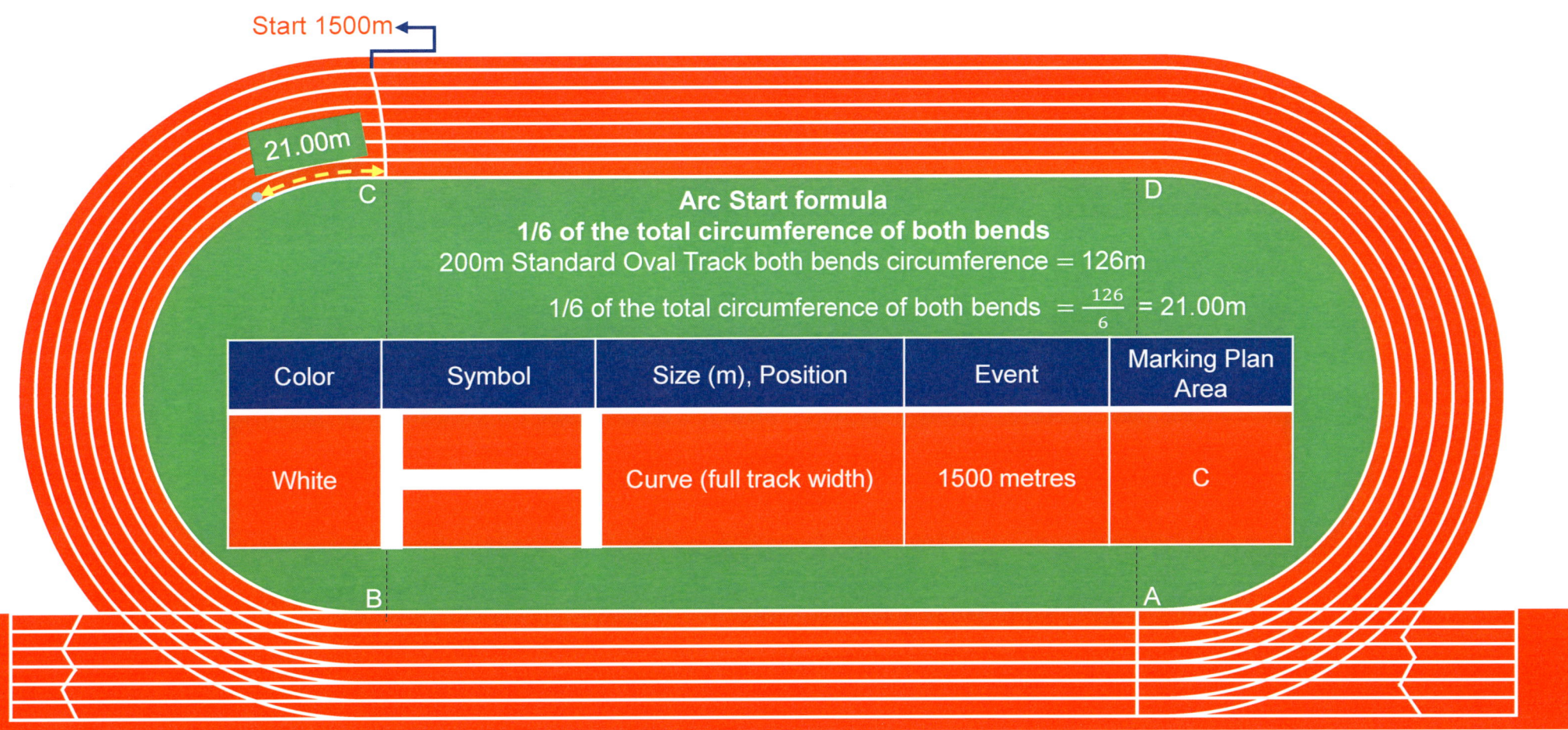

800 Metres, 1000 Metres, 2000 Metres, 5000 Metres, 10,000 Metres

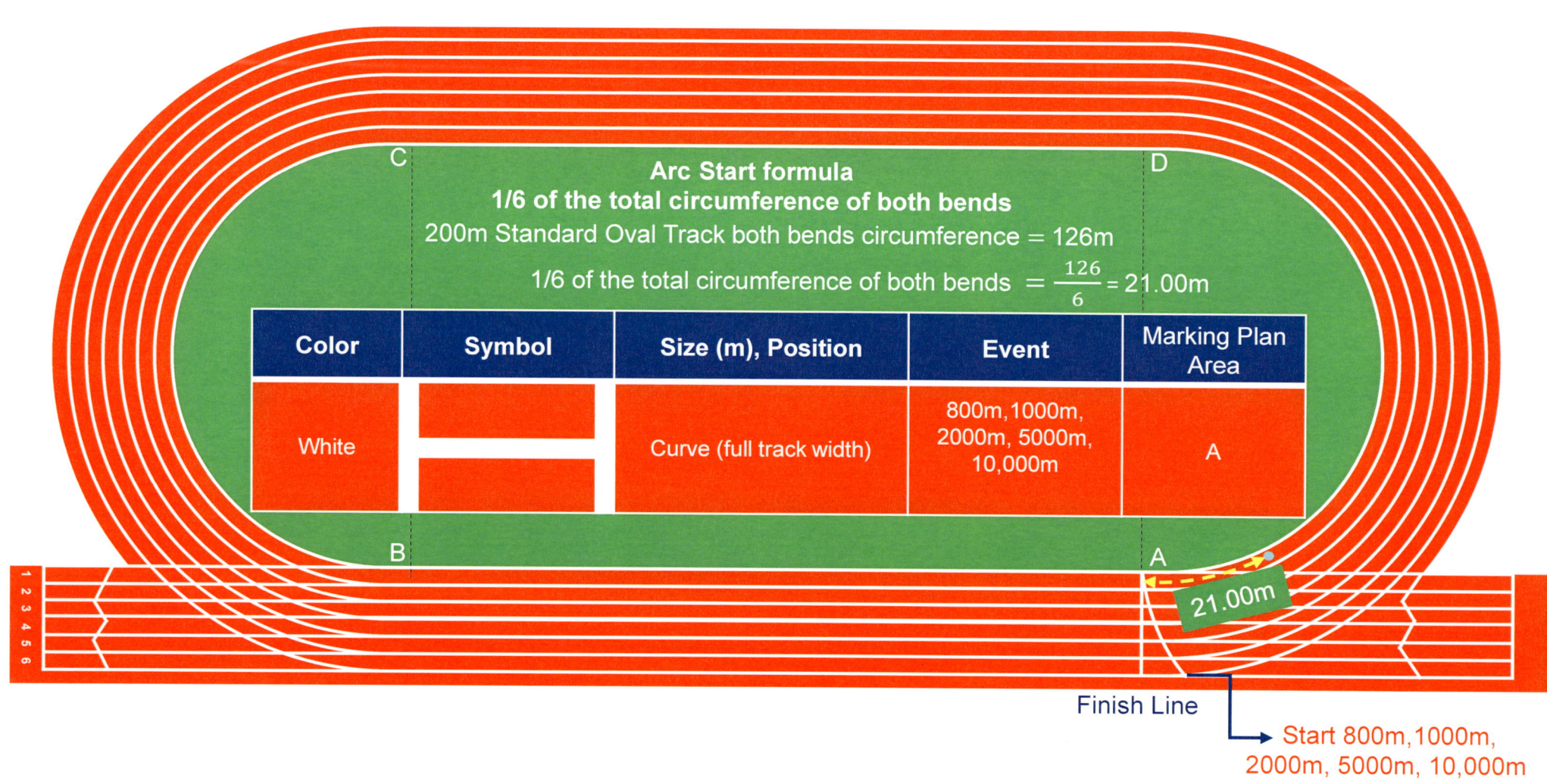

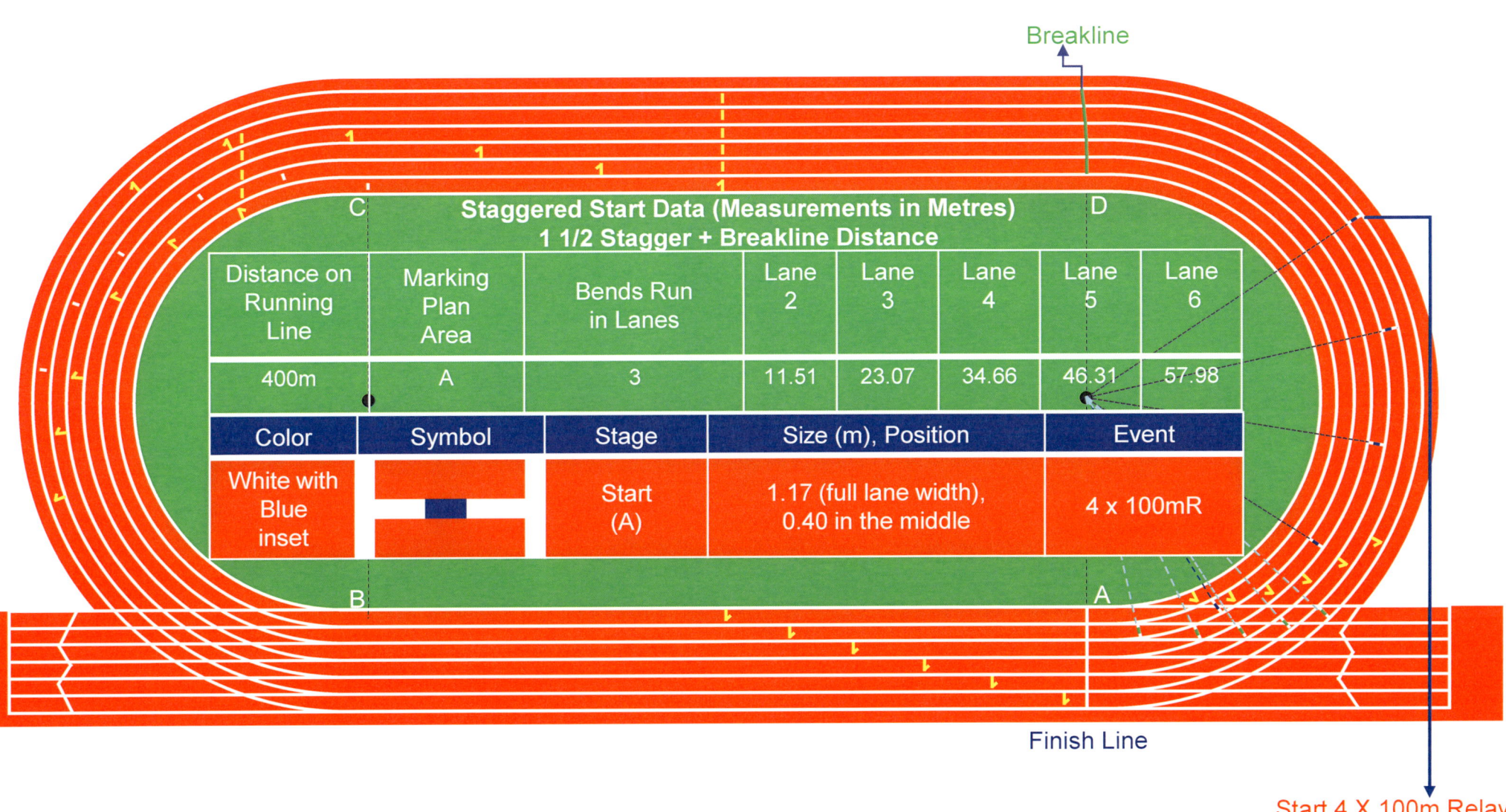

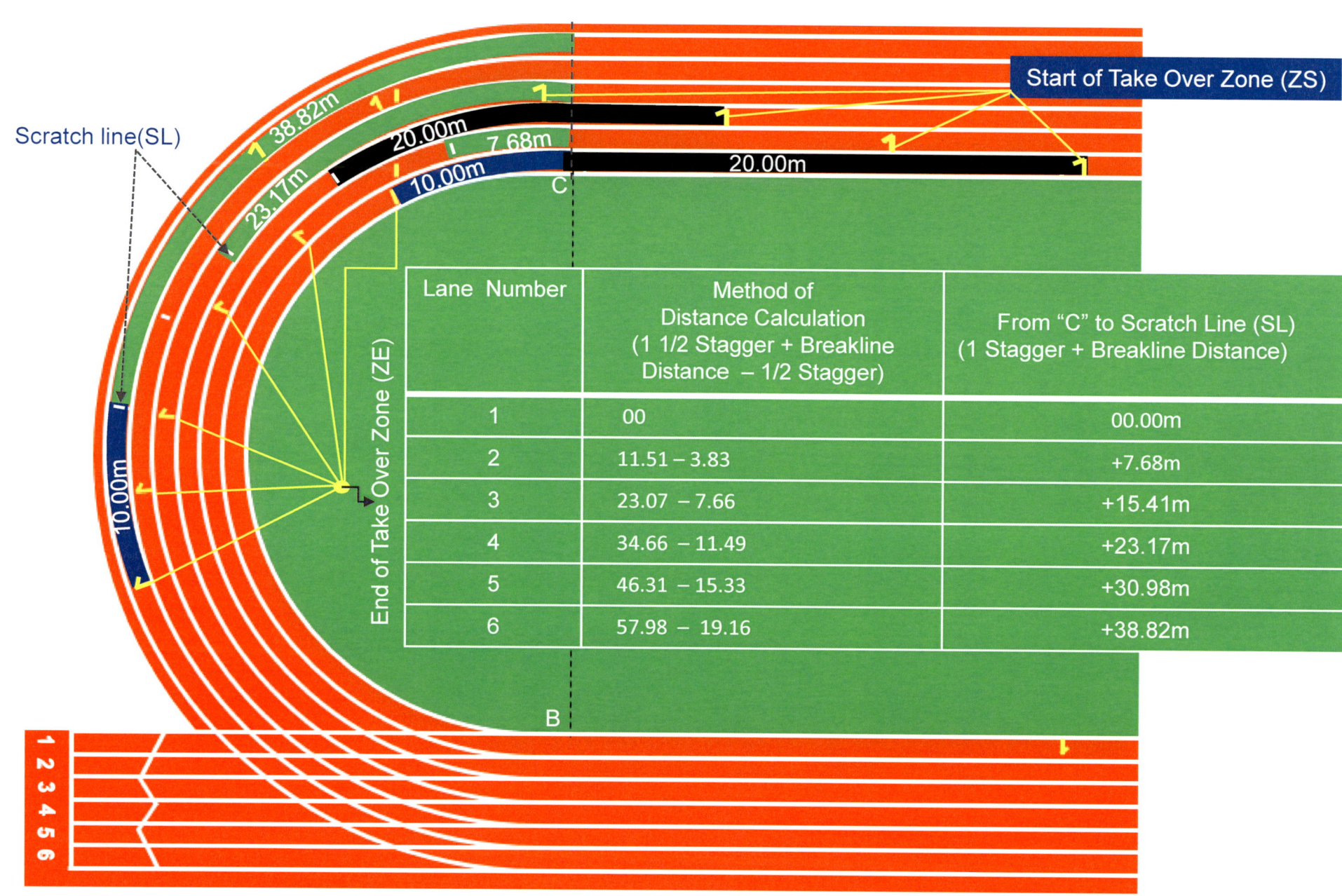

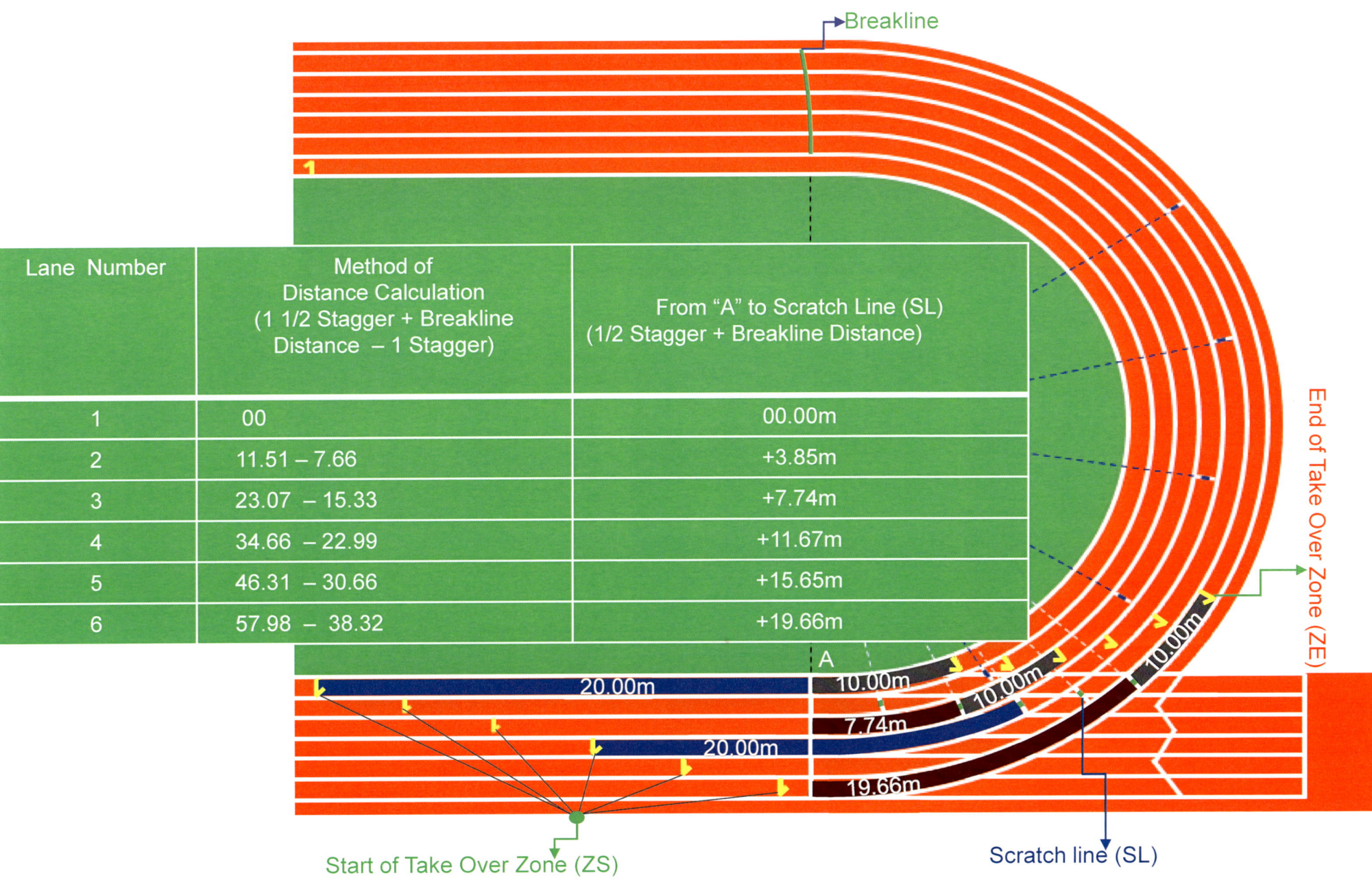

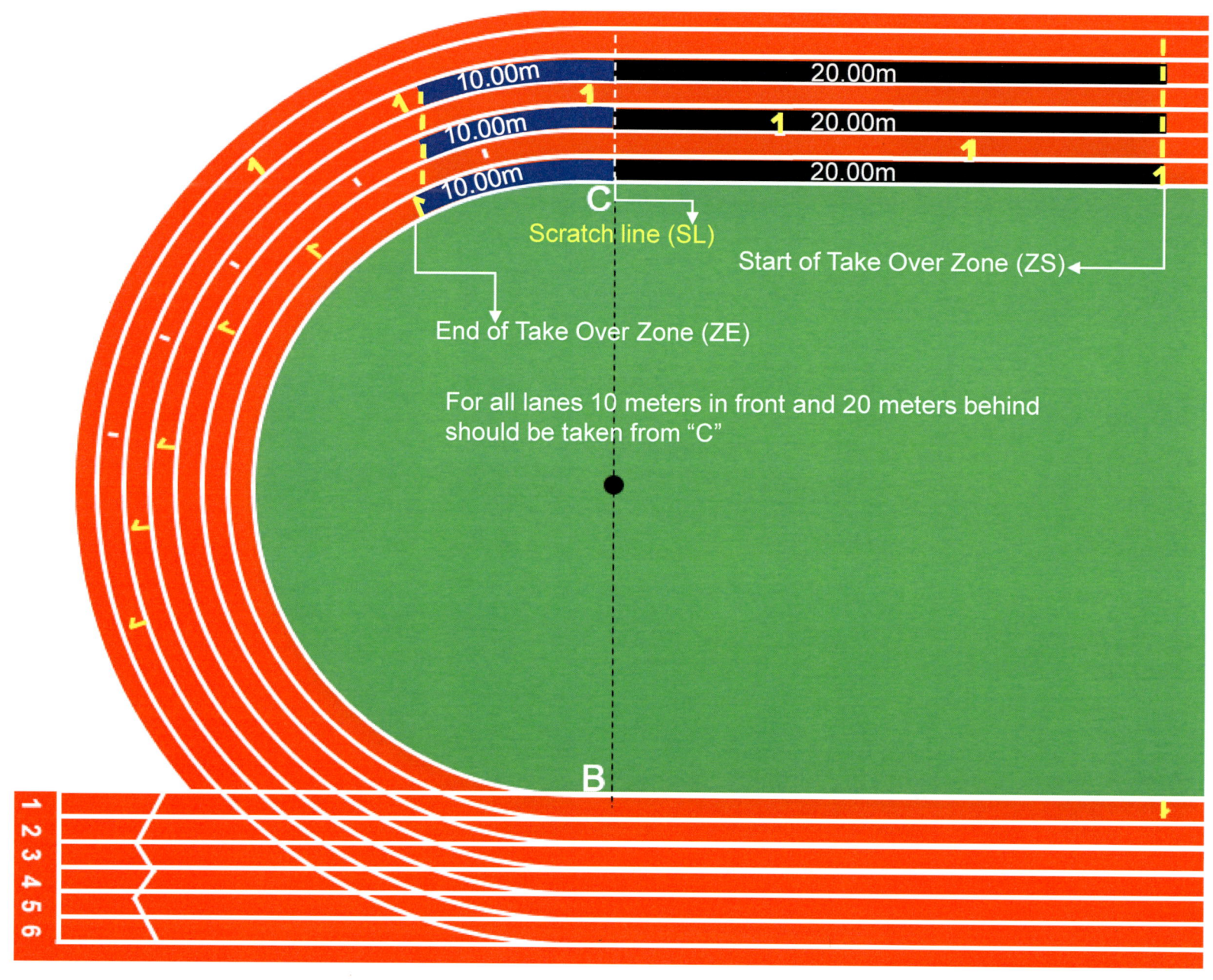

4 x 400 Metres Relay

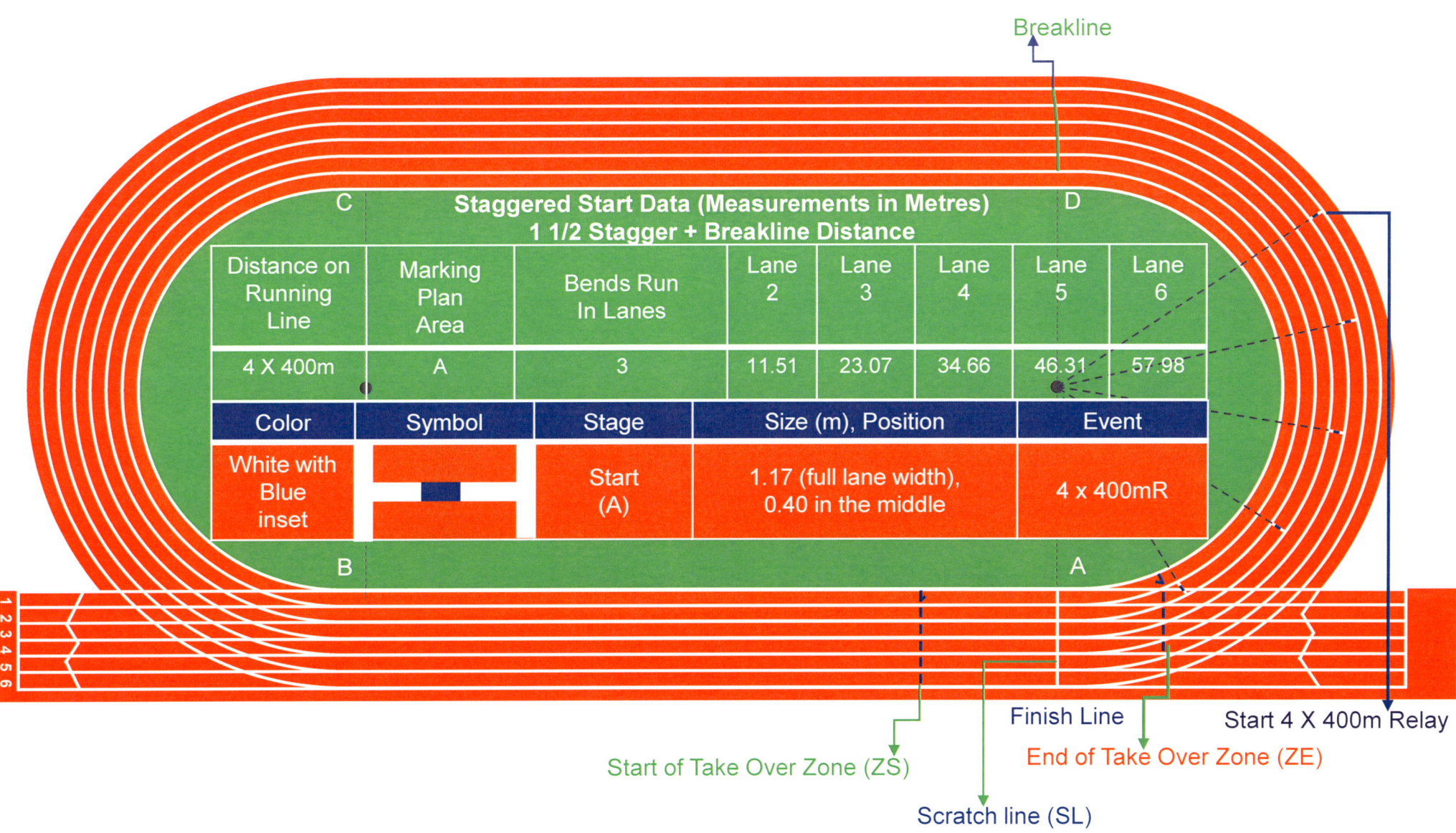

Technical Data
(from World Athletics Competition and Technical Rules 2024 Edition)

Event	Description	Senior Men	Senior Women
3000m Steeplechase	Number of Hurdles	28 (4 each lap)	28 (4 each lap)
	Height	0.914	0.762m
	Minimum Width	3.94m	3.94m
	Cross-section of Top of Barrier	12.7cm square	12.7cm square
	Number of Water Jumps	7 (1 each lap)	7 (1 each lap)
	Length of Water Jump	3.66m	3.66m
	Width of Water Jump	3.66m	3.66m
	Water Depth at Barrier	50cm	50cm
100m Hurdles	Number of Hurdles	-----	10
	Height	-----	0.838m
	Start to First Hurdle	-----	13m
	Between Hurdles	-----	8.5m
	Last Hurdle to Finish	-----	10.5m
110m Hurdles	Number of Hurdles	10	-----
	Height	1.067m	-----
	Start to First Hurdle	13.72m	-----
	Between Hurdles	9.14m	-----
	Last Hurdle to Finish	14.02m	-----
400m Hurdles	Number of Hurdles	10	10
	Height	0.914m	0.762m
	Start to First Hurdle	45m	45m
	Between Hurdles	35m	35m
	Last Hurdle to Finish	40m	40m

Technical Data
(from World Athletics Competition and Technical Rules 2024 Edition)

Event	Description	Senior Men	Senior Women
High Jump	Crossbar Length	4.00m	4.00m
	Crossbar Weight	Up to 2kg	Up to 2kg
	Landing Area (minimum)	6m x 4m x 70cm	6m x 4m x 70cm
Pole Vault	Crossbar Length	4.50m	4.50m
	Crossbar Weight	Up to 2.25kg	Up to 2.25kg
	Landing Area (minimum)	6m x 6m x 80cm	6m x 6m x 80cm
		Plus a minimum of 2m front pieces	
Long/Triple Jump	Take-off Board Length	1.22m	1.22m
	Take-off Board Width	20cm	20cm
	Plasticine Board Width	10cm	10cm
	Landing Area Width	2.75m --- 3.00m	2.75m --- 3.00m
Shot Put	Weight	7.26kg	4kg
	Diameter	110-130mm	95-110mm
	Sector Angle	34.92°	34.92°
	Circle Diameter	2.135m	2.135m
	Stop Board Height	10cm	10cm
	Stop Board Length	1.21m	1.21m
Discus Throw	Weight	2kg	1kg
	Diameter	219-221mm	180-182mm
	Sector Angle	34.92°	34.92°
	Circle Diameter	2.5m	2.5m

Technical Data
(from World Athletics Competition and Technical Rules 2024 Edition)

Event	Description	Senior Men	Senior Women
Hammer Throw	Weight	7.26kg	4kg
	Diameter of Head	110-130mm	95-110mm
	Length	Up to 1.215m	Up to 1.215m
	Sector Angle	34.92°	34.92°
	Circle Diameter	2.135m	2.135m
Javelin Throw	Weight	800gm	600gm
	Length	2.60m – 2.70m	2.20m – 2.30m
	Sector Angle	28.96°	28.96°
	Runway length min	30m	30m
	Runway width	4m	4m
Relays	Baton Length	28-30cm	28-30cm
	Baton Weight	Not less than 50g	Not less than 50g
	Length of Takeover Zone	30m (4x100m)	30m (4x100m)
		20m (4x400m)	20m (4x400m)
	Baton Diameter	4cm	4cm

Old usage	Present usage
Curve	Bend
Diagonal Excess	Breakline Distance
International Competitions	World Ranking Competitions
Curve Distance Radius - CDR	Construction Line Radius – (CLR) OR Kerb Line Radius –(KLR)
Running Distance Radius	Running Line Radius-RLR

Athletics Measurements: From 6 Millimetres to 100 Metres

SI No	Distance	Description	SI No	Distance	Description
1.	6mm	Thickness of the Rim (shot put, Discus & Hammer throw circle)	10.	7cm	Arc and extension line in javelin throw shall be 7cm
2.	7mm	Height of the Plasticine indicator board (Plasticine layer Long jump & Triple jump) 7mm ± 1mm			Control of elasticity: Hang a 3kg weight in the middle of the crossbar when in position. It may sag a maximum of 70mm in the High Jump
3.	1cm	Width of the Zero line in pole-vault is 1cm	11.	10cm	Length of the hurdle marking shall be 10cm (5x10cm) (100m H yellow, 110m H blue, 400m H green)
		Distance between upright and cross bar 1cm (at the cross bar support of high jump)			Height of the stop board in shot put 10 cm ± 8mm
4.	2cm	Height of the rim 2cm ± 6mm (shot put, Discus & Hammer throw circle).			Depth of the take-off board in long jump and triple jump (0.10m ± 0.002m)
		Cross Bar shall be never raised 2cm to 5cm in High Jump			In decathlon - pole vault the cross bar shall be raised only 10cm
		Thickness of the Finish indication mark at the finish line 2cm (2x5cm black)	12.	11cm	Control of elasticity: Hang a 3kg weight in the middle of the crossbar when in position. It may sag a maximum of 0.11m in Pole Vault
		The High crossbar shall have no bias and, when in place, shall sag a maximum of 20mm	13.	11.2cm	The stop board shall 11.2cm to 0.30 m wide
5.	3mm	Width of the All Optional line, before the finish line shall be 3cm x 80cm	14.	12.5cm	Length and width of the steeple chase hurdle marking shall be 12.5cm.
		In Decathlon and Heptathlon high jump the cross bar shall be raised only 3cm	15.	15cm	If a section of the kerb on a bend has to be temporarily removed for Field Events, its place on the surface beneath shall be marked with a white line 50mm in width and by cones or flags, minimum height 0.15m
		The PoleVault crossbar shall have no bias and, when in place, shall sag maximum of 30mm			Maximum height of the cone used in a break line (5x5x15cm)
6.	4cm	The High Jump crossbar supports shall be flat and rectangular, 40mm wide and 60mm long			End pieces of the high jump and pole vault cross bar length is 15 to 20cm
7.	4.5cm	The measurement of the Discus and Hammer Cage mesh cord centres shall be a maximum of 45mm for cord netting and 50mm for steel wire netting			Length of the hook or one side arrow in a relay take over zone is 15cm
8.	5cm	Width of all lines in a track and Field shall be 5 cm (except optional line, Javelin Arc, Pole Vault Zero Line and steeplechase marking line)	16.	20cm	Width of the Long Jump & Triple Jump takeoff board (0.20m ± 0.002m)
		Base of cone used in a break line (5x5cm)	17.	30cm	Width of the start & finish line is 30cm (if the event outside the stadium)
		Width of the Black rectangles at finish line 0.05m x 0.02m max.			Length of the relay baton is 28 to 30cm
		Length and width of 4m mark in javelin throw event is 5x5cm			End pieces of the high jump and pole vault cross bar wide is 30mm-35mm
		Size of the Break point 5x5cm (3000m, 5000m Green colour)	18.	40cm	Length of the relay scratch line 40cm
		Height of the kerb shall be 5cm to 6.5cm			Length of the check mark in 4x100m rely is 40cm
		Width of the kerb shall be 5cm to 25cm			Length of the ½ stagger and 1½ stagger with breakline distance colour marking in middle green and Red is 40cm
		Cross Bar shall never be raised 5cm to 10cm in pole vault.			
9.	6cm	The High Jump crossbar supports shall be flat and rectangular, 40mm wide and 60mm long			

Athletics Measurements: From 6 Millimetres to 100 Metres

SI No	Distance	Description	SI No	Distance	Description
19.	50cm	The height of the lane numbers marked immediately before the finish line is 50 cm	30.	1.17m	Full lane width 1.17
					Width of the Stagger line is 1.17m
20.	70cm	The High Jump Landing area for World Ranking Competitions shall be not smaller than 6m long × 4m wide × 0.7m high	31.	1.22m	Width of the lane including the 0.05m line on the outside 1.22m
					Width of the runway in Long Jump, Triple Jump & Pole Vault runway 1.22m
					Length of the take-off board in long jump and triple jump 1.22m
21.	75cm	A white line 50mm wide shall be drawn from the top of the rim extending for at least 0.75m on either side of the Shot Put, Hammer and Discus circle and Lines drawn from the extremities Javelin Arc			Height of the Wind gauge is 1.22m
			32.	1.25m	Radius of the discus throw circle 1.25m
22.	76.2cm	U18 Women 100m Hurdles height is 76.2cm	33.	2.00m	The Wind gauge shall be positioned 1.22m ± 0.05m high and not more than 2m away from the track for track events and not more than 2m away from the runway in Long jump and Triple Jump.
		U18 Women/U20 Women/ Senior Women 400m H height 76.2cm			The front pieces for Pole Vault Landing area must be at least 2m long.
23.	80cm	Lengths of the 4x400m relay second and third take over zone line marking. (blue /red)			If a section of the kerb on a bend has to be temporarily removed for steeplechase, cones should be placed 2m for the curved part of an inside steeplechase diversion.
		Length of the All Optional line, before the finish line shall be 3cm x 80cm	34.	2.135m	Diameter of the Shot Put and Hammer Throw circle is 2.135m ± 0.005m
		The Pole Vault Landing area for World Ranking Competitions shall be not smaller than 6m long (behind the Zero line and excluding the front pieces) × 6m wide × 0.8m High	35.	2.50m	Diameter of the Discus throw circle is 2.50m ± 0.005m
			36.	2.75m	Width of the Long Jump and Triple Jump landing area is 2.75m to 3.00m
24.	83.8cm	U20 Women / Senior Women 100m H height 83.8cm	37.	3.00m	Starter's Assistants must place each athlete in their correct lane or position, assembling the athletes approximately 3m behind the start line
25.	91.9cm	U20 Men 110m H height 99.1cm			
26.	91.4cm	U18 Men 110m H height 91.4cm			Minimum Distance between center of the circle to Discus cage 3.00m
		U20 Men and Senior Men 400m h height 91.4cm			A white line 50mm wide shall be drawn (usually by adhesive tape or similar material) between points 3m outside of each High Jump upright
27.	1.00m	The take-off line shall be placed between 1m and 3m from the nearer end of the landing area			Width of the Long Jump and Triple Jump landing area is 2.75m to 3.00m
		The 400m track must have an obstacle-free zone (safety zone) on the inside at least 1.00m wide and should have on the outside an obstacle-free zone at least 1.00m wide	38.	3.50m	Minimum Distance between center of the circle to Hammer cage is 3.50m
28.	1.067m	Radius of the Shot-put and Hammer throw circle	39.	3.66m	The Steeplechase water jump, including the hurdle, shall be 3.66m ± 0.02m in length and the water pit shall be 3.66m ± 0.02m in width
		Height of the 110m hurdle for men			
29.	1.10m	Length of the 4x100m relay take over zone line marking (yellow)	40.	3.94m	Length of steeple chase hurdle is 3.94m

Athletics Measurements: From 6 Millimetres to 100 Metres

Sl No	Distance	Description	Sl No	Distance	Description
41.	4.00m	If a section of the kerb on a bend has to be temporarily removed for Field Events, cones should be placed at intervals not exceeding 4m	48.	10.00m	Distance from scratch line to End of the takeover-zone in 4x100m and 4x400m relay is 10m
		Width of the Javelin Throw runway is 4m			Distance from start of the takeover-zone to scratch line in 4x400m relay is 10m
		Length of the High Jump cross bar is 4m ± 2cm			
		The distance between the High Jump uprights shall be not less than 4.00m nor more than 4.04m			The distance between the take-off line and the far end of the landing area in Long Jump shall be at least 10m and, where possible, 11m
		The High Jump Landing area for World Ranking Competitions shall be not smaller than 6m long × 4m wide × 0.7m high			
42.	5.00m	For other High Jump competitions, the landing area should measure not less than 5m long × 3m wide × 0.7m high	49.	10.50m	Distance between the last hurdle to finish line in 100m hurdle is 10.50m
		For other Pole Vault competitions, the landing area should measure not less than 5m long (excluding the front pieces) × 5m wide × 0.8m high	50.	11.00m	The distance between the take-off line and the far end of the landing area in Long Jump shall be at least 10m and, where possible, 11m
		The Judges should be placed at least 5m from, and in line with, the finish and should be provided with an elevated platform			The take-off line shall not be less than 11m for women from the nearer end of the landing area in Triple Jump
		The Timekeepers shall be in line with the finish and, where possible, they should be placed at least 5m from the outside lane of the track	51.	13.00m	The take-off line shall not be less than 13m for men from the nearer end of the landing area in Triple Jump
		It is recommended that the Steeplechase first hurdle taken in the race should be at least 5m in width, when Steeplechase Track With Water Jump Outside			Distance between the start line to first hurdle in 100m hurdle event is 13m
		For Pole Vault, the Organisers should place suitable and safe distance markers beside the runway at each 0.5m between the points 2.5m to 5m from the "zero" line and at each 1.0m from the 5m to the 18m point	52.	13.72m	Distance between the start line to first hurdle in 110m hurdle event is 13.72m
			53.	14.02m	Distance between the last hurdle to finish line in 110m hurdle event is 14.02m
			54.	15.00m	The minimum length of High Jump runway shall be 15m
					Chord distance of shot-put sector
43.	6.00m	The width of the mouth should be 6m, for Discus and Hammer Cage	55.	16.00m	The minimum width of High Jump runway shall be 16m
		World Rankings High Jump Competition, the landing area shall be not smaller than 6m long × 4m wide × 0.7m high.	56.	17.00m	400metre Standard Oval Track run-out area is minimum 17m
		World Rankings Pole Vault Competition, the landing area shall be not smaller than 6m long × 4m wide × 0.8m high.	57.	20.00m	Distance of 2nd and 3rd takeover zone in 4x400m relay is 20m
44.	7.00m	The width of the mouth should be 6m, positioned 7m in front of the centre of the throwing circle for Discus and Hammer Cage			The wind gauge is placed 20m from the take-off line for Long Jump and Triple Jump
					Distance between the start of takeover zone and scratch line in 4x100m is 20m
45.	8.00m	The Javelin throw shall be made from behind an arc of a circle drawn with a radius of 8m	58.	21.00m	The distance between the take-off line for men and the far end of the landing area shall be at least 21m.
		Length of the landing area in long jump (8.00m to 10.00m)			
46.	8.50m	Distance between the hurdle in 100m hurdle is 8.50m			
47.	9.14m	Distance between the hurdle in 110m hurdle is 9.14m			

Athletics Measurements: From 6 Millimetres to 100 Metres

Sl No	Distance	Description	Sl No	Distance	Description
57.	25.00m	Distance of shot put sector from centre of the circle	65.	45.00m	Distance between start line to first hurdle in 400m hurdle is 40m
		World Ranking competitions, where the condition permit minimum length of the runway in high jump shall be 25m			For World Ranking Competitions the minimum length of the runway in long jump, triple jump & pole vault from the relevant take-off line is 45m
58.	28.96°	The sector angle of javelin throw is 28.96°			
59.	30.00m	The minimum length of the runway shall be 30m			
60.	33.50m	For construction category I,II , and III the runway shall be 33.50m minimun	66.	48.00m	The chord distance of discus throw sector
61.	35.00m	The wind velocity shall be measured for a period of 5 seconds from the time an athlete passes a mark placed alongside the runway, for the Long Jump 40m from the take-off line and for the Triple Jump 35m. If an athlete runs less than 40m or 35m, as appropriate, the wind velocity shall be measured from the time they commence their run.	67.	50.00m	The wind gauge for Track Events is placed beside the straight, adjacent to lane 1, 50m (100m, 110m and 200m races) from the finish line.
					The chord distance of Javelin throw sector is 50m
		Distance between the hurdle in 400m hurdle is 35m			The Record for an 400mStandard oval Track Event shall be made in a track lane where the running line radius does not exceed 50m
62.	36.50m	Experience has shown that the most suitable 400m Standard oval tracks are constructed with bend radii of between 35m and 38m, with an optimum of 36.50m. It is recommended that all future tracks are constructed to the latter specification and this will be referred to as the "400m Standard Oval Track".			The Short Track standard Hurdle Races distances shall be: 50m o 60m on the straight track.
63.	36.80m	400m Standard Oval Track, Radius of measurement line (running line) in lane 1(0.30m outside raised kerb) is 36.80m	68.	54.00m	The chord distance of hammer throw sector
			69.	80.00m	Distance of discus throw sector from centre of the circle
64.	40.00m	Distance between last hurdle to finish line in 400m hurdle	70.	84.39m	The 400m Standard Oval Track comprises 2 semicircles, each with a radius of 36.50m,which are joined by two straights, each 84.39m in length.
		Minimum runway distance of long jump, triple jump & pole vault events			
			71.	90.00m	Distance of Hammer throw sector from center of the circle is 90m
		The wind velocity shall be measured for a period of 5 seconds from the time an athlete passes a mark placed alongside the runway, for the Long Jump 40m from the take-off line and for the Triple Jump 35m. If an athlete runs less than 40m or 35m, as appropriate, the wind velocity shall be measured from the time they commence their run.	72.	100.00m	Distance of javelin throw sector from 8.00m radius point is 100m

Olympic Oath

Athletes' Oath

In the name of all competitors, I promise that we shall take part in these Olympic Games, respecting and abiding by the rules which govern them, committing ourselves to a sport without doping and without drugs, in the true spirit of sportsmanship, for the glory of sport and the honor of our teams

The Officials' Oath

In the name of all the judges and officials, I promise that we shall officiate in these Olympic Games with complete impartiality, respecting and abiding by the rules which govern them, in the true spirit of sportsmanship

The Coaches' Oath

In the name of all the coaches and other members of the athletes' entourage, I promise that we shall commit ourselves to ensuring that the spirit of sportsmanship and fair play is fully adhered to and upheld in accordance with the fundaMental principles of Olympism

Olympic Games

Olympic Opening Ceremony

Main elements of the opening ceremony

1. Entrance of Head of State (HOS) and International Olympic Committee (IOC) President;
2. Playing of the national anthem;
3. Parade of athletes;
4. Symbolic release of doves;
5. Olympic Laurel Award;
6. Official speeches;
7. Opening of the Games;
8. Raising the Olympic flag and playing the Olympic Anthem;
9. Athletes, judges and coaches' oath;
10. Lighting of the Olympic flame
11. The artistic programme

Olympic Closing Ceremony

Main elements of the closing ceremony

1. Entrance of Head of State (HOS) and International Olympic Committee (IOC) President;
2. Playing of the national anthem;
3. Entry of nations' flag;
4. Parade of athletes;
5. Victory ceremonies;
6. Introduction of the IOC Athletes' Commission's newly elected members and recognition of the volunteers;
7. MoMent of remembrance;
8. Playing of the Greek national anthem;
9. Lowering the Olympic flag and flag handover ceremony;
10. Next host artistic segMent;
11. OCOG President's speech and IOC President's speech;
12. Extinguishing the Olympic flame.

OCOG - Organising Committee of Olympic Games

Introduction of Athletics at the Summer Olympics

Men	Event	Abbreviation	Women	Men	Event	Abbreviation	Women
1896	100 metres	100m	1928	1896	High Jump	HJ	1928
1900	200 metres	200m	1948	1896	Pole Vault	PV	2000
1896	400 metres	400m	1964	1896	Long Jump	LJ	1948
1896	800 metres	800m	*1928/1960	1896	Triple Jump	TJ	1996
1896	1500 metres	1500m	1972	1896	Discus Throw	DT	1928
1912	5000 metres	5000m	1996	1900	Hammer Throw	HT	2000
1912	10,000 metres	10,000m	1988	1908	Javelin Throw	JT	1932
1896	Marathon (42.195 km)	Mar	1984	1896	Shot Put	SP	1948
1920	3000 Metres Steeplechase	3000mSC	2008	1912	Decathlon / Heptathlon	Dec/ Hep	1984
1896	110 metres Hurdles / 100 metres Hurdles	110mH / 100mH	1972	1956	20 kilometres Race Walk	20kmRW	2000
1900	400 metres Hurdles	400m H	1984	1932	50 kilometres Race Walk	50kmRW	----
1912	4 × 100 metres Relay	4x100mR	1928	2028	Half-Marathon Race Walk	HMarRW	2028
1912	4 × 400 metres Relay	4X400mR	1972				

	Mixed Events	Abbreviation	
2020	4 × 400 metres Relay Mixed	4 × 400mR Mx	2020
2024	Marathon Race Walk Relay Mixed	Mar RWR	2024
2028	4 X 100 metres Relay Mixed	4 × 100mR Mx	2028

1928 introduced then IOC to drop it from the Olympic programme. It was reintroduced in 1960.

Athletics Events in the Olympics and World Athletics Championships

Olympics

Sl no	Men	Mixed Events	Women
1.	100 metres		100 metres
2.	200 metres		200 metres
3.	400 metres		400 metres
4.	800 metres		800 metres
5.	1500 metres		1500 metres
6.	5000 metres		5000 metres
7.	10,000 metres		10,000 metres
8.	Marathon		Marathon
9.	3000 Metres Steeplechase		3000 Metres Steeplechase
10.	110 metres Hurdles		100 metres Hurdles
11.	400 metres Hurdles		400 metres Hurdles
12.	High Jump		High Jump
13.	Pole Vault		Pole Vault
14.	Long Jump		Long Jump
15.	Triple Jump		Triple Jump
16.	Discus Throw		Discus Throw
17.	Hammer Throw		Hammer Throw
18.	Javelin Throw		Javelin Throw
19.	Shot Put		Shot Put
20.	Decathlon		Heptathlon
21.	20 kilometres Race Walk Half-Marathon Race Walk		20 kilometres Race Walk Half-Marathon Race Walk
22.	4 × 100 metres Relay		4 × 100 metres Relay
23.	4 × 400 metres Relay		4 × 400 metres Relay
24.	-----	4 × 400 metres Relay Mixed	-----
25.	-----	Marathon Race Walk Relay Mixed	-----
26.	-----	4 X 100 metres Relay Mixed	-----

World Athletics Championships

Sl no	Men	Mixed Events	Women
1.	100 metres		100 metres
2.	200 metres		200 metres
3.	400 metres		400 metres
4.	800 metres		800 metres
5.	1500 metres		1500 metres
6.	5000 metres		5000 metres
7.	10,000 metres		10,000 metres
8.	Marathon		Marathon
9.	3000 Metres Steeplechase		3000 Metres Steeplechase
10.	110 metres Hurdles		110 metres Hurdles
11.	400 metres Hurdles		400 metres Hurdles
12.	High Jump		High Jump
13.	Pole Vault		Pole Vault
14.	Long Jump		Long Jump
15.	Triple Jump		Triple Jump
16.	Discus Throw		Discus Throw
17.	Hammer Throw		Hammer Throw
18.	Javelin Throw		Javelin Throw
19.	Shot Put		Shot Put
20.	Decathlon		Decathlon
21.	20 kilometres Race Walk		20 kilometres Race Walk
22.	35 kilometres Race Walk		35 kilometres Race Walk
23.	4 × 100 metres Relay		4 × 100 metres Relay
24.	4 × 400 metres Relay		4 × 400 metres Relay
25.	----	4 × 400 metres Relay Mixed	----
-	-----		----

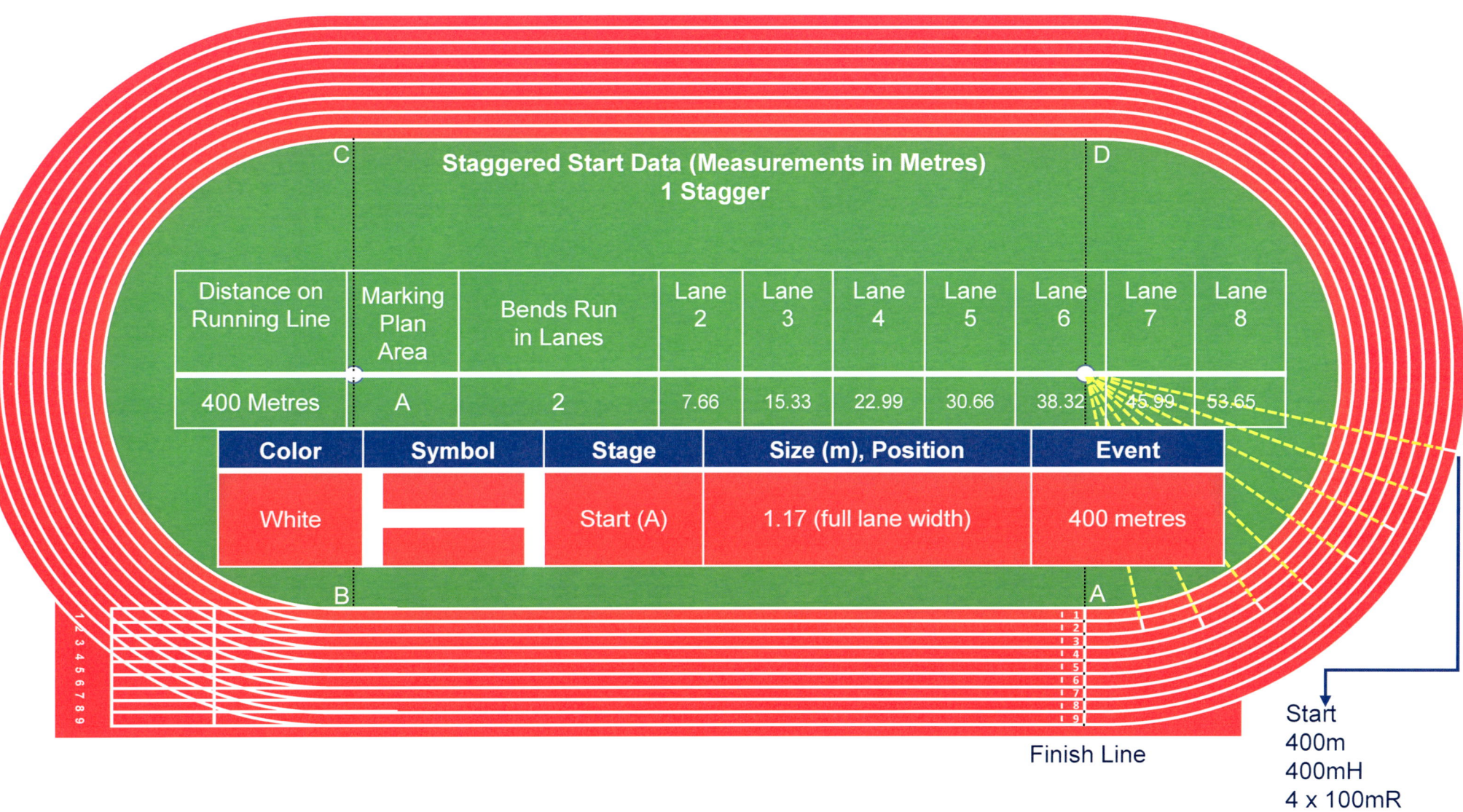

REFERENCES

WORLD ATHLETICS DOCUMENTS

1. COMPETITION AND TECHNICAL RULES 2025 EDITION
2. TRACK AND FIELD FACILITIES MANUAL CHAPTER 1 -3
3. TRACK AND FIELD FACILITIES MANUAL CHAPTER 4-8
4. TRACK AND FIELD FACILITIES MANUAL 2008 EDITION - MARKING PLAN 200M INDOOR TRACK
5. TRACK AND FIELD FACILITIES MANUAL 2019 EDITION - MARKING PLAN 400M STANDARD TRACK
6. CERTIFICATES - CERTIFIED ATHLETICS FACILITIES - 2025
7. STATISTICS HANDBOOK TOKYO 2020 OLYMPIC GAMES
8. MONDO COMPANY PRODUCTS - OFFICIAL SYNTHETIC SURFACE RUNNING TRACK COLOURS
9. OLYMPIC CHARTER

www.ingramcontent.com/pod-product-compliance
Ingram Content Group UK Ltd.
Pitfield, Milton Keynes, MK11 3LW, UK
UKRC031637240426
12048UKWH00034B/90